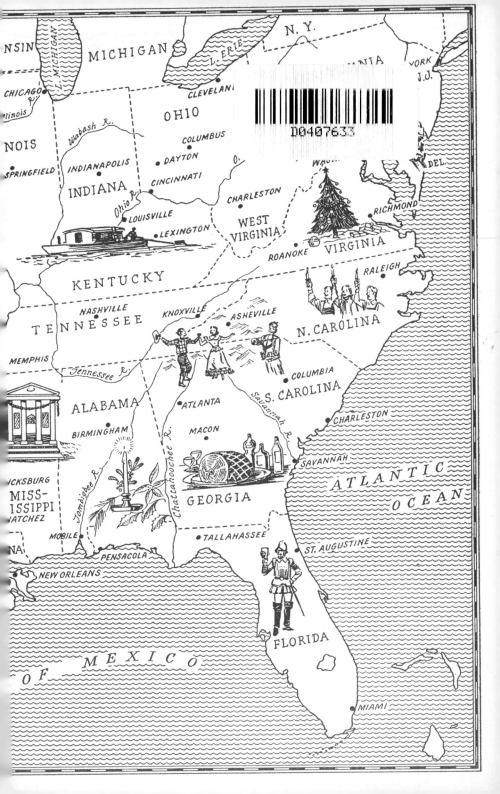

*The Southern Christmas Book*

# The Southern Christmas Book

## THE FULL STORY FROM EARLIEST TIMES TO PRESENT: PEOPLE, CUSTOMS, CONVIVIALITY, CAROLS, COOKING

by HARNETT T. KANE

DAVID McKAY COMPANY, INC.

New York

Manufactured in the United States of America.

Van Rees Press • New York

To the memories of a grandmother of Irish-Catholic
descent and another of German-Lutheran, both of whom
told me what they knew of Christmas in the Old World
and the New....

"All the music, all the laughter, all the preparations led up to Christmas."

Douglas Southall Freeman

# Contents

*The Southern Christmas Book*

# Holly in the Sunlight

THERE was Christmas in the Southern United States from the beginning days of the nation; America's first clearly recorded Yuletide ceremony took place on Virginia's soil. The area gave the embryo country its original Christmas observances, and shaped them for the generations that followed.

As the years passed, the South became a land of tradition, of customs honored through the centuries; and Christmas is above all else a season of traditions, of things done in the old-time style. "The Southern festival par excellence," one authority later termed it, and in no part of America has the happy-solemn period had so sustained, so continuing a story.

While Puritan New England shunned the ceremonial Christmas, the Southerners nurtured it and kept it ever before them.

But as there are many Souths, so there have been many Southern Christmases—festivals as different from one another as Maryland is from Georgia, and Tennessee or Alabama from South Carolina and Florida.

For hundreds of thousands of Southerners Christmas has meant the well-spiced chicken and meat dishes of Latin Texas; for others the fowl-with-sauerkraut of Baltimore; for still others the chortling Papa Noël, New Orleans' Gallic (and different) Santa Claus, or the Moravian "love feasts," North Carolina church rites of coffee and buns and lighted candles in the hands of the reverent participants.

To several Southern states—Alabama, Maryland, Kentucky, West Virginia—Christmas has brought a carnival, a survival of medieval mummering, with men in masks and costumes, serenading, skylarking, going from house to house, or marching along city streets in impromptu humor and general hilarity.

In one section of North Carolina men in sheets, wearing a steer's head, still rock about during the Christmas season as "Old Buck," a modern carry-over of medieval ceremonies. In Missouri, which has shared something of the South's civilization, bright-spirited youths follow lighthearted Creole serenading customs dating back to the French colonial regime. And in remote spots, men of the towns and villages compete, as did their ancestors of frontier days, to win, through their shooting skill, game or sections of meat.

To millions of Southern boys (up to ninety years old) Christmas has signified, as much as anything else, the firing of guns, the tossing of firecrackers, "baby wakers," and other sources of cannon-like blasts. In North Carolina little bands spend their Christmas Eve riding in automobiles to the homes and farms of friends to chant and then to aim at the sky and shoot at it with century-old muskets.

Among the isolated people of the distant ridges and coves

of Tennessee, Arkansas, Georgia, Kentucky, the Carolinas, and West Virginia can be found a mountain Christmas, observed with ancient, moving carols which have largely been lost to other Americans.

Beyond the Mississippi the long stretches of Texas bred a frontier-style holiday of high individualism and explosive content—cowboy festivities with square dancing, lusty prancing, and blasting of the heavens. In other parts of Texas the eloquent folk dramas of the Spanish Christmas are still alive. In these pageants is re-enacted the glowing story of the Christ Child and the shepherds who made their way to the Manger to pay Him homage.

Through most of the South, from Virginia to Florida, to Louisiana and beyond, there lives on a Christmas observance that some consider indispensable: the morning hunt after deer or fox or whatever game awaits in the woods. The yelp of the dogs, the pounding of horses' hoofs, the quickening of the chase. . . . In the words of one Mississippian: "That's always been Christmas for me. The rest? It's mainly extra trimming."

In the old song, "Christmas comes but once a year." For the South, however, it has come at different times, and sometimes twice. Along the remote stretches of the Atlantic coast, and in highland Tennessee, Kentucky, and Arkansas, the people observe the "new Christmas" of December 25, and then the "old Christmas" of January 5, following both the early Gregorian church calendar and the Julian one.

Among some Southerners there has been a kind of pre-Christmas in early December, when the Germanic St. Nikolaus or his helper appeared to prepare the way for the holiday. And in the marshes of lower Louisiana, a belated Christmas arrives in late February or March.

"Christmas gardens," indoor scenes depicting Christ's birth in the stable, may fill a whole room about a Christmas tree in

Baltimore; in New Orleans and St. Louis can be found the French *crèche*. . . . The South has all of them, and in some cases gave them to the emerging nation.

The last century saw Christmas surge forward as a great American celebration of a kind unimagined by the colonial people. And the special importance of the South in this development can be seen in the fact that the first three states to recognize Christmas as a legal holiday were Southern ones—Louisiana and Arkansas in 1831, and Alabama in 1836. Not until seven years later did the next, Connecticut, follow.

The Southern Christmas has become an observance different in a number of ways from that of any other region, or other country the world over. In it have merged ceremonials from many lands, with improvisations and new aspects added with the years. The wassail bowl, the gathering of greens, the general setting of the day had their origin in England and Scotland, Ireland and Wales. Carols came from a half-dozen nations, though an expert may detect a French base for many of them. The Christmas tree and Santa Claus made a late journey to the South, as they did to most of America. Arriving in Virginia hardly more than a century ago, they spread steadily to the other states. The region's Christmas of today has a somewhat international flavor—but also a clear Southern accent.

Over a period of years, moving about my native area, I have watched and studied Christmases, listened, and asked questions. I have talked to descendants of Old Dominion colonial families, to Cumberland and Smoky Mountain schoolteachers, to seventy-year-old *bon vivants* of the Carolina rice country, and to twenty-year-old Christmas huntsmen of the cotton belt, to Texas folklorists, to Latin-Southern authorities. At the same time I have worked over diaries and reminiscences and seventeenth- and eighteenth-century manuscripts. During the past five summers in Europe I have talked with people of a dozen countries about the Christmases out of which the Southern holidays have grown. And when I decided to undertake this book I was pleasantly surprised by the amount and the variety of material that was available.

From the earliest days of the nation Southerners regarded Christmas as both a holy day and a holiday—a period both of religious devotion and of general relaxation. It was and is a warming interlude that combined Christianity and older folk practices, many going back to the Druids of the British Isles, to the Middle Europeans of misty memory, to the Romans and the Egyptians, and even further.

When I was six I overheard a family helper tell my father: "I can see sperrits. Me, I was born on Christmas." It was years before I had my first slight doubt regarding the truth of the statement; even now I cannot but feel that if anyone around me does see a spirit, he will be someone who came into the world on that day.

And once a charming, sensitive French neighbor assured me: "This is the night that cattle and horses talk together. At Christmas time they have the gift of tongues. But don't you listen when you pass the stable down the street! If you do, *mon cher*, you'll be dead before the year's out." Even today I am certain that if and when I catch cows having a conversation on the holy evening, I will shut my ears before I run.

The Upper South sometimes sees a white Christmas: flakes glistening on window sills, fields and gardens pale beyond the fences. But in many thousands of miles of the South snow would be a phenomenon to remember for years. To most Southerners the snow man and the sled with ringing bells are only scenes in a book or on a greeting card. To them Christmas is usually a day of rich greenery and blooming flowers, of mild afternoons, and of evenings with the heat turned low. It can be spent on a Mississippi lawn or in a New Orleans courtyard under a banana tree; next to a Texas cactus plant or beside a fragrant tree in Florida, with fan in hand.

Nevertheless, though a red bird may sing in a tree and the sun be as warming as it is in May, it is still Christmas, a Christmas beyond climate, beyond geography. It was in Mobile, on the Alabama shore, on such a day not long ago that a quiet man took out a well-thumbed book and read to a group of us from William Shakespeare's *Hamlet:*

> Some say that ever 'gainst that season comes
> Wherein our Saviour's birth is celebrated,
> The bird of dawning singeth all night long;
> And then, they say, no spirit dare stir abroad;
> The nights are wholesome; then no planets strike,
> No fairy takes, nor witch hath power to charm,
> So hallow'd and so gracious is the time.

# CHAPTER 1

# Virginia: The First Genial Season

> Now Christmas comes, 'tis fit that we
> Should feast and sing, and merry be;
> Keep open house, let fiddlers play.
> A fig for cold, sing care away
> And may they who whereat repine
> On brown bread and on small beer dine.
>
> *Virginia Almanack*

IN Virginia, oldest part of the Old South, you may celebrate the good season in ways that encompass 350 years of Christmas-making—ways as steeped in custom as a Virginia mince pie is in spirits.

You may start the day reverently by attending services, as did the nation's first settlers, in one of several white, tall-spired colonial churches, and go on to observe the rest of the holy day in the genial fashion Virginians embraced from earliest times. If you wish, you can stand in front of a fireplace on Christmas Eve in the onetime capital of Williamsburg and watch the traditional blessing of the Yule log, the biggest and finest to be found in the woods for miles around.

As the log is set afire, you will be told that the flames are "forcing the devil out of the house" for the year ahead. And for this reason, you will be informed, the Yule log must be kept burning brightly all during the Christmas season and never permitted to go out. Perhaps you will be at the fireplace at the end of the Christmas season to help save part of the log for the lighting of the next year's flame.

On Christmas Eve you may cast sprigs of holly into the fireplace; they symbolize the woes of the year, and you will thus banish them from you. Then you will light your Christmas candles from the Yule fire and pour a little wine upon the log to protect the house from ghosts and trailing apparitions.

In all probability you will mark the Virginia Christmas by happily digging your fork into a piece of thick and dripping pie or some other richly caloric dessert, carry-overs from a more ample day of more ample waistlines. Whatever its name, the dish will possibly have been adapted from a "receipt" originally set down by Martha Washington. It was Martha whose directions for the preparation of one of the Old Dominion's classic productions, a "great cake," began: "Take forty eggs. . . ." Today in Virginia people are still taking forty eggs, or fractions thereof, and following Martha's rules.

Several times on Christmas Eve, on December 25, and on later days as well, you will be invited—commanded, perhaps, by enthusiasts—to quaff eggnog prepared from a formula devised by Martha's husband George. Here, beyond question, is a virile drink; the first President not only used both rye and Jamaica or New England rum, but he also added a liberal dollop of mellow sherry for good measure and good fumes. The men of Richmond, of Roanoke, of Charlottesville, and of other Virginia cities still emulate him.

In some Dominion households you may well hear the simplest and most famous of the South's Christmas toasts, the one with which the grave, large-framed Washington saluted those around him. Although professional orators used every toast as an occasion to make the halls ring with grandiloquent summations, rich in similes and metaphors, George Washington simply lifted his glass, let his eyes move from Martha to each of the others at his holiday table, and called out: "All our friends."

Perhaps you will hear these words spoken in a country house before a roaring old-time brick and wooden fireplace. Then you will learn the meaning of the old saying that no Virginia gentleman ever expected to be warm all around at the same time. You toast your front, turn to toast your back, turn your front again, and go slowly on and on, warming one exposure after the other.

If George Washington was the country's father, his state, Virginia, was the mother, not only of Presidents but of the Southern and, indeed, the American Christmas. First inheritor of the English holiday tradition in the New World, she nurtured it while the men of New England tried to stamp out the "pagan mockery" of the holiday observances.

In the mother country of the mid-1600's the reformer Cromwell worked vigorously to "put down" Christmas, penalizing those who sought to celebrate it with the frivolity of feasting and merriment. The Puritans of Massachusetts felt much as he did. They disapproved any special notice of the day, insisting it should be dedicated to work like any other. This mandate was enforced by fines or jail sentences for those who did anything to mark it as an occasion.

Nevertheless, for years a certain number of New Englanders honored the holidays in secret; their Christmas went underground. Later, with the shifting of currents in the old land, the region gradually lessened its opposition. But it was not for a long time—until the nineteenth century was well advanced—that Christmas became a widely popular holiday for the Puritans' descendants.

The Virginians, by contrast, took the light-humored traditions of London and Cornwall and Canterbury and kept them alive—but instituted changes ranging from fireworks to the un-British breakfast course of fried oysters, to the already mentioned eggnog, which many say is more food than drink. In the combination of eggs and cream or milk with vigorous liquors for lift and zest, some have traced a kinship to syllabub, the frothy English beverage which was popular with elderly cousins and members of the weaker sex. Yet let it be noted quickly that true Virginia eggnog is not quite the thing for maiden cousins. . . .

Although the word "cavalier" has been overused and applied too loosely to the early Virginians, it must be said that they certainly did not fit into the Puritan mold. To the New Englander, life was above all earnest. The Virginian knelt solemnly in church, and worked hard running his estate. But then he saw no reason why he should not also have a good time, and he did.

At Christmas he and his family sang carols, feasted at a well-covered board, joked, and danced. In their hands were cheering cups and in their minds the happier aspects of the holidays. From the earliest days to the present, Christmas in Virginia has been a period best described as jovial, with a light, musing note in its eye.

Even in their most cheery hours, however, the early Virginians remembered the holiday in the meager wooden chapel of their fort at Jamestown. The Dominion's first Christmas, in 1607, found fewer than forty of an original hundred alive. Famine, disease, and Indian "warres" had taken the rest; long-promised reinforcements had never materialized. Despite this bleak outlook, the hollow-cheeked men gathered before their Church of England altar and listened to the ancient message: "For unto you is born this day in the City of David a Saviour, which is Christ the Lord."

Absent and in danger was the doughty Captain John Smith, off to trade corn from the Indians, and ultimately to bring back with him, if not love for himself, at least a love story for later romancers. After the Indians killed Smith's aides, they drew up two large stones and placed the Captain's head upon them, so that they could "beate out his brains." At that moment, up darted Pocahontas, favorite of her father, Chief Powhatan, and saved him. And soon the settlers' Christmas prayers would have an answer. Just as they were preparing to give up their fort, ships arrived with the delayed supplies, and Virginia survived.

A year later Smith and his fellows had the Dominion's first real Christmas feast, a gift of the Indians. Calling on one of Powhatan's sons, they enjoyed richer fare than they had known for a long time. A chronicler reported that they were "never more merrie, nor fedde on more plentie of good oysters, fish, flesh, wild foule and good bread; nor never had better fires in England than in the warm smokie houses."

Wild fowl, fish, and oysters for Christmas. . . . This was food well removed from the roasted peacock, "ancient sirloin," and boar's head of the native land. Other differences were to appear as the new civilization expanded along the James and other Tidewater streams. Although critics called the Virginians' to-bacco a "loathsome weed," it emerged as the region's great staple, fixing upon Virginia an expansive scale of life as well as the system of Negro bondage.

People from outside Virginia who came to visit at Christmas time were full of astonishment at the mode of life on the far-spreading estates. "In most articles of life," said one visitor, "a great Virginia planter makes a greater show than a country gentleman in England, on an estate of 3,000 or 4,000 pounds a year." In 1746, the *London Magazine* declared: "All over the Colony, an universal Hospitality reigns; full Tables and open Doors, the kind Salute, the generous Detention, speak somewhat like the old Roast-beef Ages of our Fore-fathers. . . . Strangers are fought after with Greediness, as they pass the Country, to be invited."

Here was a "land of cousins"; practically everybody seemed to be related to everybody else. The colonials liked games as well as family; they liked parties, balls, visits, and hunts; and the year-end holidays were an opportunity to combine them all. More than the gavotte or the other elegant dances they enjoyed the lively Sir Roger de Coverley, which in time took the name of the Virginia reel. Accounts tell of one Virginia gentleman, Richard Lee, who gave a ball that lasted six days. On the seventh, when Lee begged his guests to stay for more fun, they claimed they were "quite wearied out"—a distinctly un-Virginian attitude.

Christmas was a convenient and appropriate season for the gathering of friends, and one ceremony invited another. At an early date the holidays became a favorite time for weddings, of which Virginia saw many. The Tidewater colonials married young and sometimes often. One planter referred to his daughter of nineteen as an "antique virgin," the most antique he knew of. Every widow, of course, was expected to take a second mate.

Virginia set the fashion for one of the South's special ways to mark Christmas, with gunpowder. In England the people rang bells, but in Virginia they turned to firearms to provide a proper noise for the holidays, welcoming the Prince of Peace with resounding blasts. Whereas other parts of the country were to take the Fourth of July as the time for noisemaking and the tossing of firecrackers, to the South of today, as of earlier days, the day for shooting is Christmas.

A Virginia guest often brought his musket with him when he went to pay a call, and joined his host in shooting while the women put their hands over their ears and the children jumped up and down in delight. When a neighbor caught the echo, he took out his own firing piece and answered, and *his* neighbor did the same. This custom was followed so enthusiastically that in time an official proclamation cautioned against the overuse of gunpowder at entertainments. After all, however much Virginians enjoyed themselves, the authorities pointed out, they still had to be prepared for Indians or other emergencies!

A French traveler of the 1680's received what he called "royal" treatment from William Fitzhugh of Stafford County. The Christmas period had arrived, and "there was good wine and all kinds of beverages, so there was a great deal of carousing. He [Fitzhugh] had sent for three fiddlers, a jester, a tightrope dancer, an acrobat who tumbled around," and, adds the Frenchman by way of understatement, "they gave us all the entertainment one could wish for." After telling them good-by, Fitzhugh added a truly royal finishing touch by sending wine and a punch bowl to the shore to help his guests on their way.

By the end of the seventeenth century Williamsburg had become the vice-regal capital of the Tidewater version of England. Planters rode there for the winter or at least the Christmas season, enlivening their days with grand balls at the Raleigh Tavern. America's first theater drew women in silks and voluminous skirts, men in powdered wigs and satin; and attendants in livery jostled an occasional Indian or simple farmer on his progress through the streets.

In his "secret diaries" William Byrd II of Westover pictures a progression of extended holiday visits from friend to friend, combining religion with an appreciation of life's amenities. On the holy day of 1709, Byrd's party ate broiled turkey for breakfast and went to church, where he "received the Sacrament with great devoutness." In the evening "we were merry with nonsense and so were my servants. I said my prayers shortly and had good health, good thoughts and good humor, thanks be to God Almighty." During many Christmas holidays his circle played billiards, drank wine, played cards, "slid and skated on the ice," enjoyed "turkey and chine," or pork, "roast apples and wine," and repeated sessions with wild goose, boiled beef, partridges, roast beef, spareribs, "tongue and udder," goose giblets, turkey and oysters, venison pastry, roast venison, minced mutton, salt fish and eggs, mutton stew, broiled pigeon, boiled pigeon and bacon, and assorted other combinations.

People of the Old Dominion also took greenery to their churches, transforming them in appearance and introducing the fresh scents of the forest. Now and then, however, the "green church Christmas" made outsiders gape. In 1712, for instance, *The Spectator* commented brightly on one interior, noting that the middle aisle resembled a "very pretty shady walk, and the pews look like so many arbours on each side of it. The pulpit itself has such clusters of ivy, holly and rosemary about it that a light fellow in our pew took occasion to say that the congregation heard the 'Word out of the bush, like Moses.' "

The colonial holiday had certain clear differences from the present one. Christmas then was a succession of observances that went on without letup from December 15 to January 6. Christmas itself was not December 25, but January 5, according to the old church calendar; it was not until about 1750 that the date was changed to the December one. For years thereafter, however, many refused to accept the alteration, and even today a number of Southerners still insist that the "real Christmas" falls on January 5.

Whatever its precise date, Christmas in the colonial period was not a day of great gift-giving. For the children there were a few toys, none of them elaborate; for the adults a generous good wish, a kiss, or a handclasp would do. Not until the 1800's did the Virginians and other Southerners take part in the custom of exchanging presents. To them the time was intended mainly for reweaving the threads of friendship; it was a season for the warming of hearts about the big fires.

Curiously, the best picture of a colonial Virginia Christmas was given by a Princeton-trained divinity student. Young Philip Vickers Fithian had heard that Virginians were "wicked" and careless in many things, and in 1773, with some trepidation, he took a place as tutor in the home of "King" Robert Carter of Nomini Hall, Westmoreland County.

At first, it is evident, Mr. Fithian blinked at the scale of life; the Carter properties were made up of a dozen or more estates, and combined nearly 75,000 acres. The suggestions of frivolity disturbed Mr. Fithian, too. Yet he came to admire Robert Carter as a man of learning and unfamiliar generosity, and before long the divinity student was drawn into a vivid life of barbecues and "fish-feats," boating days, races, and cotillions. Although Mr. Fithian himself never danced, on the Saturday before Christmas he went with the Carters and their friends from breakfast to the dancing room.

There were several Minuets danced with great ease and propriety; after which the whole company Joined in country-dances, and it was indeed beautiful to admiration, to see such a number of young persons, set off by dress to the best Advantage, moving easily, to the sound of well-performed Music, and with perfect regularity, though apparently in the utmost Disorder—The Dance continued til two, we dined at half after three—soon after Dinner we repaired to the Dancing-Room again. . . . When it grew too dark to dance, the young Gentlemen walked over to my Room, we conversed til half after six; nothing is now to be heard of in conversation, but the *Balls,* the *Foxhunts,* the fine Entertainments, and the good fellowship, which are to be exhibited. . . .

After the candles were lighted, all of them returned to the dancing room, where it was proposed that the young people play "Button, to get Pauns for Redemption." While he still did not dance, Mr. Fithian could find his way to a pair of waiting lips; "in the course of redeeming my Pauns, I had several Kisses of the Ladies!" Then followed supper in the dining room, "luminous and splendid" with "four very large candles burning on the table where he supp'd, three others in different parts of the Room; a gay, sociable Assembly, and four well-instructed waiters. . . ." Afterward came more games, with or without kisses, until ten, when the play day ended.

By this time the old English Christmas custom of "barring out" of teachers had arrived in Virginia, where it continued to be practiced for years. At William and Mary College at Williamsburg it flourished for some time, now and then to the fury of the faculty. At another plantation Mr. Fithian discovered that the tutor was "barred out" of school from December 13 to January 6. Being of a "more quiet nature," Fithian's own scholars demanded only four days off.

On December 24 the divinity student wrote: "Guns are fired this Evening in the Neighborhood, and the Negroes seem to be inspired with new Life." In the morning more gun blasts sounded all around the house. Nelson, the boy who made Fithian's fires, blacked his shoes, and did his errands, arrived early, made a "vast" blaze, set the room vigorously in order, and "wish'd me a joyful Christmas, for which I gave him half a bit." Nelson was followed by another Negro who usually made the fire in the schoolrooms; today the second man made "three or four profound Bows," expressed the same wishes, and waited for the same amount.

Next the slave who did Mr. Fithian's clothes sent a message for "a Christmas Box" or a small gift, and to him the tutor passed on a bit. The barber who shaved and dressed him also made an appearance, as did Tom, the coachman, who looked after Mr. Fithian's horse, and Dennis, the boy who waited on table. When he had given his gifts, the teacher joined the rest of the family for Christmas wishes, and at 4 P.M. the main meal was served. It was no more elaborate than usual, and still "as elegant a Christmas Dinner as I ever sat down to."

More parties, more invitations until January 6, and all in all it was a holiday season Mr. Fithian would never forget. When finally he left "King" Carter's estate, it was with expressions of regard and friendship and a promise to return, which, alas, he could not keep. He became a chaplain in the Revolutionary forces and died of exposure.

Among those Mr. Fithian met during his Virginia Christmas were a "Colonel Washington" and his wife, a couple for whom the season would always have a special significance. For they were united in marriage just as the Old Dominion's observance of the long holidays reached its end on Old Christmas (or Twelfth Night) of 1759. The scene of this event was White House, home of the widowed Martha Dandridge Custis. From the efficient Martha's smokehouse came a selection of the best hams. From the nearby waters came succulent oysters. Before the fireplace servants turned and basted enormous roasts of beef and pork on the wide spits. From the cellar came jams, jellies, and condiments. And during the last week before the holiday the mistress superintended the choice of spirits for punches and toddies, the molding of quavery desserts, the baking of rich, cream-filled, fruit-filled cakes and thickly packed pies without which no Christmas or Christmas-time wedding would be considered complete.

The great and near-great rode up to the Widow Custis's White House, alone, in pairs, and in parties, in carriages or on horseback. Years later an elderly servant recalled this holiday of holidays: "Many of the grandest gentlemen, in their gold laces, were at the wedding, but none looked like the man himself. . . . Never see'd the like, sir; never the likes of him, though I have seen many in my day; so tall, so straight! and then he sat a horse and rode with such an air!"

The next Christmas was, for the Washingtons—George, Martha, and Martha's children by her first marriage—the first of a long series of holidays to be spent at Squire George's family property on the Potomac. While at the time Mount Vernon was not one of the most imposing estates of the area—it was embellished later in the owner's life—it had a superb view of the river, and at Christmas the valley and the distant residences could be seen in a white-clad beauty.

Christmas always found George Washington enjoying one of Virginia's favorite holiday occupations—the hunt. For several centuries Virginians have considered this season one of the best times to chase the fox and to track down various kinds of game. During the Christmas period sporting guests arrived at Mount Vernon from Virginia and nearby Maryland on visits "not of days, but weeks," as Washington's grandson wrote. Since the hunt started at daybreak, the planter and his guests had to have breakfast by candlelight.

The holiday sportsmen were off before cock's crow, Washington riding "with ease, elegance and with power." His grandson never forgot him, "always superbly mounted, in true sporting costume, of bluecoat, scarlet waistcoat, buckskin breeches, top boots, velvet cap and whip with long thorn." The chase ending, the band would return to the house, and about the table members would talk over the deeds of the leading dog and the best horse.

By then Martha had her part of the Christmas ready, and over Mount Vernon there crept evidences of the delights that awaited the guests. Old Virginians say that if you lost all your senses except the sense of smell, you would still be able to tell when Christmas came near. Past and present, Virginia Yuletides descended on waves of a wonderful redolence: a union of the earthy and the exotic, of richly ripe and freshly plucked; of mellowed spirits and sharp spices and crystallized fruits, of nutmeg and steaming mincemeat, of chestnut and oyster dressings, and cakes still warm and puffed from their pans. One man summed it up as "the joyous fumes of Christmas."

Thirteen such holidays passed at Mount Vernon, until war with England broke over the colonies, and the conflict separated Martha and the new commander of the American armies. They tried to be together for Christmas, but on the historic December 25 of 1776 they were far from each other. It was then, at one of the lowest points in the revolutionists' fight, that Washington faced large forces of German mercenaries along the Delaware.

After dark on that Christmas Day, George Washington took a crucial step. Crossing the stream with its bobbing ice blocks, he scored a complete surprise and a vital success. There is another Christmas tale here; according to a number of accounts, the Germans in the British army were observing the holiday in the style of their homeland, with the Teutonic Christmas tree that was not to be adopted in Virginia until many years later.

Nor could Martha be with her husband on the still grimmer holiday of 1777, when destruction approached yet closer. At Valley Forge in this season of good will, Washington's men lay in tatters, shivering and hungry, and mutiny threatened while Congress acted as if it had become the General's enemy. Yet

Washington and his men held on, and the crisis passed. On other Christmases Martha managed to spend more or less tranquil days with George in Cambridge, Philadelphia, and elsewhere. Then the war was won, and toward dusk on Christmas Eve of 1783 the conquering soldier rode home to Mount Vernon for the best holiday he and his family were ever to know.

Bonfires lighted up the slope of the hill, and the Negroes celebrated by firing again and again into the air. After a quick inspection of his home, Washington went to bed early. Rising at 4 A.M., he gave his property a more thorough examination, looking into his stables and kennels. He returned to hear high-pitched cries from his young grandchildren—Martha's sons' offspring—and to shake hands with the attendants from the quarters, to each of whom he gave several shillings.

That day, despite harsh weather, neighbors arrived in a long file to present their warm wishes. Three P.M. brought dinner with well-cured Virginia hams, pork and beef, fish, duck, a superb turkey, and that other favorite food, oysters. It was a gathering part gay, part solemn. So much had happened . . . but now they were all together again after so many Christmases. . . . In the candlelight, and under the influence of the hour, the atmosphere relaxed, and then George Washington rose and offered his heartfelt toast: "All our friends."

Today thousands visit the shining estate of Mount Vernon at the Christmas season, and gaze from the windows or from the long porch over the sweep of the valley. Like the Washingtons, they sometimes behold a crystalline scene of half-hidden trees and a white grandeur that spreads over the Potomac below them. And this, as much as anything else, is Christmas in Virginia.

## CHAPTER 2

# A New Tree Grows in Virginia

JUST off the green in Williamsburg, the skilfully restored colonial capital of Virginia, stands a rambling house with an enormous buttressed chimney, so constructed that it seems to be a series of residences with three roof lines at descending levels. This is the Tucker home. At Christmas, when the snow falls and its wooden fence, its trees and bushes and dormer windows are dusted with a softening white, its simplicity and its air of days long past are particularly emphasized, and it looks much as it must have looked to people of the late 1700's and early 1800's.

Only a short distance from the house, at each Christmas season, Williamsburg erects its community tree which shines during the day and glitters at night against a background of imposing red-brick official structures and neat frame dwellings. There is a connection between the tall tree and the snug Tucker home. For a hundred and fifteen years ago there occurred within its walls an incident which, as much as any other, gave form to the holiday celebration in the Southern United States.

The chief figure in this incident was a young man who, more than any other single person, set a Christmas style that has continued in the South to this day. He was a member of that Teutonic race once so hated by Virginians, and he came to Williamsburg from a grim German prison cell.

When Charles Frederic Ernest Minnegerode arrived in Virginia in the early 1840's, he was an obscure youth who seemed to have little future. Soft-spoken, unforceful, he was an intellectual, and this breed has always been lightly regarded in the United States. Minnegerode came from Hesse-Darmstadt, the region that had produced the Hessian mercenaries who fought for England against the rebellious colonists in the previous century. But Charles Minnegerode, lean, sharp featured, somewhat unprepossessing, was one of those Middle Europeans who moved to America because they saw here a liberty denied in their homelands by the autocracy of their day.

Like many others, young Minnegerode had felt the club of officialdom. When he was nineteen or twenty, a student at the University of Geissen, he was arrested for membership in a society that took part in a political uprising. For five years he was either in prison or held under state control. For eighteen months he was kept without trial in a dungeon where he was brutally treated. When the scholarly boy's health failed, the government allowed him to return to his family. But the official surveillance continued and for a long time the only reading matter permitted him was the Bible. If only because of this, he developed a deep and abiding interest in spiritual matters.

Eventually the government dropped its charges against him, and Charles Minnegerode left his native land. He arrived in America with little more than the Bible he always carried with him and a much-thumbed set of the classics. He stayed in Philadelphia for a short while; then he heard of an opportunity to teach the classic tongues in Virginia, at William and Mary, the pioneer school in Williamsburg which had, as we know, figured in the early Christmas "barring out" of its faculty.

For Minnegerode, no doors were barred in 1842. As professor of Greek and Latin, he made a fine impression on the town and on his colleagues. The gentle young man showed a great feeling for children, and soon he was a favorite caller at the home of elderly Judge Nathaniel Beverly Tucker, professor of law at the college. To the Tuckers Minnegerode became "Minck," a friend who told stirring stories of castles and enchantments and of the events of olden days.

Among his tales must have been several about the peculiarly German institution of the decorated Christmas tree. Doubtless he described the night everything in creation, including the trees, went to the Stable to pay homage to the infant Jesus. The olive bent to present its green fruit, the palm offered its, but a small fir tree stood sadly apart. What had it to give the Christ Child?

Seeing the poor fir's sorrow, the story continued, some of the stars felt pity and descended to the earth to settle among its branches. As they glistened there they caught the eyes of the Child, who called out in gleeful pleasure. And ever since then, according to the tale, the evergreen has been a symbol of man's appreciation of Christ at the holy season.

With that belief went another, the warming story which told how on the night of Christ's birth every tree and bush in the world suddenly burst into bloom or gave forth its fruit. Even in the icy areas of northern Germany, the snow melted away and the branches shone forth in a glory of green. . . .

Charles Minnegerode almost certainly told the Tucker children the tale of the poor German forester who heard a faint sound outside his cabin on Christmas Eve. When he went out to investigate, he found a small boy, hungry, almost frozen. Though the man himself had very little, he took the child in and gave him food; his own son slept on the hard floor so that the child could have his bed. In the morning the family heard a soft singing everywhere about them, and when they opened their eyes they saw a strange light over the house. Their guest had been the young Christ. . . . In leaving, He had seized a fir branch and set it in the ground, where it swiftly sprouted.

Minck was a Lutheran, and he spoke, too, of Martin Luther, who, it was said, brought the Christmas tree into German homes in the 1500's. Walking toward his own house on a snowy Christmas Eve, Luther had halted at the sight of the stars glittering through the branches of a fir. The view reminded him of the shining night when Christ was born. Arriving at his door, Luther cut down a small fir, brought it inside, and placed candles on it, so that it gleamed as had the one in the woods.

And so it was, the young teacher explained, that his people still decorated their trees at Christmas as a symbol of the great hour when the evergreens glowed in the night. In Germany Christmas was not only a time of deep religious meaning but of family happiness as well. "A feast of the heart," one man called this Christmas gathering about the glowing tree, and others described it as *"Der glückliche Abend,"* the Happy Evening.

As Christmas approached in this Virginia winter of 1842, Charles Minnegerode felt a touch of sadness. He had been one of a large and affectionate family; what would his father, his brothers and sisters be doing now? Suddenly an idea came to him and he sought out Judge Tucker. Might he give a little holiday party for the children, one such as the rest of the Minnegerodes would be enjoying in Germany? The Judge agreed, gladly.

Among the small-town or rural Germans of Pennsylvania, it seems fairly certain, the tree had been introduced at an earlier date; and here and there scattered accounts indicate that ornamented firs were set up in other parts of America—one at Fort Dearborn as early as 1804; another, not long afterward, in Cambridge; and later in such places as Philadelphia, Cincinnati, and Rochester. And among small German settlements in Virginia and Maryland others might have been erected without record or comment. But by and large the South knew little or nothing of this beautiful custom.

Charles Minnegerode rode out to the nearest wood and returned with a tall fir, which he carried, probably with some help, through the entranceway and into the parlor of the Tuckers' pleasant white residence. The neighbors raised their eyebrows; a tree *in* the house? Once he had set it up, the teacher had a problem. Where in Williamsburg, or indeed anywhere else in Virginia, was he to find the objects that should go on a Christmas tree—the shining glass globes, the tinseled ornaments?

The German youth and the Tucker children improvised. Their eyes went to the puffy white popcorn that was being prepared for the season. Why not string that in loops and hang it like tinsel? Somewhere in the house they found yellow and red paper, out of which they formed globes to use instead of the traditional glass balls. In the dining room someone confiscated a bowl of nuts, which, gilded, added another kind of brightness.

Now the lights, to illuminate the whole. "There were no devices to clip the candles to the trees," a cousin recalled years later, "and it was done by twisting pieces of wire." Finally the enthusiastic Minck hung a gilded star at the top, and the tree was ready. It became a sensation among both the Tucker children and the adults; their excitement spread to the neighbors and in time to the whole town. "The dear old judge," the cousin said, "enjoyed it as much as we did." And so did little Mrs. Tucker.

The people of Williamsburg asked if they could bring their children to look at this strange and wonderful thing. Country folk knocked: Couldn't they have a peep from the door?

On Christmas Eve, under the teacher's direction, the Tucker family, children and adults, grouped around the tree and sang carols. Minck arranged games like those the German children played, and recited more stories of the tree's meaning. Judge Tucker, beaming, handed out refreshments to the young visitors, who were now pouring into the house.

Sarah Agnes Rice, a young family connection who had heard mysterious reports about the pending display, was present on the great occasion. She wrote of the small basket of candies about the tree, each with a name attached, "enriched with an original rhyming jest of sentiment," for the young ones. "A tree for the children. . . ." The Southern Christmas had taken a new turn, centering more than ever on the young members of the household. And, as in Germany, the holiday had yet another orientation—a family one—which gave it a new focus and a new unity. From now on the tree was in the Virginia towns to stay. Judge Tucker carried out the custom every year thereafter until his death; the Tuckers who followed him continued it.

Recently, Dr. Janet Kimbrough, great-granddaughter of Judge Tucker, told of the way Christmas has been kept through five generations in the Tucker House. In a Christmas card which takes the form of a booklet, Dr. Kimbrough describes the times when, as a child, she watched the pine tree arrive days early for the holidays. It was put up immediately, "as there was no furnace heat to wither it," and once it was erected, there began the serious task of decorating it.

The Tucker household had many special Christmas-tree ornaments—"the spun glass swan, the dog carrying a golden basket in his mouth, and the beautiful bunch of green grapes which came from Germany to hang on my mother's tree when she was little." Her father insisted that tinsel must never be wrapped carelessly, "any old way." The yards and yards of shimmering rope he gathered "must be hung just right." Through a keyhole the children watched, and when the last tinsel ribbon was in place, they knew the great event was almost upon them.

Although they still could not enter the Christmas room, they had their holiday tasks. "We could fill the green and red tarlatan bags with hard candies, and as soon as I was old enough, it was my special delight to fill two bowls of the best china with whipped cream." All this was preparation for the Christmas Eve tree party, mainly for the children, with the adults in discreet supervision.

At dusk the Tucker House children, wearing their finest clothes, "waited in almost unbearable expectancy" for the first guest. She was usually their next-door neighbor, whom they had seen only an hour or so earlier; even so, Susanne Garrett's arrival was an event. Soon after Susanne the other children and adults poured in. The men repaired to the Christmas room, where each received a long stick with a stub at one end, for lighting the many candles, and a sponge at the other, to extinguish any accidental blaze.

As Dr. Kimbrough observed: "We have lost something now, when we substitute electric lights for candles, but we have somewhat escaped the constant threat of fire." In the corners of the Christmas room there were buckets of water, and one of the fathers took a place nearby in case of emergency.

As soon as all the guests had arrived, the children were lined up, the youngest in front. One of the older boys or girls began the traditional: "Hark! The Herald Angels Sing," the doors swung open, and the magnificence of the Christmas tree stood before them, the scent of its greenery filling the air. Then the children marched forward and made a circle around the tree, holding hands as they looked up. "Whenever, wherever I hear

Mendelssohn's music for that hymn," Dr. Kimbrough declared, "I can shut my eyes and smell fresh pine."

As the children grew older they were allowed to go into the dining room with their parents for "hot chocolate and poker rolls, after the tree," and their places in the march were taken by new youngsters, who would halt in wide-eyed amazement before the glory of the tree, "or grab delightedly at the many mechanical toys which my father set going under it."

After a time Janet was leading the march again, but now her son, the youngest at the party, held onto her hand. When her daughter arrived, Janet escorted her; and a year or two later Susanne Garrett, once the little girl next door, brought her David who received the place of honor as newest child. As the years passed the "children of the tree" left Williamsburg for many distant points. "Those who were far away, I like to think, still returned in spirit to celebrate. . . ."

And many reappeared in person at the Tucker House. "We came, on Christmas Eve, from Norfolk, from Richmond, from Charlottesville. We came, not to a house, not to a family, not for a party, but more as one might go on a pilgrimage, a pilgrimage back to childhood, where the Christmas tinsel shines more brightly than silver, and the angels' song is really true—'Peace on earth, good will to men.' "

Meanwhile Charles Minnegerode's Christmas tree had spread from Williamsburg to other places in Virginia, from one town to the next. And four years after Minck's first Christmas another German made Southern holiday history. August Bodeker, who had arrived in Richmond only recently from the old country, faced his first December in the strange land, and he, too, thought wistfully of the customs at home.

Without announcing his intentions to anyone, Mr. Bodeker one evening set up a tree in the front part of his store, and decorated it with candles and ornaments. The children who came to see it, alone or with their parents, halted in silent wonder at the shimmering sight. From that time forward Richmond has never been without its Christmas trees.

Like the holiday itself in earlier periods, the ornamented tree was held in disrepute for some centuries and regarded as pagan and unchristian. The tree's origin, like that of various other Christmas customs, goes back to the days before recorded history when ancient races worshiped trees as spirits and set meats and other foods in their branches as offerings. Today students of folklore consider the attaching of gifts and other objects to the Christmas trees as unconscious survivals of these sacrifices.

The Druids favored their chief god by placing lighted candles on their trees, and by adding gilded apples and cakes. During their Saturnalia the Romans similarly illuminated the branches of trees. Even after the spread of Christianity many people retained the old practices and, after some hesitation, churchmen permitted the decorated tree. Yet some, both Catholic and Protestant, protested its use, or at least the way in which many eager people embraced it.

Before 1750 a minister of Strasbourg, in Alsace, declared, "Among other trifles with which the people often occupy the Christmas time more than with God's word, is also the Christmas or fir tree, which they erect in a house and hang with dolls and sugar. . . . Where the custom comes from, I know not. It is a bit of child's play. Far better were it for the children to be dedicated to the spiritual cedar tree, Jesus Christ."

Nevertheless, the lighted, ornamented tree advanced over Europe, to Alsace, Finland, Sweden, and Denmark. Princess Henriette put up Vienna's first tree in 1816, and other Austrians followed suit. Thirty-five years later, another German princess, Helene of Mecklenburg, brought it to Paris. In England, individual Germans had small trees for their intimate circles, but the custom gained little attention, until 1841, just a year before the tree appeared in Williamsburg. Albert, Queen Victoria's consort, gave the German style of tree to his new country.

About this time, too, the South, like the rest of the United States and England, was responding to the influence of another phenomenon, Mr. Charles Dickens. More than any other person in history, Dickens spread a general affection for Christmas and gave it an emphasis that proved meaningful for millions. The Englishman wrote of the season as it had never been presented before. Southerners were stirred when they read "A Christmas Carol," which first appeared in the early 1840's, and were moved as well by the holiday references in *Pickwick Papers, Sketches by Boz,* and other works. Around the plantation fires and in the towns thousands read, reread, quoted, and requoted his evocative passages:

I am sure I have always thought of Christmas time, when it has come around—apart from the veneration due to its sacred name and origin, if anything belonging to it can be apart from that—as a good time: a kind, forgiving, charitable, pleasant time: the only time I know of in the long calendar of the year, when men and women seem by one consent to open their shut-up hearts freely, and to think of people below them as if they really were fellow-passengers to the grave, and not another race of creatures bound on other journeys. And therefore . . . though it has never put a scrap of gold or silver in my pocket, I believe it has done me good; and I say, God bless it.

Certain individuals might have found irony here. For in many parts of the South those who applauded the liberal Dickens were members of a feudal group. And the irony was intensified by the fact that some called Dickens a revolutionist for his attacks on the abuses of his day—the power of great wealth and privilege, the debasing want that he observed about him. But the Southerners saw other aspects of Dickens' writings, his stress upon the warm cheer of the season, the close family life, and his pictures of such traditions as the wassail bowl:

They sat down by the huge fireplace of burning logs and a mighty bowl of wassail. Something smaller than an ordinary washhouse copper, in which the hot apples were hissing and bubbling with a rich look and a jolly sound that were perfectly irresistible. . . .

The Southerners welcomed Dickens' emphasis on family life, too, for the way in which they lived developed continuous ties of close relationship. They sighed over Scrooge, his prevision of a forgotten grave, and his change of spirit: "I will honour Christmas in my heart and try to keep it all the year." Here, and in his other works, the Englishman made many converts, at least for a time, as he pleaded for a lessening of human selfishness and a greater realization of human brotherhood.

Through the years countless thousands of Southerners have repeated favorite Dickens passages such as the one from *Sketches by Boz:*

There seems a magic in the very name of Christmas. Petty jealousies and discords are forgotten; social feelings are awakened in bosoms to which they have long been strangers; father and son, or brother and sister, who have met and passed with averted gaze, or a look of cold recognition, for months before, proffer and return the cordial embrace, and bury their past animosities in their cordial happiness. Kindly hearts that have yearned towards each other, but have been withheld by false notions of pride and self-dignity, are again reunited, and all is kindness and benevolence! Would that Christmas lasted the whole year through (as it ought), and that the prejudices and passions which deform our better nature, were never called into action among those to whom they should ever be strangers.

For others the favorite was Dickens' description of "A Christmas Tree," a masterwork of simple description:

There were rosy-cheeked dolls, hiding behind the green leaves; there were real watches (with movable hands, at least, and an endless capacity of being wound up) dangling from innumerable twigs; there were French polished tables, chairs, bedsteads, wardrobes, eight-day clocks, and various other articles of domestic furniture (wonderfully made, in tin, at Wolverhampton), perched among the boughs, as if in preparation for some fairy house-keeping; there were jolly, broad-faced little men, much more agreeable in appearance than many real men—and no wonder, for their heads took off, and showed them to be of full of sugar-plums; there were fiddles and drums; there were tambourines, books, work-boxes, paint-boxes, sweetmeat-boxes, peep-show boxes, all kinds of boxes; there were trinkets for the elder girls, far brighter than any grown-up gold and jewels; there were baskets and pincushions in all devices; there were guns, swords, and banners; there were witches standing in enchanted rings of pasteboard, to tell fortunes; there were teetotums, humming-tops, needle-cases, pen-wipers, smelling-bottles, conversation-cards, bouquet-holders; real fruit, made artificially dazzling with gold leaf; imitation apples, pears and walnuts, crammed with surprises; in short as a pretty child before me, delightedly whispered to another pretty child, her bosom friend: "There was everything, and more."...

Another literary Britisher, Sir Walter Scott, had an enormous vogue in the South. His pageantry of lords and ladies, of tournaments and chivalry, had a wide appeal in the region, so wide that critics of a later period were to describe the South as "Walter Scott-land." Scott also celebrated Christmas with ripely detailed descriptions of baronial halls, ceremonial toastings, and the much-heralded appearances of the boar's head. In Christmas matters, however, Dickens remained the Southerners' ideal. In time he grew to personify the good season, so that eventually the story, half funny, half sad, could be told of one young man's reaction to word that he had breathed his last. "Is Mr. Dickens dead? And will Father Christmas die, too?" But in the South of the mid-1800's and later, both Mr. Dickens and Father Christmas were more alive than ever.

Today in Williamsburg the Christmas customs of two hundred years ago have been revived for visitors and townspeople. Some may smile at the contrast of modern furs and topcoats with the powdered wigs and wide skirts of colonial days, but there are few places which evoke so well the spirit and atmosphere of a long-dimmed American past.

Annually the town presents a re-enactment of scenes of "hospitality and good cheer," for a full fortnight of holidays in the Yuletide atmosphere of George Washington's time, and the time, also, of Dr. Minnigerode and Judge Tucker.

A number of historic structures open their doors for Williamsburg's Christmas. One is the Wythe House, a building of striking design, dating back to 1755, with ancient brick work and a hipped roof. Here lived George Wythe, "first professor of law in America," who taught Thomas Jefferson, James Monroe, John Marshall, and Henry Clay. It was in Wythe's home that Washington made his headquarters before the Yorktown siege; and it was here, too, that the good Mr. Wythe was poisoned by his nephew. The latter was to be Wythe's heir and, as the people of Williamsburg say, he was an "impatient" fellow.

Every year Williamsburg has a "Dr. Wythe's Christmas party" at which, it is declared, the only one who does not come forth is the erudite Wythe himself. In the parlor a string ensemble, dressed in costume, plays hymns and carols, while guests sip punch made from a colonial "receipt."

Williamsburg's children open the holidays with a "Singing Candles" procession which starts the "white lighting" of the capital on December 20 of each year. From the tall palace gates the young Virginians march down the Palace Green in a candle-light progression to the Williamsburg Inn. Symbolically they "carry the flame to their homes," for candles are lighted as they pass by each window along old Duke of Gloucester Street.

All the Williamsburg buildings are hung with garlands, and wreaths decorated with cones and holly berries ornament doorways on all sides. Flames crackle in many fireplaces, and inns and homes and government structures alike glow with candles as they did in an earlier era. The Capitol and the widely known Wren building of the College of William and Mary glow with a holiday greeting.

Back in 1724 the Reverend Hugh Jones stood before the old Palace and, stirred by its beauty, remarked upon "the orna-mental addition of a good Cupola or Lanthorn, illuminated with most of the town, upon Birthnight and other nights of occa-sional Rejoicings." Today, as in the minister's day, the "lan-thorn" shines over Williamsburg.

During the Christmas season in Williamsburg there are re-ligious services in Bruton Parish Church, built in 1710-15, and said to be the oldest Episcopal church in continuous use in America. A range of other events take place morning, after-noon, and night. They embrace Christmas caroling by craftsmen in old-time dress; a pre-Christmas Mistletoe Dance; Christmas concerts, the firing of Christmas guns, an open house at the Capitol; candlelight musical programs at the Governor's Palace Ballroom; visits to plantations, re-enactments of such colonial sports as bowling, cudgeling, fencing, foot races, wrestling, jug-gling, hoop races, and "acrobatics."

The festivities also include the spirited Yule log observance. But for many the ceremony with highest meaning takes place on Christmas Eve, when a community tree is lighted near the Tucker home. Then the people of Williamsburg tell once more

the story of the young German who suffered persecution in his
homeland, and coming to Virginia, found his freedom and made
a unique contribution.

At twilight on New Year's Day there are fireworks and the
ceremonial burning of a bonfire of discarded Christmas trees.
Many Virginians believe that the trees must stand no longer
than New Year's, though others favor their continuation for a
few more days. Christmas time itself continues in the town with
a Twelfth Night festival and, on January 5, an Epiphany dinner
at which Epiphany Pie is cut.

The verse from the *Virginia Almanack* sums up the festival,
and neatly:

> When New Year's Day is past and gone;
> Christmas is with some people done;
> But further some will it extend,
> And at Twelfth Day their Christmas end.
> Some people stretch it further yet,
> At Candlemas they finish it.
> The gentry carry it further still
> And finish it just when they will;
> They drink good wine and eat good cheer
> And keep their Christmas all the Year.

# CHAPTER 3

# *Turkey and Sauerkraut*

BALTIMORE, early home of the proprietary lords, is the center of a sturdy English heritage. Yet the metropolis by the Patapsco River has also nurtured a holiday season with a difference—a German accent.

In no other Southern city, as far as I know, do the older natives ask for and get turkey with sauerkraut at Christmas time. "Why," a handsome matron blinked in surprise when I said that the combination seemed somewhat unusual, "don't you have it where you come from? It's a pretty nice dish."

Many other Baltimoreans agree with her. Frederick P. Stieff, the city's gourmet, put it this way: "Sauerkraut and turkey have long been inseparable on the Maryland table—perhaps not quite as inseparable as ham and eggs, pork and beans, and Damon and Pythias, but certainly gastronomically harmonious." When it was first presented to me, I approached the dish somewhat warily: at the end of the meal, however, I discovered that I was in warm agreement with the townfolk on its merits.

Baltimore reflects its German influence in another way; apparently it was the South's first Santa Claus metropolis. Before most of the other cities of the Upper or Lower South had even heard of the Teutonic St. Nicholas, Baltimore's children were enjoying that gentleman's appearance and helping to create what has since become a major American tradition. In much of Maryland, Santa, kraut, and turkey are all but inseparable.

Baltimore, from its earliest days a city of brick houses with neat white stoops, ornamented doorways, and mullioned dormer windows, has long had that English air. Nevertheless, as Francis F. Beirne pointed out, "If the Germans were not in at the birth they were not far behind." For the Teutonic groups who would give their names and their tastes to much of Baltimore and its environs came early to the city and the rural areas around it.

A Maryland governor of the 1750's made clear his lack of enthusiasm for these Germans; to him they were only unimportant men—weavers, craftsmen, cobblers—who could make no contribution to the development of a great colony. But he was wrong; these men were to play a large part in building the new city, and a number of them would have important roles in later years. They arrived in thick streams from abroad—from Catholic Bavaria in the south of Germany, from the Protestant north, from Munich and Hamburg and Nuremburg. Many of those who came in the mid-1800's, like Charles Minnegerode of Williamsburg, were men of intellect, fleeing injustice and repression. Before 1890 an estimated quarter of the white Baltimoreans had German backgrounds.

Trade between the Baltimore Germans and the German or Dutch elements of Pennsylvania began early and thrived for generations. The old-time Conestoga wagons swung steadily back and forth, carrying not only commodities but also a continuing Teutonic influence—language, traditions, folk practices.

As a result, Baltimore adopted Santa Claus long before he became part of the life of any other Southern city. For decades the German children talked of "old Nikolaus," his annual coming and what it meant. After a time stories of Nicholas spread among the non-Germans, and the young Anglo-Saxons shared him with his original Maryland followers.

But the Baltimoreans knew a Santa Claus rather different from the figure of present-day America; Nicholas has been a man of several faces, whose personality and purpose have changed with his stay in the New World. The Santa of today is in part an American contribution.

For there once was a true Santa, not the rotund, easygoing character of the past hundred years or so, but a Christian bishop of the East—St. Nicholas. Born in Asia Minor in the fourth century, he was known for his many generous deeds, for his acts of kindly help to those around him. He became a bishop when he was still a young man, and was credited with a series of miracles.

He also figures in numerous legends. According to one oft-told story, the good Nicholas, learning of an impoverished minor nobleman, whose three daughters lacked dowries and could not marry, decided to go to their aid and dropped three bags of gold—one for each girl—through a window.

One of the bags, the tale goes, fell into a stocking by mistake, and from that beginning developed the custom of hanging up stockings. The incident of the gold bags provided Nicholas with a symbol: three gold balls. Not only was he the patron of the pawnbrokers of the world, but he became the protector of the young, of travelers, of sailors—and of pirates as well.

Nicholas' fame spread over Europe, to Russia, Lapland, and the Arctic, where, many children were convinced, he lived; around the world countless churches bear his name. Two countries gave him special attention. To the Germans he was St. Nikolaus, to the Dutch Sinterklaas. He arrived in America with both groups and his followers settled in New York City, in Pennsylvania, and, not least, in Baltimore.

But when he first came here, St. Nicholas was still a citizen of the Old World, not a jolly, pink-cheeked sprite, but a lean, pale ascetic, carrying a dark miter and the staff of a bishop. And in Baltimore and New York and Pennsylvania he appeared, not on Christmas Eve, but on the eve of December 6, the date of his death.

For Baltimore children his arrival was always a matter of excited speculation, and of some anxiety as well. The St. Nicholas of the 1700's and early 1800's was no simple figure of benevolence. He gave the children presents only if they deserved them; if they had been naughty, they got punishments or at least sharp threats.

He brought not only smiles and presents with him, but also a set of switches, perhaps to be used on the backsides of the naughty. Those whose conduct was on the borderline vacillated between hope and terror. A toy or a whacking—which would it be? Generally, however, it was the former, even in the case of the most recalcitrant. Yet the gift was not given until after a lecture, a tentative lifting of the switch, and a promise of improvement. An elderly Baltimorean still remembers his early Christmases: "I stood there, rooted to the floor. Till the very end I never knew what was going to happen. And I think it did me some good, for a while, anyway."

Sometimes Nicholas knocked at the door with an assistant, a

strange creature from Germany who has no counterpart in modern American lore. This was Pelsnickel ("Santa in Furs"), a figure in a great cape and a fur cap. With Pelsnickel's appearance, Nicholas was divided in two: he was the one who brought good, while his dark counterpart became the giver of bad. Pelsnickel carried a great rod, with a heavy bag before him; he wore a clanking chain that dragged when he walked, and bells that proclaimed his coming and his departure.

The two figures materialized together, and the children beamed at Nicholas and cowered before Pelsnickel. Each caller spoke to the family, inquiring after the children's behavior. I have never heard of a case, in Baltimore or anywhere else, in which Pelsnickel actually doled out punishment, but often he seemed close to it, and reached out for the mischievous youth, lifting his stick. He was, however, always dissuaded by the good Nicholas or by the parents, and he would leave with a final threat: Wait till next year, and then nobody would be let off so easily!

With time came further changes in the custom: Santa was no longer a December 5 visitor; on that evening Pelsnickel arrived alone. He had become a sort of Santa spy, an advance agent, whose duty was to probe for facts. Moving about the room, the grim fellow thrust out an ominous finger and made embarrassing inquiries. So Jack had *not* been good of late, eh? Sometimes the harsh one would open his bag and threaten to grab the youngster and dump him into it. . . . But Pelsnickel never made good his threats; usually a warning was enough.

The Santa Claus legend grew and changed through the work of two writers. Washington Irving presented America with a picture of a laughing holiday figure very different from the earlier one, with his lean look and dark robes. And in 1822, Dr. Clement Moore, a teacher in a New York seminary, composed a holiday poem for his children, "A Visit from St. Nicholas." Its opening lines would soon be known all over the land:

" 'Twas the night before Christmas, when all through the house. . . ."

It was from a genial Dutch friend that Dr. Moore heard about the jolly, white-bearded Christmas saint who rode reindeer through the sky, and according to some authorities Dr. Moore's Santa was very much like that Dutchman.

Another of the doctor's friends, much taken with the poem, had it published. Neither Moore nor any member of his circle was prepared for the astonishing reception it received. For a time the author was embarrassed; he did not feel particularly proud of this effort, which had been intended only for his family. But the description of the new Santa was quoted far and wide, and the American St. Nicholas was on his way.

Then, in 1863, the widely known cartoonist Thomas Nast— himself of German descent—drew the new Santa in outlines that eventually captured the nation. Year after year Nast offered his vivid conception, and America accepted it ever more warmly. The dark-clad bishop from Asia Minor had been transformed into the bulging, booming individual from the Far North. And in Baltimore, as elsewhere, December 5 was forgotten, and the night of December 24 became St. Nicholas' evening.

Long before then, Baltimoreans had had a holiday custom of mixed English and German origin. On New Year's Day or New Year's Eve, in both countries, early villagers had formed parties, covered their faces with masks, disguised their voices, and called on friends and neighbors. The carnival-like crowd would assemble mysteriously, sing, dance, and perform stunts while their hosts and the children tried to guess their identities. Maryland continued this custom with zest, and similar celebrations were held in other parts of the South, but the Maryland version had a particular vogue among the well-to-do of the state. Amy D'Arcy Wetmore, in the Baltimore *Sun,* told how young men of the 1850's "used to go masquerading on Christmas night and during the holidays." Among those who could be seen were Sir Walter Raleigh in elaborate court attire, an organ grinder with a small boy "sewed up in a brown plush suit to represent a monkey"; a Scotch Highlander, an Indian; "Flora McFlimsey" who had "nothing to wear" and appeared in newspapers cut in rows of fringe, and a "Yankee girl," wearing a large hat and "talking in a most amusing fashion, making the ladies laugh very much." There was also an old "female" who made use of the opportunity to kiss all the women within "her" reach, particularly the younger ones.

Such elite maskers marched from house to house on Park Avenue, Mount Vernon Place, and along Charles and Franklin Streets. Ultimately, if only because of the members' increasing age, the various groups changed form. One became a chess club and later it was to be the Maryland Guard in the Confederate War.

The postwar years in Baltimore witnessed a Christmas observance without parallel then, before, or after—the movement of thousands of people to the main business district for Christmas Eve masking, skylarking, and general festivity. In the 1880's and 90's, many went to parade, shout, and prance about; the rest went to look, laugh, and perhaps to join the more active ones. Here was a good chance for last-minute Christmas shopping; big stores and little ones stayed open until about midnight. Business was good, deliriously so; people bought everything; there was so little time left that no questions were asked.

Families and groups of friends formed "promenade parties" to inspect the goings-on. Youths and their girls would amble about the streets for several hours, dividing their attention between the maskers and the shining windows of Emerich's, Rice's, Posner's, and Gutman's. The Christmas-time *Sun* of 1892 remarked that a stranger, dropped into Lexington Street at 11 P.M. that night, would see a sight "as peculiar to the city as the Mardi Gras in New Orleans or egg-rolling in the national capital."

The merrymakers carried cowbells, dinner bells, and rattlers; they dragged clanging bells on ropes over the cobbled streets. Some were dressed as Uncle Sam, others as feathered Indians, still others as nameless grotesques; bands strolled in linen dusters and white hats, or in suits made of calico, or carried violent-hued umbrellas.

Fifty young men organized a "drum corps" with ancient tin cans as instruments. A party from East Baltimore, all wearing stovepipe hats two feet high, moved up and down the street in lock step. Other revelers wore coats but no shirts, or coats turned inside out, and some had orange hair and fierce red noses; onlookers spotted "city sports" and "country-jakes." It was all, or nearly all, easygoing and bright spirited.

The custom was "not made or established," the *Sun* declared. "It simply grew. Year by year its proportions, its pranks of jollity, have increased." One explanation, the paper speculated, might be the town's climate. While Baltimore had all the "wintry accessories of Yuletide," its weather was "nevertheless so soft and mild that there is no objection in staying outdoors."

By the century's end, however, the Christmas Mardi Gras had become all too exuberant, all too spirited. The "human river" of people began to break its banks. Stores could no longer handle the excitement. Thousands milled about, knocking merchandise off the counters, and little was sold. Boys threw rotten fruit; fights broke out, windows were smashed. The police had to be called in to keep strict watch, and the observance declined.

One year Lexington Street was darkened, and the carnival had ended.

But every year, for this city whose reputation for food has always been fine, the Christmas season has brought special attractions. From Chesapeake Bay and the other waters poured a stream of fish, oysters, and other sea food. The many farms outside Baltimore yielded all kinds of meat and fowl. In the early 1830's the Fountain Inn announced it had acquired "a fat green turtle weighing eighty-four pounds," which would be served at dinner in the Long Room, at 3 P.M. the day after Christmas. "A paper is left at the bar for the signature of such gentlemen as may wish to participate."

About the same time the Patapsco Refectory spread news for housewives that its superior turtle soups would be available all during the good week, at twenty-five cents a quart. And there was, as usual, the Teutonic touch. Jendrek's drinking establishment advised its clientele that on New Year's Eve it would offer free its well-known lentil soup with German sausage. For those who had bigger appetites—*sauerbraten!*

The frugal Germans introduced goose, the favorite of many in the old country, and Baltimoreans acquired a taste for it. Among the Teutonic peoples sauerkraut was the usual accompaniment of the fowl, its tartness offsetting the strong flavoring of the goose. Was this the grandfather of the Baltimoreans' turkey-with-kraut? Nobody is certain, but on menu after menu that combination appeared.

Mrs. Ferdinand Latrobe, while not of German descent, recently described a Carroll County holiday meal which began with chilled oysters, went on to the Maryland specialty of terrapin as a separate course, and then to turkey. The big fowl was accompanied by a dressing of chestnuts or fresh sausage, and along with it went the kraut, flavored with a "large piece of fat salt pork," and served on a flat dish, "never a deep vegetable dish."

The maid, going about the table with the kraut platter, was followed by the butler with a gravy boat of thick giblet gravy, "to be poured over both the dressing and the kraut." With that, hominy, candied sweet potatoes, and spinach, and, at the end, "always a flaming pudding." As for the kraut, "it was simply one of those things that a great many people liked—almost a routine dish."

The Baltimore Christmas had its social aspects among the Anglo-Saxon elements, too. An Englishman who spent the holidays of 1866 in Baltimore felt something like war in the atmosphere, for "every ten minutes or oftener a gun or a squib was fired off." He wrote:

Christmas is not properly observed unless you brew "egg nogg" for all comers; everybody calls on everybody else; and each call is celebrated by a solemn egg-nogging. Egg-nogg is made in this wise: our egg-nogg was made so, and was declared after a good deal of nogging around, to be *the* brew in Ellicott's Mills:

"Beat up the yolks of 12 eggs with powdered sugar, then beat up with them a pint of brandy, a quart of cream and a quart of milk; lastly beat up the whites of your 12 eggs, and add them on as a head and crown. . . ."

It is made cold and is drunk cold and is to be commended.

Another account tells of a stranger to Baltimore who was waked on Christmas Day by a servant holding a tray on which reposed not only eggnog, but also ginger cake and another confection with raisins, a "Christmas cake."

For many, however, the great day for eggnogging was New Year's, and in the Baltimore of the last century a tradition of formal calls on that day reached a high point. The wise man prepared for the occasion by sipping only lightly the night before; he needed his strength and also his stomach for the happy ordeal that lay ahead. For the unmarried man the day was particularly rigorous, for he *had* to make the rounds of his friends or offend any he omitted. And he could not offer as excuse an ill mate or a baby with a cough. He might be out as early as 10 A.M., carrying with him "the list," with houses arranged geographically on a route prepared in advance.

Part of the trip, to homes nearby, could be made on foot; but much of it must be by wheel. If he had no carriage of his own, sooner or later he needed a cab, hired by the hour. Writing of "those pre-cocktail days, when liquor was 100 proof," Carroll Dulaney of the *Sun* declared: "By 3 or 4 P.M., after visiting a dozen or more homes and sampling the eggnogg, punch and apple toddy at each, you were in high gear and ready to repeat the circuit, if the flesh were strong enough to stand it."

Early and late, Baltimore offered rare Christmas-time theatricals. In 1831 the town beheld a "Grand Menagerie of Living Animals," with "a full-grown elephant of very large size and a young elephant of very small size" (only three feet); a hyena, "noted for its deformity and ferocity," and an "outrageous ourang-outang, the first living specimen ever exhibited in America." Outrageous though she might be, the orangutan was of the female gender, "perfectly harmless and playful, carries herself in erect manner; is dignified; puts on her hat; eats with a spoon and uses her handkerchief with grace." The management assured holiday customers that Miss Orang-Outang and her companions were "well secured and danger precluded"; nevertheless, no female would be admitted without a man at her side.

Even more alluring was the special "Christmas Monday" benefit at the Baltimore City Theatre and Circus. For that event Mr. Eggleston, "the American Voltigeur," would appear on the "Corde Volante" raised high above the stage and would suspend from a rope a pyramid of five men. That feat completed,

Mr. Eggleston would swerve from rope to rope through five burning balloons, drawing from the first a snake (live), from the next a monkey (also live), and from the last a "horrible dragon emitting flames"! Of Baltimore's many holiday attractions, this is the one I would most have liked to see.

In even the most hotheaded areas of the South, few men held duels during the Christmas season. In 1843, however, Baltimore witnessed one on Christmas Eve—surely the least likely time of any year. William Norris, a gentleman of Baltimore, met David Powell, another gentleman from Philadelphia.

The participants agreed, after a meeting of their seconds, to contest their differences with rifles at eighty paces. Last-minute arrangements were approved, the signal fell, and both men fired. According to Mr. Dulaney's description of the incident, one bullet struck home, removing part of the victim's magnificent whiskers. Both duelists stared in horror. A wound in the arm or the side would have been perfectly acceptable. But how could a man explain the ridiculous loss? "This was such a calamity that both gentlemen were heartbroken. . . . And they embraced and parted, not in anger but in tears." And so good will on earth and peace to all men descended again on Philadelphia and Baltimore.

## CHAPTER 4

# Christmas at "The President's House"

To the amazement of the formalists of his time, a President of the United States once celebrated Christmas by playing the fiddle for the children among his hundred guests. Another joined his young relatives and friends in an indoor fight with imitation snowballs.

Since its earliest days, the capital of the United States has had a certain Southern air. Created almost overnight out of swamp and plain, Washington bore a marked resemblance to the cities of nearby Virginia and Maryland. Yet from the beginning it has had a flavor and a character of its own.

Much of the character centers about the "exceedingly pretty little palace" which gradually became known as the White

House, although it did not acquire that name until 1902, with Theodore Roosevelt; before that, it was generally called only "The President's House." It was in this serene, columned residence that Washington's Christmas season had its steadiest focus; it was the Southerners, who made up the large majority of our early Presidents, who gave the town an observance that crystallized into the nation's "official" Christmas.

More than anything else, the White House Christmas has been a children's holiday. Whether they were widowers like Thomas Jefferson and Andrew Jackson, or beaming grandfathers like the Roosevelts and many others, or like James Buchanan, a bachelor, the Presidents of the United States have made Christmas a ceremonial for the young.

From the first days of the Federal City the holidays provided a custom which many Europeans regarded with surprise and mixed feelings: the January 1 receptions, open to all. The events that took place on that day occasionally gave onlookers a start; an Indian chief in feathers might be flanked on one side by a frontiersman, and on the other by a bemedaled ambassador. Until recent years, the capital city nearly always opened the New Year with a bustling, democratic demonstration attended by all the thousands who wished to exercise the privilege of shaking hands with their President.

The first years of the new government witnessed Christmastime levees at which George Washington received his guests. In this period the United States had no fixed capital city, and President Washington's first Christmas Day reception was held in Philadelphia. But wherever his levee took place, it always had a high polish and elegance.

The President's wife was known as "Lady Washington" by the people of her time, who were still close to the British tradition. The chief executive moved in dignity through the drawing room, his hair generously powdered, wearing a coat and breeches of black velvet, "white or pearl-colored vest, yellow gloves, a cocked hat in his hand, silver knee and shoe-buckles, and a long sword with a glittering steel hilt and scabbard of polished white leather." Even at the most festive of Christmases, George Washington remained rather aloof. Gouverneur Morris, whom the President liked, once unwisely accepted a dinner-party bet from friends who insisted that no one would dare "take a liberty with the chief." Bravely, Morris clapped Washington on the shoulder. "The Chief turned and gave him a look of such mild and dignified yet grieved surprise, that his friend shrank back repentant of his forgetfulness of respect, while the mirth of the company was instantly awed into silence."

With their grandchildren, however, the Washingtons relaxed happily. The youngsters, son and daughter of Martha's boy, Jacky, who died during the Revolutionary War, became the older couple's special charges, and at Christmas the President and his wife poured on them not only their love and affection but a stream of gifts as well. It is no wonder that the young Custises became the pets of the republic.

When the movement to create a capital city developed, there arose furious maneuvering among many localities. Finally the Potomac site received the choice. The city was laid out in full glory on paper, but only isolated buildings arose; one celebrated description called Washington a place of "magnificent distances." As one man said, nearby Georgetown was a town of houses without streets, whereas Washington was a town of streets without houses.

The capital spread only slowly over its flatlands, and by November of 1800, when John Adams took over the President's home, he shivered in the chilly emptiness of the uncompleted place. Mrs. Adams described it as "twice as large as our Meeting house" and added: "Nobody can form any idea of it but those

who come into it. No one room or chamber is finished. . . ."
Hardly six rooms were furnished. The building had no fence
around it, and water had to be carried from a distance of nearly
six blocks. The house stood at what was then the edge of a
swamp, and in cold weather the Adamses had to keep thirteen
fires going all day "or sleep in wet or dampness."

As Christmas neared, the Adamses inaugurated the custom of
White House holiday parties for children. The rooms were
lighted and heated as best they could be, and the President and
his lady stood formally in the upstairs Oval Room to receive the
friends of their four-year-old granddaughter Suzanna.

It was a pleasant affair. The chamber was hung with greens.
There were cakes and punch and other refreshments, music and
songs and, even in this season of good will, explosions of juvenile
temper. For Suzanna already had a strongly developed sense of
her rights and an instinct for retaliation. When a friend dropped,
or perhaps flung, one of Suzanna's pet sets of fine new dishes on
the floor, the President's granddaughter snatched up her friend's
doll and sank her teeth into it. By the time the Adamses inter-
vened the doll's nose was off for good.

While the next President was equally fond of children, his
inclinations were very different from Washington's and John
Adams's. Although Thomas Jefferson had visited European
courts and had, himself, a cultivated taste, he believed strongly
in democratic ways. He disturbed diplomats by receiving them
in highly casual attire, and permitting them to find any place
they could at his dinners.

With all his simplicity, however, Jefferson had a French chef
who introduced the capital to waffles from Holland, French ice
cream, and macaroni from Italy. At Christmas the President's
guests sipped vintage wines and munched on such imported delicacies as cheese, anchovies, and preserved fruits. At one of his
holiday parties his six grandchildren wandered at will among

the hundred or so guests, and on that same occasion the executive called for his violin and played for the delighted young ones. Although traditionalists may have frowned, there is something disarming in this picture of Presidential informality. "Disarming" is perhaps not quite the word to describe another evening when a White House guest drew out her tambourine and pounded it at length.

The tradition of Christmas-season receptions spread over Washington, involving government and other circles. The more famous or distinguished "received" at their homes, while the less eminent went calling on them. Hundreds rode about, carrying lists of their friends (and sometimes people they had never met) and stopping at each place in turn, from the President's mansion down. Many came to Washington for the holiday affairs, and one New Yorker left a description of his day in 1829. The Presidential mansion, he said, was "the great mart of compliments" between noon and 3 P.M. There "all the world" shook hands, bowed, and exchanged greetings; political differences were put aside for the occasion.

The squeeze was tremendous today, and after one o'clock, people began to retire as fast as others came in to fill their places. There is no ceremony, except that you do your utmost on your first entrance to make your bow to the President and his lady. If you are introduced by some public character, so much the better. After that you may go about the room, if you like, or go home, as most people do.

Presidents came and Presidents went, but Andrew Jackson, "Old Hickory" of Tennessee, gave a new excitement, a new scope to Washington's Christmas seasons as he did to many other things. This man of the border had known many troubles as a youth, and had fought his way up a steep path. After his inauguration, masses of his followers pushed and elbowed into the executive mansion on an evening of pandemonium, but later events of his administration were calmer and more decorous.

Jackson could charm and win almost anyone when he wished. A picture of this other side of the leathery Tennessean has been given by one close to him in the White House. His wife's niece, Mary Emily Donelson, told of a tense week in 1835 among the children of the household.

There were six of them, four Donelsons and two children of Jackson's adopted son; it was they to whom this invitation to other young people close to the President referred: "The children of President Jackson's family request you to join them on Christmas Day, at four o'clock P.M., in a frolic in the East Room." No party details were given out, even to the hosts; they would have to wait and see what happened.

As Christmas Eve approached they indulged in an orgy of speculation. Although Santa Claus, the fat old saint of the Teutons, had not yet really established himself in America, the young Donelsons and Jacksons talked endlessly of him to the staff. Would he really come? What did he look like, and where did he live?

The big, handsome mulatto Mammy, "saucy and good-natured, fussy and domineering," said she wished they would stop chattering about "Sindy Claws." She would laugh, she added, if the old man got tired of roaming around at nights and stayed home to roast chestnuts by his own fire.

Hans, the German gardener who talked often of Black Forest spirits and Rhine castle lore, was sure Kris Kringle would come, although he thought it odd that Santa would not be greeted by a tree. Carita, a Mexican embroidery maker who worked for the Jackson family, favored the lamps which the little ones, the *niñitos* of her land, hung on poles and bushes on Christmas Eve, and under which they would find, the next morning, presents left "by the Infant Jesus on His way from Heaven to the

Virgin's arms." To all this the coachman George had a postscript. He remembered mischievous children who reached into their stockings to discover only peach-tree switches with a label: "To be applied when spanking has proved insufficient." That had a chastening effect.

The day before Christmas word arrived that the children were to go riding with President Jackson in his carriage. They had several presents to deliver: embroidered handkerchiefs, snuff for Dolly Madison, a hand-painted mirror for the great Mr. Van Buren, said to be "on very good terms with his looking glass."

On the way they asked the President if he thought Santa would really appear. Jackson replied that they would have to wait and see. He had once known a boy, he said, who not only never heard of Christmas and Santa Claus but never had a toy in his life; and after the boy's mother died, he had no home or friends. Therefore, he went on, they should try on this day to remember those who had no mothers and fathers; this was the reason they were now going to stop at an orphanage, to give presents to the youngsters there. This visit remained in the children's memories for a long time, although it was only later, wrote Mary Donelson, that they realized the President had been talking of his own bleak childhood. . . .

That night the President invited the children to his room to hang their stockings. Several borrowed theirs from Mammy; she weighed two hundred pounds and her hose were "as capacious as the Galilee fishermen's nets she often referred to." Stockings were hung from hooks on the mantel, from curtain rings at the foot of Jackson's bed, one from a "boot jack carelessly left on Uncle's green leather armchair." One of the children had an idea: Why not hang a stocking for Uncle himself? Then the President would know what Santa Claus thought of *him.* Jackson agreed, commenting that he had waited nearly seventy years to put up a stocking.

Like millions before and after them, the young Donelsons and Jacksons begged to be allowed to sit up for Santa's arrival. Their wish was not granted and they were led off unwillingly to bed. With daybreak, they ran across the hall, asking if Santa had come. "See for yourselves," Andrew Jackson told them.

The Christmas saint had been there, after all; the stockings were filled and there were presents for everybody, including "Old Hickory." The children were drawn away for washing and dressing, but they returned promptly to examine their stockings, and to find in each one a silver quarter, cakes, nuts, candy, and fruit. Young Mary received her first boy-doll from Madame Serrurier of the French legation, a soldier in red, gray and plumes, and a minute stove with spirit lamp, for boiling water and popping corn.

As for Andrew Jackson himself, there were several gifts, a pair of warm slippers, a cob pipe, and a tobacco bag. The President of the country seemed as pleased as the children about him.

At 4 P.M. it was time for the party in the East Room, which was decorated with greens and flowers and mistletoe hanging from the chandelier. There were games, dancing, and singing; and the elders kept a careful eye on the proceedings, lest there be spats or attacks of weeping. Six P.M. signaled the opening of the dining-room doors. A band played "The President's March" and the children entered in line, keeping time to the music.

There waited the French chef's triumphs of the confectioner's art, frozen wonders all: ices in the shape of apples, pears, corn, and squash; a small frosted pine tree with toy animals around it; a reindeer pausing near a lake in which were little fish. And eyes centered on the pyramid of cotton "snowballs" covered lightly with starch. After the food, the young guests reached for these objects, with startling results. When struck properly, each ball exploded, and the East Room was a scene of snow and smoke.

At the end, after further marching, the children said good-by and started away across the lawn. Dolly Madison sighed: "It reminds me of the fairy procession in *Midsummer Night's Dream*." Andrew Jackson shook his head. It made him think, he said, of the words: "Suffer little children to come unto Me...."

During this same period a Russian in Washington gave a children's Christmas party that stirred the American provincials. Alexandre de Bodisco, his country's minister, was a beaming gentleman who went about in a white barouche, a man whose attire had "a great deal of silver," who liked brass and polish and feathers.

Jessie Benton Fremont recalled as an episode in her childhood a holiday party held in De Bodisco's ornate Georgetown residence for his two nephews, "a fete none of us had ever seen the like of." Heavy snow had fallen; the streets were not yet lighted with gas, and a line of beacon fires, flaming in the high winds, guided guests to the house. Lights gleamed in every room and window of the tall residence, and before it were roaring bonfires at which the many coachmen could warm themselves, "as in St. Petersburg."

Galleries were "enclosed, curtained, mirrored, carpeted and pictured," and two of the porches had wide swings of red and gold. Tables were piled high with dolls, toys, picture books, games, and stacks of satin bags, "and these were for us to take home."

In the dressing room sat boxes of small white kid gloves, fans and bolts of varicolored light ribbons, and there were maids in foreign-looking dress whose job it was to repair any damage to the children's hair and dresses. "We danced too—but that we did not care for—dancing was only lessons; but this world of toys and sweets and pleasant faces was the real joy." No Washingtonian could or would try to duplicate this bountiful occasion. Some may have thought it garish, a display that might spoil good democratic children; yet nobody turned back any presents that night. And De Bodisco, who stayed on in Washington for years, proved his liking for things American and also youthful when he married a Georgetown schoolgirl of sixteen.

A President of the mid-1850's, a New Englander, brought a Christmas tree to the White House on an evening that drew considerable notice. Franklin Pierce came from New Hampshire, an area which had never given much heed to the holiday; but Pierce installed a decorated tree in the mansion and entertained around it all the Sunday School of the New York Avenue Presbyterian Church. The ornamented "German tree" was winning an important status in the country of its adoption.

Following the conflict between North and South, capped by the assassination of one of the greatest of Americans, brightness returned to the capital, although only slowly.

When Rutherford B. Hayes reached the President's house, Mrs. Hayes became the first First Lady who had gone to college. A cheerful, bright-faced woman of firm ideas, she banned liquor or wines of any kind. Even so, despite the sad headshakings of many natives, she made a large number of friends. The Hayes had children, and for them Christmas became a zestful time. At the holidays young voices sounded happily in games, Christmas songs, marches, and ceremonies. During the Christmas season of '77, the Blue Room of the mansion witnessed an unusual event, the christening of Fanny and Scott Hayes.

When Benjamin Harrison arrived at the executive mansion in 1889, he brought a large family—his father, his son, his daughter, and their children. Harrison was the President who issued the oft-quoted proclamation. Calling Christmas "the most sacred religious festival of the year," he said it should mean general rejoicing among all people; it was a time for turning one's back on "cares and annoyances." As for the Harrisons, "We intend to make it a happy day . . . all the members of my family, representing four generations, will gather around the big table."

The President went on to announce that people had a "duty . . . as Christians to make merry" at this season, and declared that his own home would have an "old fashioned Christmas tree." Thus he gave the decorated German tree a still greater recognition as an essential part of the American holidays.

Not long afterward, new youth and new Christmas excitement came to the official residence with the Theodore Roosevelts. The big, lighthearted Roosevelt and his handsome young wife brought with them their six children, together with the young Roosevelts' ponies, dogs, birds, guinea pigs, pet snakes, wagons, and boats.

As outgoing as he was, Theodore Roosevelt had a strong feeling against the use of evergreens for Christmas trees. A convinced conservationist, he believed that slashing down so many growths would sadly injure the American forests. There would be no Christmas tree in the White House, he let friends know. And his face reddened angrily when he learned that two of the Roosevelt boys had slipped a tree into one of their rooms.

Their father thundered and the youths called on Gifford Pinchot, the ardent conservation authority and a close friend of the President, who tactfully pointed out that the intelligent cutting of evergreens would not destroy forests but actually aid them. Convinced, Roosevelt nodded, and the boys' tree stayed.

By the time Calvin Coolidge reached the White House in the early 1920's, the tree in one form or another was a fixture. The Coolidges had two large ones, one in the Blue Room, a second in an upstairs room. Later, using a raised platform, the family installed a Manger Scene with five or six evergreens behind it.

From this quiet corner, Grace Coolidge declared, "The real spirit of Christmas seemed to radiate to every recess of that old mansion and beyond." And in 1923 Calvin Coolidge pressed a button to light the first "National Christmas Tree," which towered on the White House lawn.

With the passing of years the White House itself underwent many extensions and expansions in keeping with the times and with the country's enlarging role in the world. The "pretty little palace," drafty and all but empty, was the home and offices of an executive whose duties widened with each generation. The building became one in which Americans took almost a proprietary interest, and in few phases of the President's life was there a greater interest than in his annual Christmas.

In the 1930's Franklin D. Roosevelt's large family gave fresh vivacity to the White House holidays. On Christmas morning the grandchildren, still in their pajamas, usually hurried to the President's bedroom to open their presents. According to a firm family tradition, after dinner that night, Franklin Roosevelt read aloud "A Christmas Carol."

By 1941 America had entered World War II and at a muted White House there arrived at Christmas time a particularly honored guest: Prime Minister Churchill, in America for a series of vital conferences. That evening, as President Roosevelt touched the button lighting the National Christmas Tree, Winston Churchill stood beside him, and both addressed the nation in solemn messages.

On January 1, the two men went together to Old Christ Church at Alexandria, Virginia, occupying the George Washington pew. Then they rode on to Mount Vernon. In the rain the Prime Minister took off his hat and placed a wreath of red, white, and blue on the tomb of the first President of the once-rebel colonies. The nation's capital had seen few more dramatic Christmas seasons than this one, which brought together the two men who, more than any others, shaped the destiny of their world.

With Dwight D. Eisenhower, young children returned again to the White House, and during the Christmas of 1955 a grandchild was born to the official family. Between the first Presidential Christmas and those of the modern century the nation had gone a long way.

# CHAPTER 5

# "Christmas Gift!"

W ITH the 1800's the Southern Christmas widened in several directions, its traditions growing with the years. All through the region—but particularly in the coastal section—it crystallized, during the ante-bellum period, into a set of customs which, despite variations here and there, followed a generally similar pattern.

One special practice was the institution of "Christmas gift," the words shouted as a "surprise" in the early morning. For hundreds of thousands this was a moment with a rare meaning. As a Georgian who went to live in Texas once told me: "The minute that message came to me after dawn, I knew I was back home, and that it was truly the big day again."

The custom was simple: Any Negro attendant who caught the resident of the big house by surprise with his call of "Chris'mas gift!" had the right to a holiday present. Many were so trapped, not always by surprise, and it was an obligation of honor to hand over a gift—perhaps a coin, perhaps another token, when they were prepared in advance for the contingency. The transfer was accompanied by chuckles and cries of delight and triumph, which signalized that Christmas had been launched in the right way.

The holiday season cast its shadow well before it. In most sections of the rural South it was a time of bright skies and winter stillness, with a trace of wood smoke in the air, and a subdued excitement hinting at the doings that were to follow. Crops had been harvested, and now work on next year's growth might be launched with the clearing of underbrush, improvement of ditches, and other preliminaries. But no matter what labor was under way, it would be dropped for the holidays; the contracts plantations owners signed with overseers often specified six or seven full days of rest, starting on Christmas Eve.

For the Negro, this was the best part of the year. Perhaps the load of his bondage weighed heavily on him; perhaps he had been separated from others of his family, or suffered under a harsh overseer. Whatever his situation, with the approach of this season his spirit lifted. "Jubilee," if only a limited one, was coming.

Some weeks before Christmas, plantations and farms were the scenes of another major event, part labor, part celebration: hog-killing day, a kind of ritual prelude to the great time itself. "I can never think of one without the other," a present-day Mississippian explains, and her brother, home from West Virginia, nods. "No hog-killin', no Christmas, is the way it always seemed to me."

For some time the best pigs were watched with care, fed, and overfed in preparation for the morning when the ax would fall.

The day had to be right—chill, frosty, cloudless if possible. The weather-wise would frown, study the "signs," and make predictions: "Next Monday, God willing." On the eve of the big day all the families, both those in the big house and those in the quarters, retired with a sense that something important was about to happen.

In the dawn bells clanged and men pounded about the grounds, signaled to one another, and went to work. From the quarters the huskiest hands were chosen to go into the pens and bring out the unwilling prey. The plantation women might prefer to remain out of earshot of the squeals that were sure to follow. They would, however, go outdoors afterward and help direct the busy hours ahead.

Each pink-white carcass was dropped into a cask of steaming water and its hair scraped off. Then up it went to a beam from which it hung for cooling and interior cleaning with new, swift knives, while tubs waited below to catch the drippings. Big fires burned here and there about the yard, while in the kitchen (always a brick building detached from the main house for safety in case of fire) others blazed away and dozens of pots and pans were ready for their part in the work to come.

The fat was dropped into great caldrons, and attendants kept an eye on it as it was turned into lard for general use. In the largest rooms in the rear there were great wooden blocks; in front of each stood an operator, wearing a white apron and a kerchief, and holding a hatchet or a knife. These women were the sausage makers; their job was to turn part of the meat into well-seasoned specialties that would be welcome as long as they lasted. Eventually, grinding machines would replace the hand labor, but not for years to come.

"Chop it some more, Tildy. . . ." "This ain' real fine yet. . . ." As the women bent forward, the scent of sage, thyme, and other herbs rose over the room. Knives clattered and scraped, and frying pans sizzled. Then the hand stuffing started, as the bits of meat were pushed into a casing twisted over a wooden holder. Hickory smoke settled everywhere, a light steam rose above the pots, and workers and watchers were enveloped in a half-dozen separate aromas.

Meanwhile children, light and dark, hovered about the fires, thrusting bits of pale-pink flesh over the flames for a true rarity—roasted pig tails. Spareribs, backbones with the meat still clinging to them . . . each type of delicacy had its partisans. For many nothing could match the wonders of "cracklin's," the crisp remainder of the skin after the lard had been removed. "Still," an eighty-year-old Floridian remembered with a smile, "I preferred pig tail any time, any day or hour."

All the children competed for one of the great prizes of the day: pigs' bladders. These were hoarded for Christmas. Blown up, they served as superb balloons, and to thousands of young Southerners of the last century no balloon of any kind had quite the magnificent pop of a hog bladder. . . .

For several weeks after hog killing the women of the house—the owner's wife, one or two maiden sisters, who were permanent guests, a cousin there for a "little visit" of six or seven months—worked over boxes and bowls with the aid of the cook and her helpers and any juvenile assistants who seemed reliable. Nuts had to be cracked and picked, raisins seeded, orange peel cut, currants washed. Candied citron appeared from the plantation supply house or from the nearest town, and the women labored to convert it and other delicacies into mincemeat, fruit cakes, and puddings.

The mistresses of the kitchen worked for hours, combining the ingredients, tasting, thinning, thickening, pouring in brandy and other spirits, then thrusting the baking tins in the ovens, peering cautiously to see their creations puff slightly and grow browner, and removing them at the proper moment. Another dousing with brandy, a cooling, and the fruit cakes were put into well-covered boxes, to "set" and "ripen" during the days that remained.

With the holidays nearer, extra cakes were made—little ones and big ones—layer cakes, wafer-like cakes, thick ones, chocolate-covered cakes, citron-ornamented ones. A few small items might be spared for the children, but the bulk went to the storeroom to be kept under lock and key. In addition to the cakes were the pies, deep, stuffed with preserved fruits, dried fruits, and custardy mixtures. Christmas without a selection of pies was never Christmas.

"Time was measured to Christmas. . . ." So a participant in the earlier holidays put it. Wagons arrived from the nearest landing; the packages they contained were pushed quickly into hiding. Children who asked too many questions were given a cryptic warning by the Negro helpers: "*Laroes catch medloes,*" or, as some explained, "Layovers to catch meddlers." This phrase, still in use in my boyhood, always intrigued and disturbed me. At its hint of mysterious entrapment, few would take the risk of opening closed doors!

From England the custom of the old Yule log had been introduced into Virginia, Maryland, North Carolina, Georgia, and elsewhere, and with the passing decades it became an essential part of the celebration. Slaves were sent out to cut down the finest and most stalwart tree in the woods, one on which they had had their eyes for some time. The best pigs, the best citron . . . the best log was a natural accompaniment.

As long as the Yule log glowed, servants were freed from work. Even if the wood burned for eight or nine days, the master usually kept his promise. In time the attendants developed a clever scheme for prolonging the delightful period: they soaked the log, so that it would last day after day. Master and household knew of the stratagem, and secretly chuckled over it, as did the servants themselves. When he came upon a tree trunk that had lain for a long time at the swamp edge a man might grin: "This one's got as much water as a Christmas log."

At a season's end the last bit of log, according to the tradition introduced directly from England, was put away for the next year, to be used then to rekindle the fire and to bring good luck. If the piece of wood was lost, all the oracles felt disturbed. That wasn't good. They knew of no specific ill fortune that might follow, "but it just ain't a right thing to happen."

In the last days before Christmas the hunters rode out to track down any game within range—wild duck, partridges, wild geese. Brought in with a flourish, the fowl would hang until it had ripened. From nearby waters—or perhaps from town—oysters arrived; but every eye turned sooner or later to the turkey, or two or three, that had been picked for the feast and was now growing plumper and more succulent with the best of feeding.

Here, of course, was the noblest viand of all, subject of speculation, comment, and aftertalk. Everybody had a turkey story; there is the remark attributed to Southern trenchermen from Maryland to Louisiana to Arkansas: fine fare that it is, the turkey is a rather awkward fowl, "a bit too large for one man, not quite large enough for two."

With Christmas in sight, women of the household had an assignment for the younger men, to go into the woods and bring back a plentiful supply of evergreens: cedar, hackberry, holly, pine. The wide hallway—larger than many chambers—was draped on both sides, and then the living room, the other rooms, and the entranceways, mirrors, mantels, pictures. The greens and the bright scarlet berries gave the house a fresh brightness and a new aroma.

Generally the hunters also sought a plant with waxy, delicately green branches and pale berries—the famous mistletoe of

British memory. It might grow on the highest boughs of the trees, far out of reach, but the plantation men, a gleam in their eyes, risked broken necks to obtain it and came home happy if they suffered only minor sprains and scratches in its pursuit.

At times the best marksmen might be chosen for the green hunt, to shoot down the distant mistletoe. Intently the others watched: one blast, two, three. . . . Success made the sportsman a hero; he would have the honor of hanging it over a door and of claiming the first kiss beneath it. Already plans had been set to entrap such luckless women as the pretty schoolteacher, too long unmarried, or the city niece who, despite her good looks, was approaching twenty and still did not have a husband.

From the city and the farm came carriages filled with relatives—sisters, their husbands, aunts, and cousins, for at last Christmas Eve was upon the plantation. Now was the time for toasts and the hanging of stockings before the mantel. If the family gathering was large, each present was marked with the recipient's name, to make certain there was no confusion. As always, the children stayed up as late as they could, then stumbled to bed.

At dawn or soon afterward the household servants would rap or thrust open doors, calling out: "Christmas gift!" "I catch you!" "I seen you first!" The present would be given, with laughter and cries of mock resentment, and if the servant was particularly privileged she would have her gift for the people of the great house: a nest of eggs she had gathered from her small chicken yard, or a hand-carved wooden ornament, or a jar of preserves.

From one room to the next the Negroes went by ones and twos, knocking or even bursting in if they thought it proper. "Christmas gift!" "I surprise you!" By now the household was thoroughly awakened, and before long the head of the house had gone downstairs, attending to the invariable Christmas service that was a proud part of his office—the preparation of eggnog.

Often he had his own particular combination, involving the addition of a special strengthener, or a certain proportion of cream, or more nutmeg than usual. In each case he would receive assurance from relatives and strangers that his was *it*, the very best they had ever tasted. ("I've said that to so many eggnog mixers that I've had to pray for forgiveness," a New Orleans matron confessed.) In many cases the drink came before breakfast. A man could eat any day; for Christmas he should go forth with the mild glow this superlative mixture induced.

In all honesty it must be admitted that a number of Southerners have never joined the eggnog admirers. They think the concoction—whether at Christmas or New Year's—too sweet, too rich, and they say that it spoils their appetite for their whole day. "A waste of eggs, and cream, too," many have said. Peter A. Brannon of Montgomery, Alabama, wrote firmly that eggs were "far better cooked. Why anyone should want to mix anything, even eggs, with a palatable spirit is beyond my conception."

Meanwhile the Christmas Day fireworks were crackling outside the house. Although nearly all the Negro children were already playing with them, the boys in the plantation home could not yet join this fun. They must first have their breakfasts and then receive their gifts. The morning meal was an unusually full one: eggs and slivers of dark-red, well-cured ham, spoon bread and egg bread and sometimes a special Christmas raisin bread; oysters to give a man's stomach a good lining, fresh fish; fruit and cheese and, early and late, coffee—particularly pungent on this day.

The meal finished, all rose from the table at a signal. Folding doors were thrown open and in the next room the presents could be seen, resting beneath the children's overflowing stockings. The gifts were dolls and soldiers, boats, grotesque figures, and skates, and always extra firecrackers and horns. By this time the custom of exchanging gifts among adults had spread in the South, and the adults as well as the children exclaimed over their new possessions. Thanks and kisses followed, and the young left, free to do what they wanted, to toss "crackers," blow horns, to pull their toy wagons behind them.

An hour or so later the first of the carriages would rock up with guests for the day, and as each approached a group of house servants darted up to greet the newcomers. "Good mornin', Mister Jack." "Chris'mas gift!" "Ah, I seen you first!" In the hallway eggnog awaited them, and Christmas wishes, inquiries, and introductions were exchanged. Frequently the mistress of the house offered only a breathless greeting and then disappeared. Her heart was elsewhere this morning, and she must be there, too.

Although she had regular kitchen helpers, she wanted to be there herself on this day, to make certain that all the delicate operations were properly meshed. And in the preparation of some specialties she trusted no one but herself. Today she looked from pot to bowl, spider to skillet to cooling cups. Gravies, white sauces, turkeys in carefully guarded dishes. . . . Earlier, she had begun the concoction of the vital plum pudding, and had gathered chopped suet, raisins, citron, nutmeg, eggs, nuts, and flour, mixed them thoroughly, dropped them into a cloth, and tied it tightly. The pudding went into one of the biggest pots, to boil for several hours under a continuing watch. Then came time for the mistress of the house to get to work on the hard sauce, a smooth mixture of butter, sugar, and brandy which would impregnate and glorify the other ingredients.

At midmorning the servants from the quarters, the field hands, gathered by prearrangement before the house to receive their annual gifts of clothes, cakes, candies, and trinkets. If the master considered himself an orator (and he generally did), or if the eggnog had had its effect, he would try a speech. No matter what its quality, the help applauded and cheered for him.

Back to the quarters the servants strolled, to continue with their own Christmas, which included calls from cabin to cabin, feasts of fried oysters, spareribs, ham, pickled pork, and the like, and joking and singing. The great meal would come later, and after that the high event, the evening dance.

If there was a church nearby, the plantation family attended the short but solemn Christmas Day services. On the way there and also on their return, they called on neighbors for brief greetings, their holiday appetites enhanced or sated according to what they consumed.

Dinner was at about three in the afternoon, the climax of long planning, long hoping. Every available chair was crowded about the big table, whose leaves were extended as far as possible. Nevertheless, the children often moved to a second, smaller table in the next room. Seldom would there be a first course; everything was placed on the table, to be eaten at will—main dishes, side dishes, seasonings, preserves.

On this day grace had a particular solemnity. "Father in heaven, we thank Thee for the bounty that we are about to receive. . . ." At once an attendant or attendants materialized with the turkeys, done to a smooth-skinned, almost polished brown, surrounded by potatoes and stuffed vegetables, and filled with a highly caloric dressing—of oysters, or chestnuts, or a corn-meal mixture. With all the dignity of his rank, the master lifted a sharpened knife and got to work.

With the brown meat or the light (preceded by the usual question about preference) went a dark gravy, pickled mangoes, brandied peaches, and other savory accompaniments. At the end of the table stood one or two hams, dark and inviting; a large roast, cold or warm; and a heaping platter of oysters for those who had not had enough of them at breakfast.

Potatoes in two or three styles, vegetables in butter, vegetables with egg, with a flavoring of ham or bacon or meat. . . . The meal continued for two hours or so, with second helpings or third ones, and heads turned discreetly if a fourth were taken. Toward the end the hostess slipped away and from the kitchen marched a helper, picked for his strength of arm, who beamed as he presented the *pièce de résistance,* the plum pudding. It had been ignited so that the blue flame played around the heavy ball of promised delight.

Applause, cries from the children, calls of approval. . . . As the fire burned down, sections or spoonfuls went to all the adults and some of the older children. Now a lull, and the women left the table, taking their young with them. On came decanters of wine and plates of nuts and raisins. For another hour, perhaps, the men would talk, and then heads would begin to nod and one after another would drop out of the conversation. Those who stayed regaled one another with recollections of former years, news of neighbors, crops, and conditions, plans for the year ahead, tales about eccentric relatives who collected old silver or young wives.

At length even the most garrulous had had his say, and the company rose. Even though more guests were arriving, some climbed drowsily upstairs to recoup their strength with an hour or two of sleep.

In the quarters the Negroes had their meal, a smaller replica of the one in the dining room, with additions such as raccoon and possum. Here hilarity and good will were unlimited; the master might call, and if he did he seldom failed to exchange a toast with his workers. Then the Negroes returned to their cabins, to crackling fires with popcorn for the children and apples circling on a string, which made the air redolent with their tart-sweet fragrance.

After dark the big house reverberated to music at the piano, to songs and the dancing in which grandmothers and teenagers took an equal part. Proceedings were interrupted by laughter, squeals of surprise, and protests as one girl after another (and some beyond the girlish stage) were seized beneath the mistletoe. . . . Understandably, supper was light that night: more turkey and stuffing, warm or cold; more ham and roast meat. Conversation was light—comments on the day and talk of the event that awaited, the Negroes' annual Christmas dance. Already sounds echoed from the quarters, a distant thumping, an occasional high note.

The plantation people attended in a body, to be given places of honor at the front. Here, beyond question, was the day's most enthusiastic observance. Fiddlers, thumpers, shouters, callers of the turns. . . . "Salute your pardners!" . . . "Top ladies cross over!". . . . "Sides forward!" The hour was buoyant and zestful.

Not until midnight did the planter's family finally get up to leave. The dancers would continue for many hours; they could go on until dawn if they wished, and spend the next day recuperating. The guests who were leaving that night started on their way, exchanging handclasps, kisses, and good wishes; those who lived too far off would stay on for another day or another week. A last smile at the door, a tired sigh, the lowering of a final flickering light in the hall, and Christmas had gone until the next year.

Such was the day as it came down in the memories of dozens of participants. In retrospect, matters took on a softened gloss. There were many accidents, of course: a turkey overdone, a mincemeat pie that did not come off, lost tempers between cousins, sometimes a shadow of bankruptcy. Nevertheless, in most cases it was a good day. Too many people wanted it that way; too many worked to make it so.

It was the Negroes who gave the Southern Christmas the distinctive music which still lives on. Thousands of Negroes, and later other thousands of whites, sang the simple and touching "Rise Up, Shepherd, an' Foller."

> There's a star in the East on Christmas morn,
> Rise up, shepherd, an' foller.
> It will lead to the place where the Savior's born,
> Rise up, shepherd, an' foller.

> *Chorus*
> Foller, foller, rise up, shepherd, an' foller,
> Foller the Star of Bethlehem,
> Rise up, shepherd, an' foller.

> If you take a good heed to the angel's words,
> Rise up, shepherd, an' foller.
> You'll forget yo' flocks, you'll forget yo' herds,
> Rise up, shepherd, an' foller.

> *Chorus*
> Foller, foller, rise up, shepherd, an' foller,
> Foller the Star of Bethlehem,
> Rise up, shepherd, an' foller.

For the Christmas feasting and revelry were only one phase of the slaves' Christmas; the other was the devout, plain faith of the people. As John Esten Cooke saw it, Christmas was to them "what it was in the pious Middle Ages—a solemn mystery as well as a joyful reality. With the rejoicing of the season is inseparately connected in his mind what this rejoicing arises from." The Virginian long remembered a song an elderly Negro woman had sung him when he was a boy.

> Oh, chillun, Christ is come
> To heal you of yo' danger;
> Pray that you may be reconciled
> To the Child that lays in the manger.

Men and women of later days might have smiled at the words. But for Mr. Cooke the last lines had a "strange and subtle suggestion of a mysterious sanctity," which stayed with him through all his life. And from the minds and mouths of the plantation workers came a Christmas spiritual which many consider to be among America's finest songs: "Go, Tell It on the Mountains." It was sung on many occasions, at small gatherings just before the holidays, as a dark mother chanted her child to sleep, or by a lone Negro man as he worked over the tobacco or cotton or rice crop.

When I was a learner, I sought both night and day.
I asked the Lord to aid me and He showed me the way.
Go, tell it on the mountains,
Over the hills an' everywhere,
Go, tell it on the mountains,
Our Jesus Christ is born.
*Go over the hills an' everywhere,*
*Go, tell it on the mountains, go.*

He made me a watchman upon the city wall,
An' if I am a Christian I am the least of all.
Go, tell it on the mountains,
Over the hills an' everywhere,
Go, tell it on the mountains,
Our Jesus Christ is born.
*Go over the hills an' everywhere,*
*Go, tell it on the mountains, go.*

# CHAPTER 6

# "The Christmas City"

THEY were a quiet people, the Moravians, a people who believed in peace and sometimes suffered for that belief. From middle Europe and generations of persecution they came to this country, largely to Pennsylvania. Some remained there, while others emigrated southward to North Carolina, to leave a continuing mark on the life around them. Every Christmas for generations the eyes of other Southerners have turned to them and to their center at Winston-Salem.

They are a musical folk, a singing folk, and in the holiday season their city—originally Old Salem—has always rung with reverent melody. "The Christmas City," some have termed the community; in very few others in the county has the feeling of Christ's presence been so strong. Here also is a children's Christmas, planned to give the young a particular part in honoring the Baby who lay that night in the Manger. And on Christmas all Moravians—of whatever age—join in a symbolic rite, meeting together, like the early Christians, and breaking bread. The buns and mugs of coffee they have on this occasion emphasize the bonds of fellowship that hold together all believers, members of the family of Christ. Then, in the dim church, each person is given a lighted candle, which serves to remind him that Christ said: "I am the light of the world," and "Ye are the light of the world—let your light so shine before men, that they may see your good works, and glorify your Father which is in heaven...."

The Moravians of North Carolina are not a large denomination but have remained true to their special ways. Their *Unitas Fratrum* or Unity of Brethren began in the 1450's in old Moravia (now part of Czechoslovakia), Bohemia, and Poland, developing out of the evangelical movement of the reformer Jan Hus. Hus was burned at the stake, and his associates were imprisoned or driven from their homes. But in spite of persecution, the society grew and in 1720 a small group, escaping from Moravia, came to the estate of the pious young Count Zinzendorf of Saxony in central Germany.

The count, a man of education and wide interests, took the Moravians under his wing, planning to instruct them. But instead he himself was instructed. He joined the organization, was chosen bishop, and proved himself remarkably zealous in propagating the society's beliefs. A person of great charm and earnestness, he was particularly successful in finding missionaries for the society. He would meet a stranger, inform him enthusiastically that he had "a place for him," perhaps in the Far North. Then he would hold long conferences with the amazed prospect and often win him to the assignment!

From the time Count Zinzendorf became a member, the Brethren's church had a predominantly German tone. Its services are held in that language. The Moravians remained a "plain" people, who believed in the simplest of attire. To church the women wore the *haube,* the distinctive cap which came down slightly on each side of the head. The church became an institution of great music, with choirs and general singing accompanied by trombones or French horns and other instruments.

Again the Moravians suffered; Count Zinzendorf was banished for some years, but his interest in the church remained firm and, indeed, grew even stronger. He helped extend the movement to the American colonies, and a group of Brethren made its way to Georgia, where it met unexpected problems. War was raging between the English and the nearby Spaniards, and the Moravians wanted no part in fighting of any kind. Leaving Georgia, they transferred to Pennsylvania, where they formed the thriving settlements of Bethlehem, Nazareth, and others. Then in 1752 a pioneer party made the long, harsh march through the Shenandoah Valley to North Carolina, to start their work there.

The Moravians were a striking band, different from those among whom they passed; they wore severe dress, unornamented in any way, and they had a look of determination, of dedication. In their slow-moving Conestoga wagons they struggled over dangerous streams, huddled in wet tents, and fought on through mud up to their knees. Their vehicles slipped toward the mountain edge; repeatedly the Moravians saved them by locking wheels and helping the animals back to the course. Again, as the wagons rocked downward, the Brethren fought to avoid crashing into the trees and rocks in their paths.

Reaching North Carolina, they took possession of a 100,000-acre property that lay beyond the already occupied areas. The members of the group—men only, because of the hazards—had been chosen carefully for the skills necessary to make a pioneer community function: there were a doctor, a miller, a carpenter, and several tradesmen. In mid-November the first temporary center was established and given the poetic name of Bethabara, "House of Passage" in the Hebrew. In a small log house, the lone men celebrated Christmas Eve with two services, the first at 9:30 P.M. and the second a "love feast," a deeply felt testimonial of fellowship.

Then and many times later, as animals prowled in the wilderness outside and Brethren kept guard against savage attack, music rang out in the night. A hollow tree limb served as a wooden trumpet; there was a small organ, and there were French horns and violins. On special church days or when callers approached, the horns sounded to summon members and to welcome newcomers.

Among these first Carolina Moravians no one owned land; all formed a company in which each stockholder received shares and assumed his part of the costs. Here and at other settlements they erected their buildings in a Central European style with steep roofs and many dormers.

When they first met the Brethren, other North Carolinians would blink in surprise, but nearly always they got along well with the peaceful folk. Often the only doctor and minister available for many miles were members of the Brethren and they were generous with their assistance. In times of need they gave freely of their food and supplies. The newcomers also made friends with the Indians, who never attacked them and spoke of their Bethabara as a place of "good people and much bread."

Other Carolinians, however, had Indian troubles and a few years after the Brethren located there, clashes sent a stream of refugees to Bethabara. The Moravians permitted the displaced people to put up huts in their settlement and at their mill, and when Christmas arrived the kindly Brethren sent an invitation:

Would the other families like to join them that day? Gladly the refugees accepted. . . .

From their beginning in North Carolina, the Moravians have been magnificent keepers of records; each January 1 they have read a journal of the past twelve months. This remarkable account of their experiences describes that early holiday occasion:

On Christmas Day the English children from the mill came to see our Christmas decoration; they were so poorly clad that it would have moved a stone to pity. We told them why we rejoiced like children and gave to each a piece of cake. In Bethania Brother Ettwein held a Love-feast for the twenty-four children there; at the close of the service each received a pretty Christmas verse and a ginger cake, the first they had ever seen.

To the refugee children of the English element the Moravian Christmas, with its boughs and garlands and candles flickering in the dusk, must have been a stirring thing. In their isolation the Brethren had created the kind of Christmas they had long known. There were the Bible verses in careful German penmanship and, not least, the Moravian holiday cakes that many others were to enjoy through the decades.

Within two years, at Bethabara and also at the settlement of Wachovia, the Brethren held the first of their Christmas Eve love feasts for children. In each place the young "rejoiced over the birth of the little Jesus" and at the end received lighted candles which they held high as they sang. Then, as on many subsequent Christmas evenings, the children carried with them the ministers' words: "As Jesus came that He might be a shining light for us in a black world, so let each of us bear a light for Him."

Additional Moravian towns grew up as new members of the Brethren arrived in the latter years of the eighteenth century. Soon after another New Year's Day the men cut the first logs for their largest center, Salem, or Peace, a name suggested by Count Zinzendorf; they sang hymns as they worked.

In the succeeding years the Moravians met new problems. They would not fight in the Revolution, though they did provide material help for the rebels. They were heavily fined for their pacifism, and ordered to pay triple taxes in lieu of service. After the war, the bad feeling died away and George Washington himself paid a call at Salem. There he accepted an invitation to attend a singing meeting with the Governor and others, "to their great edification."

The colonists and later Carolinians who visited at the Christmas love feasts found that the unmarried women lived in one hall, the bachelors in a "brothers' house," and the couples and families in other quarters. They noticed, too, that ribbons of different colors marked the women's white headdress: blue for the married, white for widows, pink for unmarried women, dark red for the young girls, and light red for the youngest.

Some of the Moravian structures remained in place through the generations, weathered and sturdy, with their steep stairs, stone-paved basements, and trim brick walks. In time, some communal features of the earliest settlements were discontinued, and the method of dress became less austere, but the Brethren continued their basic beliefs. One of their principles was a thorough education for both boys and girls, and eventually the Moravians' neighbors asked if their children could be received for similar training. The Moravians agreed.

A girls' school was started in 1772; in 1802 this became a boarding school, the second such institution in the United States. (The celebrated Ursuline Nuns of New Orleans had established the first in 1727.) To this school came children of other faiths, to receive the dedicated teachings of the instructors, and to look on at the annual Christmas services and the love feasts.

One such outsider was the daughter of a Presbyterian minis-

ter of North Carolina, Mary Anna Morrison, later Mrs. Thomas
Jonathan (Stonewall) Jackson. Throughout her life Mrs. Jackson spoke of this busy, pious world—the steady assignments, the
hours of work in the girls' small gardens, the atmosphere of
high devotion at Christmas, and always the music. Then and
later, in times when so many American pressures have tended
toward a rigid conformity, the Brethren have maintained their
separate ways, their special traditions.

Today, for those who go to the Christmas City, music seems
to be everywhere, in echoes around the corners of the brick
houses—a distant instrument, a murmur of voices chanting six-
teenth- and seventeenth-century hymns and even more ancient
ones from Bohemia and Moravia.

For days the mothers and grandmothers have been preparing
the holiday confections, using recipes little changed from those
long-ago days in North Carolina. There are brown Christmas
cakes, white ones, molasses cookies, nut drops, pepper nuts.
After the batter for these delicacies is mixed, it is generally
kept for several days in the refrigerator. In that way, the Moravian *hausfrau* explains, the result will be crisp and paper-thin.

In the meantime, the men have been laboring on the *putz*,
decorations for the Christmas tree, whose base has a decorated
scene of Christ's birth. Winston-Salem has many such versions
of the mystic drama, from tiny ones to enormous ones that
cover most of a room, with dozens of variations in between. No
matter what the variations, always there is the central group,
the Christ Child in his cradle with the people and animals
about him. Additional scenes may be constructed—meadows and
fences, castles on mountainsides that recall the Moravians' original homes; windmills that move, meadows and fences, lines of
soldiers and ponds.

Long thought and effort go into the creation of the *putz*.
Some families have beautifully carved figures which they bring

forth every year, while others add new ones each season. Childless couples, or those whose children have gone to other places, continue the custom, and even men and women in their seventies will have a *putz:* "without it, Christmas would not be right." Formerly the Christmas tree with its *putz* was shown to the children for the first time on Christmas Eve. Now they help make it and look forward to that pleasure. In this way, say the Moravians, the young learn good lessons in a pleasant fashion.

The women have still another task at this season, a task which begins in October and continues into the holiday month. They make thousands of Christmas candles, one for each person who will attend the festival ceremonies. First the candle wax itself must be prepared. Enormous cakes of beeswax are melted in vats built into the whitewashed brick oven of the old Brothers' House, which dates back to 1786. Then the beeswax is mixed with tallow; for every 50 pounds of wax, 12½ pounds of tallow are used. After the mixture is melted and stirred, it is strained and poured into large pans to cool. Then it is cut into small blocks.

Now the candles themselves can be made, some of them in molds fashioned long years ago by the grandmothers of the present-day Moravians. The beeswax and tallow mixture is melted again, and the lightly scented material is poured into the molds, in which a long wick has been inserted. Then the molds are put aside and after the proper interval, with almost reverential care, the women draw out the yellow-green tapers and set them aside.

Elsewhere other women, wearing aprons and traditional Moravian caps, make red-frilled holders or "petticoats" which are placed at the bottom of the candle to prevent the dripping wax from burning the fingers.

Big, many-pointed Moravian stars that will hang on porches, in doorways, and windows are a beloved part of the community scene. The hollow parchment stars are made by an intricate process, in which thirty-two tapering sections, each three-sided, are fashioned into a graceful whole. In former days candles illuminated the star; today electric bulbs are used. In early December the women of the church hold a "Candle Tea" to launch the Christmas season. At the old Brothers' House the "elbow latch" swings wide in hospitality and thousands enter to see the moss-covered *putz* that covers two rooms. In the House are the fragrances of pine and cedar boughs, of Moravian "sugar cake" (a coffee cake from an early recipe), and of coffee.

Christmas is near, and on the afternoon of Christmas Eve adults and their young gather for the children's love feast. Long before the church doors open, hundreds have taken their places near the entrance; in the group are couples in their seventies and children of no more than a year, held by their mothers or grandmothers. Quickly every seat is filled, and a light, subdued murmur hovers in the air. The church is hung with greens, decorated with many natural growths. The afternoon sun shines through a window picturing the Mother and the Christ Child. The lights have not yet been turned on, and the window glows in its rich colors.

Outside, a band is playing hymns; it stops and a hush falls. In the high belfry a summons sounds, a trombone sending out the notes of the ancient music signaling the start of the ceremonial. The organ peals, and the service begins. "Hail Thou Wondrous Infant Stranger" is the first hymn, and the minister reads the scripture and offers a prayer. "Hark the Herald Angels" . . . "The Night Is Sleeping". . . . The hymns are simple, familiar ones, in which the children join, their voices subdued at first, then lifting with the others.

A pause, and the doors open to admit a line of women in white, bearing baskets of soft buns. Behind them are men with wooden trays holding mugs of pale coffee. A homey scent spreads over the assembly, the good, warm smell of the coffee and sweetened bread. The Bishop is served first, then the others, quickly, gently. When each person has his bun and his beverage, the Bishop raises the mug to his lips, drinks, and the others do the same. The coffee is very mild, and most of the children enjoy it as they join in the rite.

The choir sings: "Today we celebrate the birth of Jesus Christ who came to earth. . . ." The children are earnest, reverent. The men and women reappear to remove the coffee mugs, and voices rise again: "Come hither, ye faithful, triumphantly sing. . . ." After a moment the chorus begins the familiar words: "O little town of Bethlehem. . . ."

Gradually, as the sun fades, the church has been growing darker, and now the only bright point is the lighted transparency of the Nativity picture which hangs in front of the organ. This is the time for the Moravian hymn which many consider the loveliest of all, and which dates back to the 1600's. The choir chants:

> Morning star, O cheering sight!
> Ere thou cam'st how dark earth's night. . . .

The doors open again and the women in white step forward, lighted candles in their hands; behind them are men holding trays of other lighted candles, which stand out in hundreds of circles of illumination. The women hand the candles to the Bishop, the choir members, the children and adults. The church glows with the many flickering points, small hands carefully clutch the tapers with their red paper bases, and the voices of the choir sing out:

> Morning star! thy cheering light
> Can dispel the gloom of night;
> Light divine, come and shine
> In this darksome heart of mine. . . .

Morning Star, O cheer-ing sight! Ere Thou
cam'st how dark earth's night! Je-sus mine, In me
shine; In me shine, Je-sus mine; Fill my
heart with light di-vine. A-men.

As the words die away, the Bishop talks simply and briefly to the children. He tells of the way the Child was born in the Manger, with the cattle around Him. He pictures Jesus' love for children, and appeals to them to be worthy of that love. Jesus had come to earth to be a light in a darkened universe, he says, and now all of them should bear a light for Him.

The members of the congregation hold their candles aloft in a demonstration of faith, and the Bishop gives his blessing. Now it is time to leave, to walk home, still holding the candles, now extinguished. This night the same candles will be placed in many windows where they will cast their circles of gold into the surrounding dark. With each lighting, by tradition, goes a prayer that the Christ Child may enter the home on the holy evening.

Before long, the time comes for the viewing of the tree and the shining scenes about it. The yellow lights and rays of blue give the *putz* a dramatic glow, and the children stand there, caught by the beauty and the mystery of this re-enactment of the central moment in the Christian story. The family talks of the *Christkind,* the Christ Child, and on this night he seems very close. Then, of course, the presents are waiting, and young and old open them and give thanks. . . . Later the older people return to the church for their own love feast, and again the rich music pours from the choir, from the instrumentalists, and from the congregation. For a second time coffee and buns are distributed, and in the heavy dark the illumination is even more striking than before. When the services are over the throng goes through the night past the ancient houses and fences, the trees and the ivy on the walls. And, as they did on another evening, in Bethlehem, the stars look down.

## CHAPTER 7

## Old Buck, John Canoe, and the New Year Shooters

RODANTHE is a little-known village on the Outer Banks of North Carolina, an island jutting a mile and a half into the Atlantic. The people of its sandy, wind-driven shore have always led an isolated life. But even though the children of Rodanthe—like its adults—have been cut off from the mainland and its benefits, they enjoy one advantage over the youngsters of Raleigh and Charlotte, Greensboro and Asheville.

In Rodanthe Christmas comes not once but twice a year. The island observes the Yule holidays in two sets of spirited ceremonies, one on the "New Christmas" of December 25, and the other on the "Old Christmas" of January 5. And the residents of Rodanthe have something else, a good-natured January 5 mummers' festival whose star is "Old Buck," a four-footed creature who has ridden down a long path out of ancient English mumming. Old Buck, folklore authorities say, is a unique survival of a custom that most modern Anglo-Saxon Americans have given up or forgotten.

For a long time, as we have seen, Christ's birth was observed on January 5, but when the British changed their calendar, most of the colonists followed suit and accepted December 25 as Christmas Day. Yet here and there beyond the well-settled areas, in isolated spots or among people who are perhaps simply "too independent," the January date still holds sway. In conversation with the natives of more remote areas, I have several times been informed firmly, almost angrily: "December 25 just *ain't* Christmas. My grandpa said it, and I say it, too; and my folks'll go right on having it on the real day." In a small number of outlying sections, the January 5 celebration is still the only one. For years it was the only one in Rodanthe, too, with the result that some intolerant mainlanders called the Rodanthians "pagan" and "un-Christian."

Eventually the islanders conformed, at least to a degree, by observing both the December and the January date. But generally the latter is the more important occasion. "Which is just as it should be," says a Rodanthian.

On December 25 there are church rites, a Santa Claus, and gifts—the standard Southern festival. January 5, Old Christmas, is different, and it is honored in more ancient ways.

Traditionally the day began soon after dawn with a distant sound of soft music, "real Christmas music." A visitor described it as "faint, eerie," bordering at first on the supernatural. "The early morning atmosphere," he wrote, "lent a peculiar sweetness." The music came from the homemade fifes and drums of a band of serenaders, whose instruments had been passed down from father to son.

The gentle, worshipful procession went from house to house; on some years, it is said, there were prayers at each residence. The march continued for hours, until by dark every home had been reached.

At midday there was an intermission. The musicians, who had been joined by others during the course of the morning, arrived at the spot at which their holiday dinner was to be served. This was a hearty meal in which roasted oysters, the succulent specialty of the coast, had a large part. Then came more visits to homes, and about dusk Rodanthe's contribution to the Southern Christmas, mummers' night.

On this Old Christmas evening people stepped out in costume, simple, gay-spirited bandannas, colored stockings, ancient furs, even more ancient hats. They made their own masks of cloth or paper with grotesque noses, long chins, and overhanging brows, or hid their faces inside dark stockings into which holes had been cut for the mouth and eyes. They wandered wherever the spirit moved them, hailing friends, laughing, joking, skylarking.

Then the high moment: the arrival of Old Buck, an animal half frightening, half hilarious. Old Buck, said the Rodanthians, had once been a monstrous scourge, the terror of the Hatteras Woods, who left his retreat only once a year, on January 5, galloping forth in majesty and also awkwardness. He consisted of a pole covered with bed quilts or blankets, and a steer's head with a fine pair of horns. At his neck hung a bell. The two men beneath his quilts cavorted and danced in a way that made the very young shudder and their elders giggle. Old Buck's rider, perched atop his quilts, directed the monster's wanderings. "Caper, Buck. . . ." "Straight ahead, now." "Right over there, fast!" As Buck approached, the crowd swerved, screamed, and called out encouragement: "Get 'em, Buck, get 'em!" Not until everybody felt tired, including Old Buck, did the Old Christmas end.

Whether the Rodanthians knew it or not, their custom went back to earlier English folk ceremonials. From Cornwall comes a description of "a hobby horse represented by a man carrying a piece of wood in the form of a horse's head and neck, with some contrivance for opening and shutting the mouth with a loud snapping noise, the performer being so covered with a horsecloth or hide of a horse as to resemble the animal whose curvetings, biting and other motions he imitated." Much earlier, Staffordshire had a horn dance at Christmas, with men carrying stag horns on their shoulders. Clearly Old Buck has English ancestors.

Old Christmas is homecoming time, and many men and women who have left Rodanthe return every year for this event. Last year they were joined by a few outsiders from North Carolina and Virginia. Although the Old Christmas had been modernized in its details, the ceremony still retained its light-hearted flavor. In the afternoon the Rodanthians, in casual costumes like those of earlier times, drove their automobiles up and down the road. It was all most good-natured, neighborly, and simple. As dusk approached excitement grew in Rodanthe and the neighboring settlement, Waves. From nearby Avon, Salvo, Buxton, and Hatteras came men, women, and children who still spoke with the "toime and toide" brogue of the Outer Banks. Along the beach, parties of men gathered driftwood and wreckage to be used for the outdoor oyster roast.

As a large moon rose over the ink-black Atlantic, the people gathered in their old schoolhouse. At one end was a stage, at the other benches for natives and guests. The curtain parted and the program began. There were singers, dancers, musicians, and declaimers, most or all in masquerade and blackface. Then a pause, and out pounded Old Buck, as fearsome as ever. The audience fell away in mock fright as he clattered down the aisle, turning to left and right, tossing his head, threatening those around him. But Old Buck had been changed and modernized. On his back rode Santa Claus, impersonated by a youngster. Here was the new American Christmas wedded to the old.

Then the benches were pushed back and it was time for dancing, in square and other styles. Outside, a fire had been lit. It was covered with tin sheets on top of which the oysters would be roasted. The people danced, walked out for oysters, and went back to dance again and to greet one another with the cry of "Merry Christmas."

In the words of an observer: "There was nothing 'quaint' about all this, nothing self-conscious. It had an honest look; these people were having a good time out of their own resources, a wonderful time. At 49 I can recall evenings when this happened in the country, and I was seeing it for the first time in many years. I hope the Rodanthians never turn 'dignified' or 'picturesque' on us!"

For many generations before and after the Confederate War bizarre celebrations of somewhat similar origin were held among the Negroes in other parts of coastal North Carolina. Here was mumming with an African and West Indian flavor. Nowhere else in the United States have I been able to find a parallel to the "John Canoeing" or "John Kunering" of several Carolina settlements.

For days before Christmas in such towns as Wilmington, major port of the area, Negroes whispered their plans for "John Kuner," a ceremony whose followers were supposed to keep their identities well hidden. White children, remembering the event from previous years, talked of it no less.

On Christmas morning there rose the distant sound of rhythmic chanting, accompanied by instrumental music. A procession appeared down the street, its members crying out as they went, and the children of the town ran to their porches or to the street, to view a line of blacks with strips of bright-colored cloth attached to their clothes, or any one of a dozen kinds of grotesque garb. Each had a "Kuner face," a mask with a great nose and beard. Many wore horns, and all moved in a wild, fantastic style.

With them the celebrants carried musical instruments: animal bones, jew's harps, triangles, cows' horns, all played with an air of "gruesome mirth." Dougald MacMillan, whose description of the event is most authoritative, explained that even though all the masqueraders were men, a few wore women's clothes, and their high-voiced screeching added to the merriment. A leader, always an especially horrendous figure, carried a rawhide whip which he snapped back and forth, to keep the bolder youths at a distance. As the procession moved on, its members sang their traditional chant:

> Hah, lo, here we go!
> Hah, lo, here we go!
> Hah, lo, here we go!
> Kuners come from Denby.

On and on the singers went, the rhythmic instruments pounding, the voices rising and falling. Now and then the songs varied, with a soloist followed by a chorus.

> (Soloist): Young gal go *round* the corner!
> (Chorus): My true love *down* the lane!
> (Soloist): We on the grass where the dew been poured.
> (Chorus): *Hey*, me lady, go *down* the road. . . .

With their streamers and tatters whirling around them, the Kuners stopped at the houses of white people, or before groups they met on the street, and sang and danced for them. One of the party held out a hat to collect money, and then the band strolled on its way. As Louis T. Moore declared, "Some of the younger ones were somewhat frightened at the sight, but it did not take them long to learn that they had nothing to fear from the Kuners, and from then on this particular feature of Christmas was looked forward to with as much eagerness as was the arrival of Santa Claus himself."

At one time, the same North Carolinian observed, there was a single Kuner group in Wilmington, but it did so well in passing the hat that others were organized, until there were eight or ten, each trying to outdo the others, in costume and music. All of them appeared on Christmas Eve and throughout the Yule season, the bands moving nightly up and down the streets.

Nobody could be certain of the custom's age; some of the oldest North Carolinians said they had "always known it." It thrived at Edenton, at Hillsboro, near Wilmington, and spread to a number of other places. In 1824 Dr. James Norcom pictured it at Edenton. There, he said, the slaves were "in the habit of enjoying a State of comparative freedom; of having dances and entertainments among themselves; and of celebrating the season in a manner almost peculiar to this part of the world."

Had the whites not supported the John Canoeing, as it was termed at Edenton, it would not have continued, Dr. Norcom declared. He admitted that at times drinking was heavy, and "trifling evils" followed. But, he added, the "angel of humanity" whispered that the slaves were entitled to "a part of those blessings which their labor has procured us."

Where did John Kuner or John Canoe come from?

North Carolina's great port, Wilmington, was for a long time in contact with Jamaica and the Bahamas, areas in which John Canoeing of a style close to that of the North Carolina grotesqueries has thrived for many years. And almost identical ceremonies have flourished in Africa. There the old people talk about a real person, one John Connu. John Connu, who lived in the early 1700's on the Guinea coast, was a zesty character who became a folk hero, and in his name groups of men have long gone about during the Christmas season in "fantastic manner, with cow horns . . . masks and boars' tusks on their faces."

Although the custom began to decline in North Carolina after the Confederate War, it continued in reduced form into the opening years of the twentieth century. Richard Walser has called my attention to descriptions of it in these later days, but only a few people seem to have bothered to record what they saw of the custom. The disapproval of strait-laced individuals finally sent John Canoe home.

Strangely enough, the white youths of Wilmington and other sections of the coast adopted "coonering" in their own fashion. As late as the 1890's and early 1900's, groups of boys in their early teens would go from house to house to indulge in restrained skylarking and to receive little gifts from friendly families. Although they wore masks, it is presumed that those on whom they called generally guessed who they were.

Henry Bacon McKoy has told how he and his contemporaries would don sashes, shawls, topcoats and long trousers ("most of us being in short pants at that time"), red bandannas, shirts, or dresses. "Everything had to be old and ill fitting." He did not recall a single refusal; the hosts always appeared pleased to see him and his friends. The white "Cooners" would talk with the family, do "plenty of giggling," receive fruit and candy, and go on to the next place.

Mr. McKoy became a Cooner because his older brother had been one, and his father had gone coonering in his youth. At the time he did not know there was any name for a mask other than a "Cooner-face," whether it was worn at Christmas or any other time. And he had never heard that the custom had been originated by the Negroes. He and his friends did not know even how to spell the word. "We just did it," he writes.

Miles away, in the rolling western hills of North Carolina, a last band of descendants of old-time settlers carries on yet another survival of an all-but-forgotten ceremonial. These are the New Year Shooters of Cherryville, a group of men of assorted ages who engage in a marathon-like undertaking that goes on for eighteen uninterrupted hours.

Using antique muskets, packed heavily with powder to give the greatest possible noise and smoke, the old members and the young ride by car around the area, from house to house, to blast and salute some fifty or so residences. The observance is now rough-house in nature, now moving in its archaic ceremony. Its high point is a stirring recitation or chant in honor of the season and of each family whom the Shooters hail.

The "crier" stands in the cold night, intoning a set address which men of this piedmont region have been chanting, in one form or another, for more than a century and a half. A stranger who once joined the group said: "I'll never forget the evening. It was like something out of an old, old story. Every once in a while I felt as if I were listening to people of another age, in another land."

For many years a leader of North Carolina's New Year Shooters has been a man now in his middle eighties. Some of his associates are his own age, others ten years or so younger, and still others in their twenties and thirties. Each autumn the group meets to select a route to be followed; once it is set, all householders on the way can be certain that, barring catastrophe, they will be hailed at some time between midnight and 6 P.M. the next day. This is the way the Shooters' grandfathers and great-grandfathers conducted matters; that is the way, they say, it will always be.

The Shooters assemble on New Year's Eve. Most of them

wear hunting or other informal dress. Puffing on cigars, chewing tobacco, leaning on muzzle-loaders dating back to the Confederate days, they spend the last interval before midnight in chuckling conversation about the events to come.

As the moment approaches the band grows more intent, clustering about its two leaders, the venerable A. Sidney Beam ("Uncle Sid" to the town), a man with a quiet dignity, and the burly Howell Stroup, the active manager. For sixty-five years Uncle Sid has served as a crier, reciting over and over again the speech that has become a legend in the locality. As midnight comes nearer, watches are taken out and the men prepare their blunderbusses.

"All right. One, two—"

A bell clangs. Midnight has arrived, and with it a roar which echoes through the area, sends heavy smoke over the town. Someone shouts, others cry out in approval, and Manager Stroup motions to the boys. They jump into their cars and set out for the countryside. Their grueling schedule has begun.

At the first stop the ritual starts. Halting before the house, Mr. Beam calls in a loud, clear voice, "Halloo . . . Halloo. . . ." If the third cry brings no response, the Shooters move on. But seldom does the party's appearance mean anything but an eager welcome, a door flung quickly open. And then Uncle Sid steps forward, to give the chant that he knows by heart. Few who have heard it, the Carolinians say, can forget it. Clearing his throat, Uncle Sid intones:

> Good morning to you, Sir.
> I wish you a happy New Year,
> Great health, long life,
> Which God may bestow
> So long as you stay here below.
> May he bestow the house you're in,
> Where you go out and you go in.

Time by moments steals away,
First the hour and then the day.
Small the lost days may appear,
But yet they soon mount up to a year.
Thus another year is gone,
And now it is no more of our own,
But if it brings our promises good
As the year before the flood,
But let none of us forget
It has left us much in debt,
A favor from the Lord received
Since which our spirits hath been grieved.
Marked by the unerring hand,
Thus in his book our record stands.
Who can tell the vast amounts
Placed to each our accounts?
But while you owe the debt is large,
You may plead a full discharge.
But poor and selfish sinners say,
What can you to justice pay?
Trembling last for life is past
And into prison you may be cast.
Happy is the believing soul.
Christ for you has paid the whole.
We have this New Year's morning called
You by your name
And disturbed you from your rest,
But we hope no harm by the same.
As we ask, come tell us your desire
And if it be your desire
Our guns and pistols they shall fire.
Since we hear of no defiance
You shall hear the art of science.
When we pull trigger and powder burns
You shall hear the roaring of our guns.

Oh, daughters of righteousness, we will rise
And warm our eyes and bless our hearts,
For the old year's gone and the New Year's come
And for good luck we'll fire our guns.

The words issue in a monotone, with the voice rising often at the end of the line; the effect, said one listener, was "weird and great and beautiful, like something out of old England." A brief silence, and the Shooters, ready for the moment, let out blasts that rock the house, shake trees, and make dogs bark. In firing, each man holds the gun from him at about knee level; if it were placed against the shoulder, the recoil would knock him over. But even at this distance, the shooter swings with the recoil much as "a square dancer swings his partner."

As the roar dies away, the householder invites the band in for refreshments—a drink, a little food, or cigars. The visit is a short one, for the hosts know that a long route lies before the Shooters. A good-by, a last expression of good will, and they roll off. Eventually they halt at the home of Mrs. Viola Carpenter. For many years "Aunt Violet," also in her eighties, has given the Shooters their first meal of the New Year, a real man's feast— meat, fowl, big sandwiches with the crusts on, condiments, cakes, and pies.

Even here the band cannot stay long. A few more felicitations and it chugs away through the moonlight to make stop after stop. Then comes time for a brisk breakfast, after which the Shooters rock off again. It is a point of honor, as the big-framed manager, Howell Stroup, explained, that no house on the itinerary be missed. Occasionally the men yawn, stretch, shake the sleep out of their eyes, but none drop out. That, too, Mr. Stroup observed, is a matter of honor.

As a result of increased interest in the New Year Shooting,

a second band has recently been organized, with Lloyd Stroup, Howell's cousin, in charge. The two groups converge at some homes, but largely they follow separate routes. At certain houses the Shooters salute the women who live there with "The Ladies' New Year Speech." Vance Sellers, authority on this ceremony, has set down the words:

> Good morning to you, Miss.
> I wish you a Happy New Year,
> Great health, long life which God may bestow
> As long as you are here below.
>
> I wish you part in ev'ry ease,
> And God will 'stow you luck and peace.
> God will preserve the house you are in,
> Where you go out and you go in.
>
> I wish you lovers of every kind
> To suit your heart and please your mind,
> Whose hearts are pure, whose hands are clean,
> Whose tongue still speaks the thing it means.
>
> No slander dwells upon your tongue.
> He hates to do his lover wrong,
> Or should we trust in ill report
> And venter to our lover's heart.
>
> And then my hopes and wishes meet
> And make my meditation sweet.
> The very frost that spews the ground
> And the hail that sends a dreadful sound.
>
> Icy bond the river hold
> Our tender arms the winter's cold,
> Board the vine your face to see
> And dwell forever in love with me.

If our branches are in danger, shoot
From Jacob's staff to David's root.
False are the men of high degree
To a better sort of vanity.

Laid in a balance both appear
Light as a puff of empty air,
The sun and moon with bearing light
And all the sparkling eyes at night.

What we begin or what we do,
Let this be right and prosperous, too.
Or let this in our names be done
Until our earthly race is run.

Now here we are standing in your yard,
Just a little distance all apart.
When we pull trigger and powder burns
You shall hear the roaring of our old guns.
We hope this may be your desire
That all our guns and pistols, they shall fire.

Much as the riders enjoy the conviviality, the event has a basic seriousness. One member thought the occasion had "something religious about it." As the men stand at the edges of the hills among mists from valleys and lowlands, the observance takes a solemn tone. In the view of reporter Bill Sharpe of *The State*, the ceremony seems a combination of country joyousness, faith, and fellowship, suggesting both the charivari and the carol.

Also, as Mr. Sharpe noted, the New Year Shooting is a kind of family reunion. Most of the participants are related to one another and to their neighbors; in many cases their grandparents had lived in the hills and farmed the land side by side. Generally, too, they are plain folk—farmers, plumbers, carpenters. "We don't want 'society' people, ever," an earnest youth insisted.

At last, some time after 5 P.M., the Shooters arrive at the end
of their route, to be met by friends for a final hail, congratulations and good wishes. Then, exhausted, most of them go home
to sleep for hours.

In this area—Gaston, Lincoln, and Cleveland counties—New
Year's has been "shot in" since the earliest recollections of man.
Uncle Sid learned his chant from his older brothers, in days
when there were five or six bands of Shooters in the area. While
the others eventually gave up, the Cherryville group has remained strong. "I suppose we'll never have a really big bunch
of Shooters," Howell Stroup declared. "Most people couldn't
or wouldn't stick to it. But for those of us that keep it up, it's—
well, something mystic, our way of showing our loyalty to our
friends."

In this observance authorities see traces of English mumming
customs, and also a strong element of the German. Many of the
natives of the region are of Teutonic descent; their ancestors
arrived about 1770 from Germany or other parts of central
Europe, or from the German and Dutch sections of Maryland,
Pennsylvania, and parts of highland Virginia. The folklorist
Arthur Palmer Hudson has noted that in Germany men assembled for generations to "shoot the old year out and shoot
the new year in." Bohemian youth used to gather on New Year's
Eve to fire into the air in a custom called "shooting the witches,"
designed to frighten away evil spirits. In most cases these ancestors of the present-day Shooter were invited into homes for
refreshments.

In earlier days traces of similar or related rites were found
in various parts of the South. In Missouri, Mr. Hudson learned,
the men used to chant a New Year's sermon, with many identical
words, in much the same fashion as the Cherryville band, their

behavior paralleling in many respects that of the Carolina Shooters.

But today this ceremonial, once known to thousands, is followed by only a few. . . . From Old Buck to John Canoe to the New Year Shooters, the strands of connection have been dimmed by the years; yet they are there, far back in the European past of America.

# CHAPTER 8

# Low Country: Opulence and Rice

CHARLESTON realizes the English idea of a *city*...." The
traveler who said that was offering a tribute, which a
Charlestonian would promptly have acknowledged, to a man-
nered place, a town of grace and style which, from its earliest
years, had a certain fashion of doing things. In this capital of
South Carolina and the low country which lay tributary to it,
there was always a particular "way" which was often considered
more important than the things to be done. Understandably,
Christmas came to Charleston and its rice plantations with a ceremonial flourish.

But the Charlestonians and the low-country people could
also laugh. A caller who went there shortly before the Revolution declared its folk "the gayest in America," and a later

analyst judged theirs "perhaps the most urbane of American cities." Charleston believed in a calm life, and the casual tempo was appropriate to a region whose climate bordered the semi-tropical.

The low country was and is a section of rich beauty, with a fecund soil that has supported an agricultural empire: properties of thousands of acres along seaside salt flats; lines of azaleas and oleanders, crepe myrtles and fig trees with moss-hung swamps in the distance; and always stately town houses, high galleried, walls flush with the sidewalk, with, as the phrase had it, their "shoulder to the street" and semi-enclosed gardens behind brick walls and iron gateways.

Charleston has long had a cosmopolitan touch. Her original settlers included a sizable group of West Indians. Experts have traced a "West Indian look" in the houses, as well as a hint of southern France. The port was crowded with brigs and schooners, the seaside streets lined with the offices of merchants who served the great planters. South Carolina growers had to have large estates; the crop demanded enormous expense in the building of levees, water gates, and reservoirs. It demanded a sizable labor force, too, and large numbers of Negroes.

Secure, ever certain of themselves, the South Carolinians could smile at the statement that, to the native, B.C. meant "Before Charleston." They did not bother to raise their eyebrows at the story that their children were taught this town was "the place where the Ashley and Cooper rivers meet to form the Atlantic Ocean." They could even shrug at the hoary remark that they were the Chinese of America, because they worshiped their ancestors and ate so much rice.

It was Mrs. St. Julien Ravenel who told my favorite South Carolina rice story, about the elegant butler, Jack, who, when serving a Charleston family dinner attended by an upcountry senator, had to be asked twice for a helping of rice. At the first request Jack looked stonily ahead. Only when the senator asked a second time did the butler lean down and whisper to him. Later the senator laughed and repeated what Jack had told him: "That wouldn't do, sir; we never eat rice with fish!" In any case, when Christmas came to Charlestonians or their low-country relatives, rice was never far away. . . .

Charles Lanman, describing his "Adventures in the Wilds of the United States," in 1856, gave a detailed picture of Christmas on a plantation in South Carolina. He arrived shortly before the holiday began, in time to see the festival in full swing. Early in the morning of December 24 the slaves began their holiday making. The field workers rode out to take to market the products they had harvested or gathered from their own plots of ground. All methods of transportation were commandeered to get them to the neighboring town.

Excitement accompanied the hundred or so men, women, and children as they started off along a winding road through shadowed forests. The leader's wagon was drawn by two horses; in it were several cotton bales which would net him about a hundred and fifty dollars. Then came another vehicle, in which a group of older women kept guard over an assortment of trussed-up poultry. A few carts and a wagon, pulled by a pair of mules, also held a mixed load, "a supply of rude-wrought agricultural implements, a few bags of corn and other grain, and a neatly-dressed hog, with his hoofs pointing to the sky."

A venerable Negro went by on a no less venerable horse, his only saddle a bag of seeds the plantation owner had allowed him to glean from the fields at harvest's end. A band of boys and girls pressed forward on foot, "more for the frolic or freedom of the thing than any desire to obtain money," though some had stowed in the wagons an occasional fox- or coon-skin processed

from the catch in their traps. At the end of the procession a mis-
cellaneous group rambled along, in smiling, joking mood.

All of them stayed in town for hours, bargaining, collecting
payments, enjoying whatever the place offered in low-priced
fun. About dusk the party moved homeward, "and although
some of the more indiscreet may have imbibed an undue quantity of the intoxicating beverage, the majority of them are as
circumspect in their deportment as could be expected," Lanman
wrote.

Now began "the long-anticipated frolic of Christmas Eve."
Out came fiddles and banjos, and the people of the quarters
launched a party for young and old alike. They talked about
their sales that day and their purchases, about what they would
do with their new possessions, about the good times they intended
to have for the rest of the holidays; they sang and danced until
day approached.

Only two hours after sunrise, Lanman continued, they were
out of bed again and going about "with considerable activity,
considering their loss of sleep." House servants and field hands
who thought they might be wanted at the residence "placed
themselves in the way of the master and mistress" and performed
whatever small services were needed.

Then the field people returned to their cabins for a wide range
of holiday making. The old women and the other religious folk
hurried into wagons to "hear the story of the Saviour" at a
neighboring church. A second group, whose relatives belonged
to a nearby owner, obtained passes to go to visit them. Men with
a passion for shooting had bought or borrowed guns and powder
and blasted away through most of the day.

But a few particularly energetic slaves, who already possessed small properties of their own, worked for themselves even
on this festive occasion. They were pressing toward their goal of
buying their freedom. And since some of the plantation opera-

tions could not be put aside, the slaves took turns, doing the necessary work until Christmas time ended.

A native of the rice country, daughter of a governor of the state, has filled in the story of a Carolina Christmas in intimate style. She was Elizabeth Allston of Chicora Wood, who spent a privileged childhood along the Pee Dee River, in a two-and-a-half-storied white frame house with a piazza on three sides, in a setting of tall oaks. Elizabeth's father was to become a secessionist, while her uncle, James L. Petigru, a famous attorney, stayed firmly loyal to the Union—remaining in South Carolina until his death in the middle of the Confederate War.

But Elizabeth Allston's mind was on other matters when, years later, she wrote of a prewar Christmas at Chicora Wood. The girl, then in her teens, had left Charleston for the rice estate, her arms heavy with presents for the blacks, "fruit and candy and dolls and nuts and handkerchiefs and stockings and head-handkerchiefs." For hours she and her mother and aunt selected and prepared the gifts, then decorated the house with holly.

On Christmas Eve she looked in on the ritual of eggnog making (carried out here in advance of the day itself), helped the children hang their stockings, and later assisted the grown-ups in filling them. The great morning began early, with the servants slipping into the house with their cries: "I ketch you!" Streams of such laughing callers converged on the house, a new group every few minutes. With all these interruptions the Allstons were, as expected, late to breakfast; the cook and her helpers, too, had had to tiptoe up with their calls of "Christmas gift!" and talk over the Allstons' own presents at considerable length.

After many false starts the family went in to breakfast and the house servants assembled with them for prayers. The meal that followed was heavier than usual: "sausage and hogshead, and hominy, and buckwheat cakes, and honey and waffles, and marmalade, which mamma made from the oranges which grew all around the piazza."

Meanwhile the field Negroes appeared before the house to begin their Christmas dancing. This took place, with Mr. Allston's approval, on the piazza itself, with the family looking on. One man played the fiddle and two others used heavy sticks to beat out the time. Triangles and bones rattled steadily, with "all the young Negroes on the plantation, and many from the other plantations belonging to papa, dancing, dancing, dancing." The planter regularly saw to it that some of the younger lads were taught to play the violin, and there were always one or two capable of leading the rest. "The way in which they mark time with the sticks," wrote Elizabeth Allston, "has always been a wonder to me. They beat them in syncopated time, the accent always being on the second beat. I have tried in vain to get the motion, and yet very little children do it in perfect time."

On this Christmas Day the Negroes' music hardly stopped from morning until night, except for meals. The dancers would shift, one set going home to refreshments while another took the floor. The fiddler, stick knockers, triangle player, and bone rattler would change, and the fun continued on and on with endless zest.

That night, with the help of one or two others, Mr. Allston set off the long-anticipated fireworks, while the blacks and whites stood around and applauded. The next day and night were much the same; the only work to be done was to feed the cattle, pigs, sheep, and horses—"just three days of pure enjoyment and fun." It was also a period of feasting for the Negroes; a beef and several hogs had been provided for them and extra rations of sugar, coffee, molasses, and flour were given out, with "great quantities of sweet potatoes."

An interval of work, and then followed three more days of

relaxation at New Year's. January 2 brought another rite, the distribution of new clothes for the slaves. Early in the morning, "Maum Mary," the brusquely efficient household assistant, strode forth to pile the supplies in neat hills of cloth about the piazza. For the women she produced rolls of red flannel, calico, and white homespun or unbleached muslin, while the men received rolls of dark colored material for jeans, and rolls of white for shirts. Much of the cloth was imported from England; the English fabrics had strength and warmth beyond anything obtainable in the United States.

Maum Mary also had a supply of buttons, threads, and needles suitable for the thickness of the goods. It took nearly a whole day to read out the list of names and to distribute the clothes. The next day went for the distribution to the young—a still longer process. Each child took his or her place before Maum Mary, who sat surrounded by clusters of material. The dark woman lifted the homespun to the top of the small head, brought the material down to the floor, then up again to the head, and then cut the bolt at this length.

Mrs. Allston read out a name; up stepped a small girl, who dropped a curtsy to each member of the family and to Maum Mary. The latter was "sometimes inclined to be very impatient . . . and jerk the timid ones around a little; but if papa was there he would say quite sternly: 'Gently, Mary, gently.' The little girl, as she went out loaded with her things and the things of her little brothers and sisters, would drop another curtsy of thanks. The boys were taught to 'Tech dy furud,' as Maum Mary called it; being really just what the military salute is now; but they were generally very awkward about it."

A major problem was always shoes. A month or so earlier, all the servants had been summoned to "give their measure," a procedure which involved marking a light strip of wood with the length of their feet, and having the name fixed to each marker. Measurements went to a reliable shoe dealer in Charleston, who boxed the shoes and dispatched them to the plantation, for arrival by the third day after New Year.

But vanity, alas, often made trouble. Some of the slaves sent too short measurements, "and then what a disappointment and what suppressed groans and lamentations when the new shoes were tried on!" Repeatedly the cry went up: "Somebody change my measure." But the original markings were very clear, and those who had provided their proper lengths could guffaw. "Remember," the anxious ones were told, ironically, *they* "had small feet," and so they would have to suffer. "Me, I got big foot and I kin run een my new shoe!"

In the rice country, as Elizabeth Allston remembered, the Christmas season brought visit after visit to and from the neighbors, and since most planters also had city friends, from them as well. The rice plantations were extremely large, and consequently even neighbors lived far away, but excellent dirt roads extended over the flat country, and there were always plenty of horses and vehicles. The scale of everything was big; when a family made its annual transfer to Charleston, its own members plus the servants, a small army shifted base. In one case a friend of the Allstons counted heads: the cook, the coachman, the butler, the laundress, their mates and children, the owner's own family —and the number reached fifty.

Years later, Mrs. Elizabeth Allston Pringle returned to the rice country to find a scene unaltered in a number of ways: the stretches of old, moist country, houses against the gray-draped trees, thousands of birds winging about the greenery. There were the same "cooters" or terrapin, that emerged from the river to lay eggs; the partridges and snipe, wild turkey and deer were still there, and in the many waters were the perch, bream, and trout she had never forgotten.

In other respects, however, by the early 1900's decay had set in. Rice cultivation was in a long decline; the earth banks that had protected the crops had washed away, and the homes, big and small, stood neglected. Elizabeth Pringle, determined to bring back something of the former Allston crops, moved into Cherokee, a family property which she had bought with the funds left to her when the division of her father's estate had been made. There she would live an isolated existence, in a country she had known from childhood.

For some years Mrs. Pringle struggled against storms that devastated her property, against fluctuating prices, and, not least, against human nature. Her tribulations are recorded in her chronicle, which has many moving moments.

January 1, 1904. On the rice plantation the first of January is the time for the yearly pow-wow, which the Negroes regard as a necessary function. It is always a trial for me, for I never know what may turn up, and the talk requires great tact and patience on my part, not more, I suppose, however, than any other New Year's reception. One is so apt to forget that the *patte de velours* which everyone uses in polite society is even more of a help...and makes life easier to all parties.

Elizabeth Pringle's New Year at Cherokee began with a funeral. For years "hands" had been quitting the rice area for Charleston, anxious for a more rewarding life. In death, however, they wished to be taken "home," to their old plantation. Mrs. Pringle met an oxcart bearing a long wooden box, with the chief women mourners, veiled in crepe, sitting on the coffin; behind it rattled several buggies, each bearing more people than it was intended to carry, and behind them walked a long line of friends. Although the trip had required a great deal of money, everyone had "thrown in" to make it possible.

The same day, another sad sight. Mrs. Pringle found water

rushing through a broken riverbank on her property, and she had to order repairs. "It will cost a lot, and I do not know where the money is to come from; but if I do not make the stand against the water, I shall not be able to plant anything."

The next months saw more bad news. Yet there were to be occasional good tidings. On the following Christmas night Mrs. Pringle wrote: "Had a peaceful, happy day, many loving tokens of the blessed season of good will." She had always enjoyed the opportunity to give small presents to her Negro helpers, and this time she "included the Zs, in my offerings." The Zs were a white couple who had just signed a contract to use some of her land, and she had strong hopes that the experiment would work out for their benefit and hers. She was taking particular pains to get the Z. family well started.

Nevertheless, Mrs. Pringle was disturbed by one conversation with Mr. Z. Moved by the holiday spirit at Cherokee, he confessed to her that he had shot two men in his time, had been shot twice, had stabbed another man nine times, and had been "all cut to pieces myself." For two years, however, since meeting Mrs. Z., he had stopped drinking and was trying to live a good life. They would find out. . . .

Besides many little things to eat I presented them with a pair of Plymouth Rocks, a beautiful pullet and cock, as they are anxious to start a poultry yard. This afternoon she came in with an offering for me, a necklace of fish scale flowers made by herself, which she had told me the other day she sold for fifty cents. I was quite touched by it and by her happiness over the fowls. Altogether I feel very thankful that I have found such satisfactory people. . . .

January 1, 1905. Sat up last night to see the old year out, the year which has brought us sorrow and distress, yet there is great sadness in seeing it go. In the last moments of the dying year I sank to my knees and prayed that this whole land might be blessed and guided through the coming year.

The day is brilliantly beautiful, and we went to our simple little service in Peaceville. Dear, frail Mrs. F. has made a great effort to get to church "to return thanks for her many blessings." Eighty-five years have passed over her, the first half surrounded by all the comforts and conveniences that money can give. She now has the bare necessities of life. . . . She is always cheerful, always dainty and beautiful to the eye, and one never hears of what she lacks or needs, nor of the possessions of the past.

Today Chloe came to tell me Elihu is very sick with pain in his side. I sent her out at once with some tea and milk, a mustard plaster I made, and told her to see it put on. . . . With all his faults, he is one of the best men on the place. . . .

January 4. I am puzzled beyond measure to know what to do for another year. It is impossible to go on planting rice if it is to sell at 40 cents per bushel. It is an expensive crop, and if one borrows money, as I did last year, at a high rate of interest, and puts a mortgage on the plantation, it very soon means ruin. . . . Instead of being anxious to have the usual first of January pow-wow over, as I generally am, I shall do all I can to put it off, for how can one do one's share in a pow-wow when one does not know what to say?

Somehow the year went on. Mrs. Pringle lost her foreman, the finest worker she had. Mr. Z., the white tenant who was "trying to lead a good life," became more difficult, sullen, and careless with her property. Once he lost his temper when she spoke to him and might have killed her with a shovel. Nevertheless, she faced him down, then and later. Sadly, Mrs. Pringle broke her contract with him and paid him much more than she could afford. More losses, more disappointments, and still an occasional happy surprise, a sign of some progress.

With the next Christmas at Cherokee she received a windfall —a dollar a bushel for rice! If only, she reflected wryly, she had used less of it for food and feed. . . . For the holidays, she rehearsed the Negro boys and girls of the area in the Creed, the

Lord's Prayer, the Ten Commandments, and the singing of "While Shepherds Watched Their Flocks by Night."

After four hymns they stand in order of size on the piazza and I hand them around two pounds of candy, which just gives each child a stick, and they depart. But today little fellows shot out from the row and four with much serious unwrapping of handkerchiefs handed me each an egg. I was much surprised and thanked them with effusion.

Preparing a parcel for a good Negro boy who was away, Mrs. Pringle provided a suit, cap, suspenders, and underclothing. "To my intense regret I could not put even a nickel in the pocket. I generally put a quarter and I know he will search every corner." On Christmas Eve she wrote that the mail had delivered "loving offerings from my dear ones," but her spirits were low. "I had not the heart to accept the many invitations I had to spend Christmas, and so I am alone and have time to realize the one great Christmas gift made to our humanity once for all time."

This Christmas Eve at Cherokee Elizabeth Pringle stayed up until 1 A.M., rummaging for presents to give the servants. "I cannot bear to have nothing for them, but my dear father's constant injunction, 'Be just before you are generous,' is indelibly impressed upon me. I owe money to several and so I have not been willing to spend even a quarter for Christmas preparations."

From her own gifts from her family she drew out six boxes of candy, including her prized home-made nutted chocolates. She had two pounds of common stick candy in the house, and she gathered apples and similar items. Hunting in the garret, she discovered five fair-sized boxes, filled them, and attached Christmas cards and ribbons for each of her household helpers. Only when she finished did Mrs. Pringle notice that the containers had somewhat inappropriate labels: "best carbolic soap" and "finest mourning paper"—this latter with black bands all over the box! Nevertheless, she had done her duty, and now her mind went back to the helpers of her childhood holidays.

In the olden time there used to be such crowds coming in to the upstairs hall to wish the Merry Christmas, and one must have a gift for each. Long after the war they kept it up, and I used to have a hamper of little gifts all wrapped to pitch out of the door as I heard each voice. Now I had only Chloe, Dab, Betty, Bonaparte and Gibbie to provide for. . . .

On this Christmas when Elizabeth Pringle went to church she found only three or four others worshiping there. The day was cloudy; the font, filled with holly, provided the only sign of festival. When the organist did not appear, Mrs. Pringle learned to her dismay that she herself had to "raise the hymn," singing without accompaniment, even when they reached the elaborate "Shout the Glad Tidings, Exaltingly Sing!" Despite 'all this, she left the service in improved mood; "all my depression and discouragement floated upward in the quavering shouts of glad tidings."

But the year was not a good one. The old banks of earth about one of her main fields sagged away, and she gave up rice as a crop. She tried cotton; it grew well enough for a time, yet she could not count the experiment a success. On the next December 31 she ended her diary: "Spent this last day of the old year writing letters of thanks and affection, and after dark I made up a bright fire, Chloe and Patty Ann having gone away on their Sunday outing, and sat in the firelight without lighting the lamps and reviewed the mercies and blessings of the past year. God forgive me for my mistakes and sins therein, my blindnesses and lost opportunities."

On this night of stocktaking, Elizabeth Allston Pringle had much to ponder.

I have so loved the freedom and simplicity of the life, in spite of its trials and isolation. The living close to Nature—the trees, the birds, the clouds, and all the simple loving dumb things. But it almost seems as though I was meant to give up. . . . I cannot sit idle in the midst of all this fertile soil. But I must wait, and watch, and listen, in silence, for the still, small voice, which comes after the storm and the earthquake, and brings the message. . . .

By the next Christmas she had finished her experiment, and over her Cherokee a deeper silence than ever had fallen.

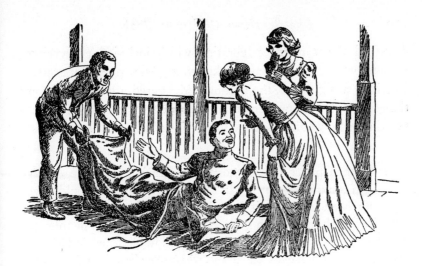

## CHAPTER 9

# *Himself for a Christmas Present*

IN MOST places Christmas arrived with a smile; to Georgia it
came with a chuckle, a long series of them through the years.
Early and late, the people of Atlanta, Savannah, and other parts
of the state have regarded the holidays with a quick, bright eye.
The Georgians had parades of masked "fantastics," "wrestlings
for geese and turkeys," "chicken fights," "Roman-candle battles," "buckboard riding parties," "shooting for prizes," bonfires that lighted up whole towns, and some of the liveliest individual merriment on record.

They ate and drank well, too; writing of Christmas in the
1840's on a Georgia plantation, Richard Henry Hutchings

described the standard celebration which included everything from mincemeats to fattened turkey to striped peppermint candy. Reaching a high note, the authority delivered a dissertation on the eggnog and its proper preparation. The ritual drink, he assured all who would heed the voice of wisdom, must *not* contain milk.

In heathen places farther north, even then this sacrilege may have been committed, but not in Georgia. The master would have hung his head in shame if it had been necessary to eke out the quantity by diluting it with milk. Never! As soon would he tolerate the mint being bruised in his julep as to allow anything in his eggnog but well-beaten eggs, sugar and whiskey or brandy, mixed with rum. And he drank it from a silver spoon, as a gentleman should.

To show that he knew whereof he spoke, Mr. Hutchings volunteered a prime recipe, a lusty combination of several varieties of spirits. Obviously the eggnog was the prewar dry martini of the South; every man had his personal method of creating its joys and yielded precedence to no one else on earth.

Into an earthen bowl place the yolks of six eggs. Add six level tablespoonfuls of granulated sugar and stir with a silver spoon until the sugar is thoroughly dissolved and the mixture smooth. Add six tablespoonfuls (some would add a seventh "for the pot") of whiskey or half rum and half brandy. Stir well. With a silver fork whip the six egg whites stiff. Fold in the yolks, sugar and liquor mixture, but do not agitate more than necessary for thorough blending. Serve in a silver cup or glass goblet with a silver spoon. The recipe serves four.

A contrast to the plantation observance was the city-style one in Atlanta, as different in mood as it was in setting. Few have written of it so well as has Lollie Belle Wylie in her picture of the New Year's celebration in 1867. Atlanta was poor in this year just after the war, she said, and "there was not much furniture left in the homes after Sherman's march." Nevertheless, the town had a zesty New Year's Day.

The holidays of '67 brought few firecrackers to light Atlanta and hardly a handful of noisemakers could be found to liven up the city in these straitened times. Christmas saw only quiet family meals, church services, and candles in windows, signs of good will toward passers-by. But on the first day of the New Year, Atlanta threw open its doors.

The women had fewer supplies to work with, and therefore labored harder than usual for the occasion. Greens were used to cover empty corners and ornament otherwise drab rooms. Long garlands of cedar were draped over the walls; ivy vines clung to the chandeliers with their many candles, and over chromos between the windows fell tendrils of bamboo "which came all the way from Peachtree Creek, or further on from the banks of the Chattahootchie River."

On New Year's Day Atlantans opened their houses at noon, and kept them open until 10 P.M. "No one was invited," Mrs. Wylie explained. "The humblest man had the right to hand in his card at the door, walk in and have a glass of wine and a piece of cake, wherever he chose to go." Although most of the homes were bare of silver flower holders, crystal vases, and the other elegancies of an earlier day, the Atlanta hostesses provided substitutes, simpler but adequate.

Nor had they lost the art of concocting rich confections, and though the ingredients were plainer than they had been, most people said they noticed no difference. There was no cake, yet in a few cases hostesses managed to satisfy another New Year tradition: sliced Georgia ham and beaten biscuits. (At least a hundred strokes—if the biscuits were to be worthy of their name.)

Love, we are informed, also played a part in the city's New Year doings. The ladies planned craftily; older hostesses asked the younger and better-looking girls to assist in receiving, in order to "make the occasion more attractive for the younger set." Which meant, of course, the male half of it. For handsome girls in a receiving line, New Year's often produced a bridegroom. The day was relaxed and easygoing, "and if one happened to see more than was visible to the normal eye, no one criticized, for taking cake and wine at every house had the strange effect of muddling the vision sometimes." Few of the men arrived alone. For economy or for protection from the less attractive females, they came in twos or threes or even larger parties, riding in carriages hired for the occasion.

In the sixties and seventies the custom of sending Christmas and New Year cards had still to reach Atlanta and many other places in the South. But many of the men callers had highly decorated personal cards. The names were "illuminated by the finest pen of the Spencerian artists"; birds, baskets of roses, and cupids surrounded the florid signatures. "The young men who were more sentimental had small silk ribbons tied on their cards in love knots." The postwar times might be bad, but the Victorian era was in full flower.

When a hostess fell ill, or if her family had suffered a loss, she contented herself with hanging a basket at her door on New Year's Day. People understood at a glance; they left their cards and went on their way, and each side felt it had done its duty.

Writing of this aspect of the New Year at a later date, Margaret Stiles told of a childhood holiday in Savannah, when two of her aunts whose widowhood prevented them from receiving, followed the tradition by tying a neat basket on the bell. (The ladies, while bright and cheerful, observed another custom of the time by wearing long crepe veils to the day they died.) That afternoon carriages rode up again and again. The young Georgian and her sister watched through the shutters as people ascended the steps and dropped their cards. "We wondered why such charming ladies could not receive the handsome gentlemen who came to call, and we decided that if ever we were married, we would not be widows."

In a little-known early writing effort, Margaret Mitchell, author of *Gone with the Wind*, has re-created later Georgia doings of New Year's afternoon. Picturing the reception days of 1900, "Peggy Mitchell" described an Atlanta that had recovered from its postwar troubles.

In a story that appeared in the Atlanta *Journal* of 1923, Mrs. Will A. Speer of Peachtree Road recalled for Miss Mitchell the time when "methods of entertainment were old-fashioned and Atlanta was small enough for everyone to know everyone else. . . . My mother handed down to me the tradition of keeping open house on New Year's day." The house, Margaret Mitchell noted, was open for a long period—from 9 A.M. to midnight, and one year Mrs. Speer shook hands with fifteen hundred people. Noon and 6 P.M. brought hot food, "and in between times, eggnog and a plate." The hostess found it "a little wearing," but admittedly it was a happy way of growing tired.

Another Atlantan, Mrs. Bates Block, told of her mother, who "never issued any invitations" to her New Year's receptions, "but expected all her friends to call—and they all did! That was one occasion when you could see all of your friends at one time."

In another part of Atlanta several families arranged to give their parties at the same hours, "so that our guests could go from one house to another and make the rounds within two or three hours. Then when our neighborhood parties were over, we would all go to other parties ourselves."

In the early 1900's, Miss Mitchell tells us, decorations at these parties were lavish. Mistletoe was twined around cutglass chandeliers. Stairways were draped in holly, with vines and greenery along the banisters. Eggnog bowls had holly wreathed along the sides and were surrounded by fruit or flowers encircling a central bowl piled high with whipped cream. With a sigh Margaret Mitchell thought of her own era of 1920, when "there is nothing to do but go to a movie or play golf (which one can do any week day), and when you pay half-hearted calls on friends who obviously aren't expecting any company."

Another contrast is provided by the Christmas account of the brisk-humored Georgia countryman, "Bill Arp," the character created by Charles H. Smith of Rome, who appeared in the Atlanta *Constitution* before the opening of the twentieth century. Cloaking himself as an unlearned rural fellow, Bill had a great deal to say, both lighthearted and penetrating. Once he declared that in the Confederate War he had killed as many of the Yankees as they had of him.

Bill's creator, Charles Smith, was gentle and sharp by turn, a family man who regarded Christmas and its manifestations with an occasional wry grin. Gray-bearded, with a bald head and string tie, he luxuriated in the holidays. His daughter has described his habit of arising early to wake the children by playing the flute or by serenading them at the piano in a highly special fashion; he hit only the black keys.

"Christmas on the Farm," Bill Arp called one of the pieces over which I—and many others—have chuckled. He began it sentimentally:

A happy New Year ... I don't mean just the first day, but all the year round. I wish from my heart everybody was comfortable and contented and everybody lived in peace. I was ruminating over that kind of a millennium which would come if there were no bad folks—no lazy folks, no envy nor spite nor revenge—no bad passions, but everybody took things easy and tried to make all around them happy. I wasent thinking about a religious millennium for

I have known people to make mighty good, honorable citizens who dident have any religion to spare, and some who had a power of it on Sunday but was a'juggling with the devil all the rest of the week. I was thinking about that class of folks who gave us no trouble and was always willing to tote fair. . . .

Let's have a Christmas all the year long. Let's keep the family hearth always bright and pleasant. Fussing and fretting don't pay. Solomon says it's like water dropping on a rock—it will wear away a stone. The home of an unhappy discordant family is no home at all. It ain't even a decent purgatory. The children won't stay there any longer than possible. They will emigrate and I don't blame 'em.

Now, getting to the heart of the matter, Bill made illuminating comments on the respective roles of husband and wife in Christmas arrangements.

We've had a power of fun at my house the last few days. Mrs. Arp said she was going to town. She had a little passel of money hid away—nobody knew how much or where she got it, but sometimes when my loose change is laying around or left in my pockets, I've noticed that it disappears very mysteriously. It took about two hours to arrange herself for the expedition and she left us on a mission of peace on earth and good will to her children.

"Now, William, you know the Christmas tree is to be put up in the hall. You have very good taste about such things and I know I can trust you without any directions. Put it in that large square box in the smoke house and fasten it well to the bottom, and put the top on the box for a table, and the girls will cover it nicely with some curtain calico. But I will not direct you, for I know you can fix it all right.

"There are most too many limbs on the tree. There is a lot of pop corn already threaded and you can arrange them in festoons all over the tree, and the oranges that Dick sent us from Florida are locked up in the pantry. Thread them with a large needle and tie them all about on the limbs. The little wax candles and the tins to fasten them are in the drawer of my bureau. I've had them for several years and we will light up the tree tonight.

"The milk is ready to churn you know. Set the jar in the large tin bucket before you churn. It will save messing the floor. There are two turkeys in the coop—take the fattest one—you can tell by holding them up in your hands. Ralph will help about the turkey.

"If you think one turkey will not be enough you had better kill a couple of chickens to go with it. I do hope all the children will be here, but I am afraid they won't. It does look like we might get together once a year anyhow. Now do attend to the turkey just as nice as you can, and leave the butter for me to work over when I come back.

"The front yard ought to be swept and the back yard is an awful mess. But I will just leave everything to you. Keep the hall doors locked, for the children mustent see the tree until Santa Claus comes. That mistletoe must be put over the parlor pictures. Hunt up a few more eggs if you can find them. Don't disturb the mince pie in the closet—never mind about that either, for I've got the key in my pocket."

Surely thousands of Georgia husbands, and husbands from other states as well, had a merry hour over this portrait of a housewife. To it Bill Arp added a chronicle of Christmas at his house: "How the little folks had lived on tip-toe for many days waiting for Santa Claus, and how that humble parlor was dressed in cedar and mistletoe, and the big back log put on, and the blazing fire built up, and the little stockings hung by the mantel. ... How that blue-eyed daughter played deputy to him, and was the keeper of everybody's secret; and shutting herself up in the parlor, arranged everything to her notion."

Then a new Christmas note. When supper ended, one of the Arp boys, his cornet in his hand, darted up the ladder to the roof to blow the signal that Santa Claus had arrived. With such a blast from above, what child could doubt St. Nicholas's reality?

The young ones raced into the room, crying out in surprise, and gladness "gleamed and glistened all around, and the big bucket of family joy ran over. But everybody knows how it is hisself, and don't hanker after a history of other people's frolics." In closing, Bill commented on New Year's resolutions which, he said, were "kept about three weeks."

That's all right. Keep 'em as long as you can, but don't repent of this year's sins too much at once. Don't get too much religion at a revival, for by and by the snow will be gone, and the spring will open and the birds begin to sing and flowers to bloom and man's conceit and independence come back to him and make him forget the winter and his promises, and strut around like he was running the whole macheen.

In Savannah, Georgia's great seaport and older social center, the 1870's, '80's, and '90's beheld a more sophisticated Christmas funmaking. During this period thousands of people poured into the main streets on Christmas Eve to make merry, to inspect the sights (including other people there to inspect *them*), and to toss and dodge firecrackers. The evening's stars were the "Fantastics," a lively organization whose members masqueraded and held formal processions for the public.*

The Fantastics had their own blaring band. Some maskers went on foot while others rode fine mounts. Their dress was elaborate, with feathers, spangles, silver, and satin. Crowds lined up to watch and follow them. At times the Fantastics turned to satire, poking a finger at town foibles, at politicians and at other leading lights.

In 1870 their "funny, grotesque costumes provoked a roar of laughter . . . in every direction, and their whole route was one of triumph." A year later they emerged in garb representing

---

* A full picture of Savannah Christmases of the period is obtained from excellent separate studies by Alfrieda De Renne Barrow and Edith D. Johnston.

"many persons, distinguished for their virtues and follies and vices." Such characters included "Punch, the Prince of Fun," "King William of Russia," and an individual who "carried his tail over his shoulder," stuck out a fiery tongue, and darted a long fork at the throng—His Highness the Devil, a big-bodied fellow in shiny black dress. Behind him was a little red imp on a horse. The sight inspired a newspaper to political comment: "If the defunct Governor had appeared, the trio would have been complete, but there is only room for one Bullock on earth and one in the lowest place of all."

The cult of the Fantastics thrived for decades. Rival groups developed, and one holiday witnessed a "Fantastics No. 1" parade at 10 A.M., a "Fantastics No. 2" at 2:30 P.M., and a tripping of the "light fantastics" that night. Fireworks and noisemaking were a major part of the Fantastics' proceedings. On one occasion, "at the junction of Bull and Broughton streets, the regular annual bombardment took place . . . opened in the usual manner by a few young men throwing firecrackers at each other." Again, said an ironic note, "some 4823 tin horns of all shapes and sizes were purchased, and it appeared by common consent they were all blown at the same time without intermission."

An equally jaundiced observer declared at another time that "the sidewalks could not hold the people, so they bulged into the street and half-filled the asphalt pavement with an aimlessly straggling mass. They were four blocks of bedlam, of tooting horns, of shrieking cornets, of loud laughter, loud talk and senseless gabber." Yet a native of modern Savannah looked back nostalgically to these days when every square had its boys' Christmas clan "and the city was alive with bonfires."

The townsmen also enjoyed such entertainment as turkey-shooting at the Isle of Hope; a chicken fight "between two chickens of local celebrity on Christmas morning in Yamacraw, in the presence of a large number of lovers of the sport of the cock-pit"; trotting and running races at the Park Course, with special trains back and forth; and "buckboard parties" that rode out to the track, returned to town for lunch, and went thundering off again.

In these days before automobiles, "everybody seemed to think that nothing better than a ride to Thunderbolt (the track) could be had, and the streets and roads were enlivened by many hand-some equipages. . . . It is seldom that there is such a run on livery stables, and by two o'clock the proprietors were telling those who called for teams that they had nothing left in their stables."

But not all Savannahians celebrated Christmas in this style. In 1879 a "Drew Temperance" gathering was "largely at-tended" during Christmas week, with "undoubtedly the best meeting of the series." And repeatedly newspaper editors com-plained about Christmas cannonading. In 1878 one noted that while churches were well attended by "the staid and thought-ful," great sums were spent "in the useless and dangerous display of fireworks," and that "many pronounced these 'roman candle battles' on a public thoroughfare as simply abominable."

Apparently Savannah preferred to be abominable. A few years later, in one of the city's parks, young men and boys collected six hundred barrels of wood for fires and the mayor, "with his usual liberality," contributed a hogshead of resin and a wagon-load of fireworks! Other fires in other parks kept the town glow-ing all over. A fireworks vendor presented a nine-inch list of offerings including cannon crackers, Roman candles, skyrockets, "Colored Fire in Bags," "Geysers," "Giant Torpedoes," and others which, it was promised, would give a magnificent effect after dark. All of these, the brochure went on, were "enter-taining to children and perfectly harmless."

Savannah, always a city of gourmets and a center for social

travelers, professional men, and other sojourners, provided many a Christmas-time fulfillment at the table and bar. Its hotels and restaurants had shining reputations, and at the holidays their proprietors competed in the range and succulence of their fare. The Gem Saloon of 1875 proclaimed a "novelty for Christmas," a glass of eggnog for every customer, with fried oysters, free. That same year brought tributes to the "annual punch" prepared in the editorial rooms of the *Morning News* by Franz Bergmann, the "well-known mixiologist."

The punch was said to be similar to one that had been brewed recently for the King of Sweden. An expert asserted that its "component parts were most admirably proportioned, the result . . . one of the most exquisitely flavored we have ever tasted . . . mild and yet not insipidly so, and the aroma of each ingredient was well preserved." According to the same authority, the mixiologist completely surpassed "his famous effort in New Orleans where he brewed a bowl for the ladies . . . the merits of which were discussed for months afterward."

In 1876 the proprietor of the Cotton Exchange Restaurant pledged "a magnificent bill of fare for the Christmas dinner . . . Sol Smith Russel's great dish of 'goose stuffed with sage and "inyins." ' " Yet nothing could match the De Soto Hotel's gala gentlemen's free lunch of 1891, which "exceeded anything of the kind ever seen in Savannah . . . Chef Xavier Heller's crowning work of art since the opening of the season."

On this night of splendor the centerpiece "represented a team of suckling pigs harnessed to a wagon driven by Santa Claus, and loaded with boned turkey garnished with quail. . . . The second piece was an immense salmon, decorated in green, red and black and lying upon a bed of green moss made of frozen suet and butter." At the head of the table sat two wild turkeys with their wings and feathers "on as if alive," and at the foot there rested two proud hams, "one figure in sugar representing a vase of flowers, and the other checkered like a chess board." For hotel guests, as noted before, it all came free. At least a hundred gourmets, gourmands, and trenchermen paid the chef the compliment of consuming everything, down to the last edible ornamentation.

One Georgian gave a special rural or small-town flavor to his Christmas yarn about the courtship of "Major Jones." For a long time William Tappan Thompson amused Americans with his tales based on observations of the state and its people. The Major had hankered for many months after his "Miss Mary," but now he could write that he was engaged. He had done it, "slick as a whistle, though it come mighty nigh being a serious undertakin."

More than twenty times the Major had made up his mind to "come right out with the whole business," but whenever he "got whar she was, and whenever she looked at me with her witchin' eyes, and kind o' blushed at me," he always felt "kind o' skeered and fainty. . . . It's a mighty great favour to ax of a right pretty gall," he thought.

Nevertheless, on Christmas Eve Major Jones put on a new suit, shaved his face "as slick as a smoothin iron," and called on the Stallinses, Miss Mary, Miss "Car'line," and Miss Kesiah. After the amenities had been taken care of, the Major declared he wished to give Miss Mary a Christmas present "to keep all her life." With many blushes at such bold language, the young woman indicated she would accept it.

"But it would take a two-bushel bag to hold it," the Major warned, and that evening she must have such a bag, like a Christmas stocking, on the back porch. When she waked in the morning, he announced, the gift would be there.

Then Major Jones took his leave. At midnight, however, he returned to Miss Mary's and slipped up to the porch, where, sure enough, an old meal bag was hanging to the joists. Although it was "monstrous unhandy" to reach, he had determined not to back out. He set chairs on a bench, climbed up, caught hold of the rope, and let himself into the bag.

His entrance into the bag made it swing against the chairs, which toppled over with a crash. The eldest Miss Stallins' big cur dog awoke, startled, and went "rippin and tarin through the yard," trying to find the source of the trouble.

The Major in his bag tried not to breathe "louder nor a kitten," and after a time the dog stopped barking. But now a new hazard developed. A stiff wind rose, and the bag swayed violently in the icy air. The Major was frozen and he began to feel seasick. Afraid to move too much lest he break the rope, he stayed there hour after hour, teeth rattling.

It seemed to him that morning would never arrive, and only the thought of Miss Mary kept him from freezing. In the early hours the dog returned and, sniffing about the bag, barked as if he had treed something. "Git out!" the Major muttered, very low, so that no one else would hear. "You abominable fool!"

An ever-growing alarm swept him; the animal might nip him at any moment, "and what made it worse, I didn't know whar bouts he'd take hold." Neither a wheedling approach nor a low whistle seemed to please the dog and he stayed there, whining and barking, until finally the chickens crowed, and the oldest sister came out on the porch.

She summoned Miss Mary. What on earth had the Major left there? "I'll lay it's a yearlin or some live animal or Bruin wouldn't bark at it so." Soon the three sisters stood, puzzled and a little frightened; they had seen the thing move. Finally they called their helper to cut the bag down. "Don't hurt it for the world," Miss Mary cautioned.

Cato, the helper, "let the bag down easy," and the Major tumbled before them, covered in corn meal from head to foot.

Miss Mary cried out in astonishment, and the Major reminded her: "You know you promised to keep my Christmas present as long as you lived."

The other women "laughed themselves almost to death," brushed the meal off him, and vowed to hang up that bag every Christmas until they, too, got husbands. Miss Mary blushed "as beautiful as a morning-glory" and announced she would stick to her word. The Major thawed himself out, Miss Mary said he must call her Mary now, and the two families gathered for what he proclaimed one of the greatest Christmas dinners ever seen in Georgia, "and I don't believe a happier company ever sot down to the same table."

# CHAPTER 10

# Under the Quiet Palm Trees

CHARLES DICKENS once declared, rather pontifically, that, "after all, a Christmas without snow . . . is only half a Christmas." In Florida, the state that juts far down toward the tropics, the author of "A Christmas Carol" would not be regarded as a very good judge of the matter. When I quoted Dickens to an aging, kindhearted native of Jacksonville, an enthusiast of Florida's holiday season, he snorted.

"The Christmas we have down here looks more like the Bible Christmas than anything anybody's ever seen. Palms and sand, and—and vines and roses in December. . . . It has the Holy Land atmosphere, and the people that started Christmas would feel a lot more at home here than up there with the English fogs.

When you see that Mr. Dickens again, you tell him so for me!"

I promised, agreeing that, as far as Christmas goes, Florida need feel no inferiority to any part of America. Though "newest" of the Southern states in one sense, it is the oldest in another. Europeans landed in the vicinities of Pensacola and St. Augustine, Tampa and Miami, St. Petersburg and Key West, decades and even as much as a century before they went to Virginia or to New England; and it seems certain that the first American Christmas rites were held along the Florida shores.

On the other hand, many parts of Florida were not settled until the 1840's, and some hardly saw real development until about fifty years ago. In the sections where sugar estates flourished, a plantation Christmas was celebrated; while only a short distance off, the observance was closely related to that found on the frontier. Florida, like Texas, also had cowboys who led a casual life, and whose ways of celebrating seemed somewhat explosive to the town neighbors they visited during the holidays. Latin Christmas or Anglo-Saxon, ancient or not so ancient. . . . A Miami resident explained: "Whatever the rest of America had for the holidays, we've had it, too." And other things as well. In few other parts of the South have I seen a Florida innovation —Christmas trees in the patios and beside the swimming pools.

Although a long file of early Spanish explorers ventured to the breeze-swept Florida coasts, many left scant record of their adventures. But beyond doubt some spent the holy season on shore with the priests who accompanied them, the long expanse of ocean behind them, hostile Indians ahead. As they knelt before improvised altars, they must have added to their devout celebration of Christ's birth a request for a Christmas favor— deliverance from these dangers.

In October, 1539, a group led by the strong-willed Hernando De Soto, and including twelve priests, camped just southwest of modern Tallahassee, remaining there until March of the next year. Tallahassee patriots, therefore, claim the "original" American Christmas ceremony as their own. There is also an account of a Christmas observance in 1565 at St. Augustine, before the wooden altar of the Mission of Nombré de Dios, presided over by Father Francisco Lopez de Mendoza Grajales. Today the shrine of Nuestra Señora de la Leche stands there.

The St. Augustine settlement of 1565 was the first permanent one established by Europeans in what later became the United States. For St. Augustine has continued to exist, despite raids, overnight destruction, plagues, and other hazards; while Jamestown was abandoned by the Virginians and other early ports underwent transfers of location or complete rebuilding.

The armor-clad Spaniards who clanked about the palmetto clumps gave the place a stamp that is still recognizable—stuccoed walls, arched gateways, overhanging galleries with Iberian ironwork. In the patios, with their banana plants and their smell of flowers, the people had Christmases that were Latin in their religious reverence yet at the same time free spirited and free moving.

The British took over St. Augustine and Florida for twenty years, but the Spanish returned and even after the United States assumed ownership in 1821 the area continued to have a Latin look. Two decades after American rule began, a caller set down the Latin Christmas-time enjoyments. The Presbyterian Bishop Henry B. Whipple of Minnesota stayed in St. Augustine in the 1840's, watched drowsy alligators in the vicinity, and admired the "groves of wild oranges" and the luxuriance of the greenery. But he did not admire all things Floridian: January 1, "delightfully warm and pleasant," brought a large ball with much the carnival flavor of those held in French Mobile during the holidays. That night one party of maskers dressed as Indians and re-enacted "the war dance of the Seminoles."

The people of St. Augustine, the Bishop wrote, start their mummering at Christmas "and continue it until Lent." At least some of the Americans had joined the Latins and clearly enjoyed themselves. "These masquers select their own disguises and then visit from house to house, acting their several parts. At times these disguises and the acting is excellent, but many times it resembles the fantastics seen on military training days."

Now and then maskers sent word to someone that they would "dance at his house in the evening." Obligingly the host provided refreshments, while the merrymakers produced their own music. After acting their parts, they remained for a social evening. One night in early January three separate masked companies called at Bishop Whipple's temporary residence. The first consisted of three Spanish girls, dressed as elderly women, who "danced beautifully." In the second group were a supposedly "hideous old man and a would-be-fashionable woman"; and in the third "a barber, his sweetheart, a homely black woman, a little decrepit old man." Generally the bands brought tambourines and violins and danced about the house.

Night after night the maskers paid calls; by this time many of the Anglo-Saxon elite had been drawn into the Spanish custom. "The Hon. Mrs. Bronson disguised as an Indian squaw, Lieutenant Runford as Billy Bowlegs, Miss Spafford as an old Irish woman and Lieut. Lee as her son, Miss Hernandez, Miss Worth and Miss Humphreys as nuns." The Bishop expressed doubt that "this kind of amusement well suited the dignity and standing of some of the parties concerned. It is certain it would be deemed a letting down of dignity among our northern people, but among the Romans some do as the Romans do."

Despite all this, Bishop Whipple concluded that the Christmas masking, like other Spanish customs, was "fast disappearing . . . giving way to American tastes and American amusements, much to the benefit of morality." And yet, from his own descriptions, the observances were mild and harmless, and thirteen years later another Anglo-Saxon at St. Augustine, Charles A. Lanman, discovered the Carnival-Christmas still in full sway. The masqueraders, accompanied by bands of musicians, were parading the streets every evening until midnight.

The "forbearance" of the Anglo-Saxons, as Mr. Lanman described it, enabled the Latin celebrants to "enter their dwellings without ceremony" and cut their capers. Later, they retired to rendezvous in the Spanish quarter and "spent the remainder of the night in dancing and festivity, to which they are universally addicted."

Latin Christmases thrived at Tampa, Key West, Pensacola, and other Florida places; much of the Spanish flavor can still be traced in each of them. From Cuba thousands of men and women have moved to the nearby Florida peninsula, to work in the cigar factories and follow other callings, and introduced their own version of the Spanish holidays.

Meanwhile the Anglo-Saxons arrived in Florida in irregular numbers, clustering at one point after another on the shore or inland. A later Christmas visitor, noting how magnificently the tea roses usually held their own in the Florida December weather, remarked that they possessed "the feminine trait of exposing pink and white beauty to the inclement winds without growing goose flesh." For the most part there were few goose bumps during the state's holidays. And among the settlers of 1850-60 in the east central section, at Orlando, which eventually became the largest inland Florida city, a simpler, rural American style of Christmas developed.

It was the Seminole Wars that had brought the first settlement of central Florida. Men assigned there, liking the area, stayed on, and cattle growing sprang up and prospered. At the beginning, however, as E. H. Gore has noted, "money was scarce" and Christmas comparatively meager. The main presents were red hair ribbons for the girls and red-streaked candy for all the children. "The men laid in a store of tobacco and the women had their snuff."

The quieter Orlando settlers went to church, and had their holiday meals at home with friends; however hard the times, they ate well at Christmas. Mr. Gore reports so many wild turkeys in the woods that hunters often killed more than they could eat. Since there was no ice in which to preserve the birds, the housewives dried the breasts and threw away the rest. For Christmas the men occasionally barbecued a steer or a hog, and bear and deer meat were also served, with sweet potatoes, home-made cheese, corn bread, and "surrup" made from sugar cane.

Christmas evening in Orlando proved a time for the menfolk to kick up their heels. "It was more like Halloween," one pioneer said, in understatement. On one well-remembered night boys piled heavy boxes in a barricade across the main street, so that everyone had to detour. The higher-spirited ones caught a calf and turned it loose on the second floor of a hotel. When a man from the East Coast slipped heavily and lay down to rest in an empty lot, the town celebrants "built a fire around him, and he thought he was in hell, especially when his coat caught on fire." At about that point, the boys rescued him and dressed his burns. All this, clearly, came under the heading of good, clean fun.

That same night Billy Bowlegs, the Indian leader, and some of his men came into town, seeking firewater. The townsmen knew "just the place" the red men wanted—the church ladies' Christmas bazaar. The ladies paled when the Indians appeared, but bravely took them in and fed them. "They had a good time," Mr. Gore notes, "but disappeared into the forest the next day." Later in the evening the cowpunchers took over the town and the marshal hid out, "as there were too many of them for him to handle." Firing wildly into the air, they rode their ponies up and down the streets, and then up the steps and into the saloons, where they drank at the bar without getting out of the saddle. When one cowboy "saw something fancy on the wall" he shot three times at it. Lassoing a cow, they dragged her through the streets. Having decided that lassoing was fun, they began to lasso each other and anyone who happened to venture by. (Most citizens stayed home.)

By 1885 Fort Myers on the West Coast, which was to become a center for the shipment of citrus fruit, cattle, and winter vegetables, had reached a quieter stage. Small boys, "the destroying angels," used up practically all available fireworks at Fort Myers before Christmas arrived, and so the town was not so noisy as expected. As Thomas Gonzales notes, there was talk of a "serenading party" to go from house to house on Christmas Eve, but it did not materialize. Determined fun-makers nevertheless marched up and down the streets, beating tin pans, pots, kettles, washboards, and the like.

And Christmas morning saw an old frontier-type observance: "Shooting for the beef," said the announcement, and the best riflemen gathered to fire a hundred yards for an excellent beef. First-prize winner would have the choice of cut he wanted, and four others would follow according to their ranking. The men had practiced for weeks, and the day was bright—perfect weather for shooting.

Nevertheless, many were disappointed at the showings, and the day after Christmas, perhaps to prove how much better they could do, the shooters assembled for a second contest. This time the prize was something less glamorous, a pair of boots "offered by Towles and Hendry." The scores that day were even worse than they had been the previous morning, but that might have been blamed, of course, on the night's celebrations.

By then Fort Myers was debating its major event of the season, a joust or tournament in the pattern of medieval days to honor a Court of Love and Beauty. Such tourneys thrived all over the South in the 1850's and also after the Confederate War, with men riding on to the field under such names and banners as Sir Launcelot, Ivanhoe, and Richard the Lion-Hearted.

Horses were groomed until they shone, and bright ribbons and assorted decorations were braided into their manes. The riders' costumes included sashes or trailing robes. Bugles sounded, and often a professional speechmaker, chosen for the volume of his voice, flung his arms in the air and in a tremolo paid tribute to the glory of Southern ladies and the gallantry of Southern noblemen.

Many blamed the phenomenon on Sir Walter Scott. Mark Twain chortled over these high-flown theatricals. Critics have noted that, whatever some Southerners said, the South of the nineteenth century was rather unlike the England of King Arthur's court, if, indeed, England itself had ever been quite that way. Nevertheless, generations of men and women went misty-eyed at the glamour of the day as "knights" with Southern accents galloped out and ladies reviewed their champions. And the Floridians, like most Southern men, had to ride so much that they qualified as excellent horsemen.

While tournaments were held at various times of the year, at Fort Myers, as in some parts of Texas and other places, they eventually became part of Christmas.* As Thomas Gonzalez re-

---

* In the Lone Star State, Frank Dobie (whose mother was once crowned a Queen of Love and Beauty) listed tournament tilters with the proud titles of "Knight of Shanghai Springs," "Knight of Dry Branch," and "Knight of the Bragg Wright Thickett." And he has quoted a Texan, once of Alabama, who honored his queen with these remarkable lines:

> Fair lady, take this wreath,
>   And though its flowers may fade upon thy marble brow,
> The day on which I gave it thee
>   Shall ever be as fresh within my memory as now.

Although Mr. Dobie does not say so, it might have been verses such as these which eventually did in the Texas tournament. In any case the custom died.

ported, rules were simple. Holding their lances, the participants would ride across the field at full speed, aiming for three rings that hung in a line from horizontal bars about ten feet off the ground. Each had a fair opportunity to show his skill.

On this Christmas occasion of 1885 the weather was chillier than usual, and windy, but the knights provided moments of strong excitement. A certain amount of humor crept into the exhibition, for one J. C. Jeffcott, "our Irish comedian," took part by bestowing a title on each nobleman, "and the appelations in most cases were very significant."

The winner had the right, as usual, to select the Queen of Love and Beauty to rule over the Court a night later. When the tilting ended, the contestants held a second competition, a less lustrous one, for a prize of "a pair of fine blankets," offered by the ever-present firm of Towles and Hendry.

Cowboys firing into the Christmas night, Indians at ladies' church socials, knights tilting for the right to name a queen and also to collect blankets ... Out of them evolved a Florida Christmas with survivals of the old and a number of latter-day additions. In 1935, for instance, a settlement in the piney woods beyond the Atlantic coast learned how correct Dickens was when he said there was "magic in the very name of Christmas." In that year the Florida town of this name celebrated its hundredth anniversary.

In 1835 American soldiers labored to build a new fort against Seminole attacks, and as Christmas approached, the men were struggling to complete a stockade of cabbage-palm logs. By December 25 they had finished their work and to the fort came settlers who rejoiced in their refuge, and who helped the soldiers name the stockade: Fort Christmas.

Later the "fort" was dropped from the town's name and it

inched along as a small market center in a locale of citrus groves and cattle. Then, with its centennial, the world took notice.

Today about 300,000 pieces of mail pass every December through this town of 300 people. Men and women from all sections of the United States send cards and letters to be stamped with the mystic postmark and remailed. Others write in from Mexico, Canada, France, England, Scotland, Italy, Korea, Japan. One impressed Swiss sent two hundred letters.

Dozens of visitors to Florida arrange their trips so that they can call at the Christmas season and mail their holiday cards and letters in person. Few postmasters in the country are as busy during this season as is Mrs. Juanita Tucker, who has served for more than a quarter century in a one-room office. To the town's regular postmark she adds a bright, special cachet. A recent one had a green Christmas tree, decorated with candles, and the words of the carol: "Glory to God in the Highest."

Christmas, Florida, has a year-round open-air Christmas tree, and soon after Thanksgiving the town holds a community "Christmas shower" to gather ornaments for the handsome growth. Before it stands a sign: "The permanent Christmas tree at Christmas, Florida, is the symbol of love and good will: The Christmas spirit every day in the year."

Regardless of what Mr. Dickens said about the need for snow at his favorite season, he would have liked that. After all, the thought is his own.

Every Christmas week thousands head toward the Bok Singing Tower near Lake Wales, center of a musical observance which has stirred countless Americans during the past quarter century. Here is Florida's highest elevation, Iron Mountain, a retreat for endless flocks of birds and also a place of serenity for people who seek the South in winter. On top of the mountain, in a region of thirty or more lakes, stands the majestic tower, 230 feet high, of soft gray-and-pink rock and marble.

On this mountain, it is said, the Indians convened annually for their ceremony of the Rising Sun. Near the present tower early searchers discovered a large stone with thirteen smaller ones, symbolizing the Indians' great sun and the year's thirteen moons. Today the spot is the setting of a tale that is a kind of legend in itself.

Born in the Netherlands, brought to the United States as a baby, Edwark Bok found opportunity for achievement, and felt a profound gratitude to the country. A man with a remarkable perception for beauty, he never forgot the story of his grandparents. Grandfather Bok, assigned to guard a bleak, treacherous sand island off the coast of Holland, had first coped successfully with wreckers who preyed for years on trapped vessels. Then he had gone to work with his wife to turn the large sandy waste into an oasis.

Steadily, year by year, the Boks put down trees and bushes, created parks and winding walks. Flights of migrant birds went by, settled tentatively, then continued to come as annual callers, until the island won fame among Europeans.

As each of her thirteen children reached maturity, Grandmother Bok called him, gave a full acount of her husband's labors, and urged the young Bok, when he went into the world, to carry with him something of that spirit, and make the place around him a more beautiful one. In America Edward Bok became a distinguished editor, a benefactor of music at a time when most Americans regarded it as a European luxury, and also an earnest laborer, although some snickered at his efforts, for the thing called world peace. One winter, while he was staying in Florida, he made his way to the peak of Iron Mountain, and as he looked about at the green earth and silver lakes below him, he again remembered the family tradition, and resolved to turn this place into a monument to his grandparents.

Today, in the nearly sixty acres of Mountain Lake Sanctuary, there grow unending varieties of vines and shrubs, plants and trees, thousands of azaleas, iris, amaryllis, callas and magnolias, oak trees and palmettos.

As they once went to Grandfather Bok's sandy island, birds by the tens of thousands have come here, winging their way about the tranquil setting. From Europe sanctuary officials have imported others, including a continental nightingale to sing beside the Florida mockingbirds.

The delicate Singing Tower crowns the area, occupying a small island with a moat in which its outlines are reflected. Far above, eight Gothic windows, thirty-five feet long, have a delicate tracery, from which issues the music so many people hear during each Christmas season.

The notes come from one of the greatest sets of carillons in the world, with seventy-one bells covering a range of four and a half octaves. The largest weighs nearly twelve tons, the smallest twelve pounds. With each Christmas men and women arrive at this place of superb bird life, of a surpassing beauty of many vistas, to hear concerts of music of the holy season. Over the soft air goes a flood of deeply moving notes: carols, hymns, songs of holiday significance.

## CHAPTER 11

# "Watching for the Coming of Christ"

IN THE rural stretches of Alabama, thousands of men and women gathered together every Christmas Eve to sing, to pray, and, on bended knees, to "watch for the coming of Christ." His return to earth, they felt certain, would take place on this night, some time after midnight on the anniversary of His birth.

They began to assemble about nine or ten o'clock, and remained together for hours. There was no regular service, no sermon, during this half-solemn, half-joyous event, and their voices rose as they chanted hymns or in halting phrases affirmed their faith on a night of supreme significance.

While it was not confined to the Negroes, this custom found its strongest expression among the former slaves, and although it was followed in other states, for generations it was especially common in Alabama. Peter Brannon, the state archivist, remembered it from his own boyhood years.

The tradition, Mr. Brannon noted, was "not superstition, but really a reverent homage to the occasion." It was less a church than a folk observance. In Russell County, for example, the Negroes did not gather at the church itself, but at Riley's School.

Most employers knew of the custom, and realized that their servants would not leave the school building until daylight. Accordingly, the Negroes were not expected to be on duty for an early breakfast Christmas Day. The worshipers would make their appearance later in the morning, after a few hours' sleep, tired, but filled with the meaning of their earnest ceremonial.

In South Carolina there was a similar belief, which continued for many years. Elizabeth Allston Pringle noted that on Christmas Eve, in the opening years of this century, all her servants went to the "setting up." Carefully they explained to her that attendance at this ceremony was one of the strongest articles of their creed. "They must not be found in their beds on this mysterious night when the King of the world was born and laid in a manger."

Once Mrs. Pringle warned a feeble servant that she was not strong enough to be up so long. The old woman's response was immediate. Did Mrs. Pringle think she would let the Lord catch *her* in bed on the night when the very cows fell on their knees? * "No, Ma'am, dis night is fer pray, en shout, en rejoice." The Alabama Negroes would have said precisely the same thing.

Alabama has always been a state of diversities, from the mountainous and rural northern area to the elegant French-

* For this Christmas belief see the later chapter, "The Night the Animals Talk."

English-Spanish-American Mobile; from the thriving industrial region of Birmingham to Montgomery, the "Confederacy's Cradle," with its nearby cotton fields. An old plantation civilization flowered in one area; the steamboats rolled from river landing to market. In another, a comparatively short distance away, there grew up the bustling business towns of the newer South. It is not surprising, then, that Alabama's Christmases should have ranged from the homespun to the urbane, from the folksy to the cosmopolitan.

One of the region's first recorded holiday episodes involved both whites and Indians, and, as in other places, mixed romance with Christmas. William Bartram, the botanist, had left Mobile in late November of 1777 in the company of an English trader who had married an Indian girl, and a helper who was part Mustee Indian, part white. Although the latter's father had taught him reading, writing, and mathematics, neither the boy's education nor his experience among the English-speaking peoples had prevented him from falling in love with an Indian girl, the daughter of a chief.

Bartram spent the Christmas holiday season among the Creeks in what is now Montgomery County. To his delight, he learned that a wedding ceremony was about to be held. The first day was one of "rest and audience," the second would be "devoted to fasting." And that night were held the festivities uniting the Mustee youth and the chief's daughter.

The red men danced, played solemn music, and feasted for hours. As morning approached, the newlywed couple quietly went off to a pavilion of green boughs, in front of which grew two tall magnolia trees. They stayed in this chamber through all of the next day, "no one presuming to approach the sacred, mysterious" dwelling place. Thus one of Alabama's pioneer Christmases. . . .

Two decades later Benjamin Hawkins, a Creek Indian agent,

went to this Indian region as guest of a Macon County trader, a man who had a true trencherman's taste. The Christmas meal of 1796 included pork, a pair of fowls, a pair of ducks, rice, potatoes, "cole-warts" or artichokes, both Indian bread and white bread, homemade butter, coffee, rum—and, for good measure, tea.

The Negro slaves in the settlement had their own holiday good time, dancing and drinking, while the whites and Indians enjoyed theirs each in a separate set of festivities. The red men might not have accepted the white men's faith, but they heartily approved of their celebrations.

Four years later—again on a Christmas—love blossomed unexpectedly in Alabama's Indian land, in the community of Sam Mims on Tensaw Lake. In this area of hard-working settlers, then remote, there were neither ministers nor law officers, and, we are told, many young couples "took up housekeeping" together, planning to get married later, when and if an official turned up. Such an informal arrangement, however, did not satisfy Elizabeth Linder, daughter of a well-to-do native of Switzerland, and young Daniel Johnson. He was as poor as she was rich, and although her family disapproved, the couple had been in love for a short time, and decided to find somebody who could make them legally man and wife.

Keeping their secret from all except a few of their closest friends, Elizabeth and Daniel went to a breezy Christmas Eve party. At first they joined in the dancing, but soon they disappeared and, with several sympathizers, slipped to a canoe and paddled on to Fort Stoddart, which, while many miles off, was the nearest place that suggested itself. The settlers rowed for hours, and dawn had come and gone by the time they reached their goal. Although they were able immediately to locate the officer they sought, he clearly did not agree that he was their man.

Captain Shaumburg of the army's Second Regiment was mixing his Christmas-morning eggnog, we are informed, when the anxious couple arrived. He was only an army man, he informed them; he knew nothing about marriage rites, and who said he had any authority to preside at anything of any kind?

Elizabeth and Daniel had their arguments ready. The United States had sent Captain Shaumburg there as protector of its people and the supervisor of their welfare; in the absence of anyone else, he had to serve. Reluctantly the Captain gave in. Everybody toasted the bride and groom, and the officer said a few words. "I, Captain Shaumburg of the Second Regiment, United States Army, and commandant at Fort Stoddart, do hereby pronounce you man and wife." And then, it is said, he added: "Go home. Behave yourselves, multiply and replenish the Tensaw country." The area smiled over the episode, and it was generally agreed that Elizabeth and Daniel were "the *best* married pair they had known in a long time." This Christmas wedding ceremony is believed to be the first marriage performed in Protestant Alabama.

At Mobile, Christmas produced, in a curious fashion, the phase of the town's life for which thousands have known it best —the Carnival doings which have set a model for many other cities. Certain aspects of Mobile's large-scale Mardi Gras preceded even those of the South's Carnival capital, New Orleans. From the early 1700's, when the French settled on Mobile Bay, the colonial Alabamians held carnivals. Sometimes they took place on New Year's, with the "Boeuf Gras" or Fat Ox, but they were also held on other dates.

Then, on New Year's Eve of 1830, a band of light-spirited Mobilians enjoyed a round of festivities which took them, eventually, past a darkened hardware store, and Mobile's New Year's Eve organization, the Cowbellion de Rakin Society, had its birth. In front of the shop, in the fashion of the day, stood several symbolic rakes, hoes, and cowbells. The gay group snatched them and, brandishing them, paraded up and down the streets. Their mood growing ever brighter, they serenaded the homes of friends, pounding and clanking as they went, and they wound up their festivities by waking the mayor, who invited them in for another few sips. From that day on, the good-natured band was a major element of the holidays, growing louder, larger, and, in general, funnier with the years. Still carrying rakes and ringing cowbells, participants added masks and costumes and floats—and eventually the gaiety evolved into impressive parades with a different theme each year.

The evening always finished with elaborate tableaux in a theater, with a grand march, and with dancing for members and invited guests. At midnight, as Caldwell Delaney has explained, a whistle shrilled, the masked men who had been part of the festivities disappeared, and the rest of the crowd kept on dancing. Membership in the Cowbellion de Rakin was secret, and even the members' wives did not know their identities, it was asserted. If Mobile women were less given to curiosity than others of their gender, it is possible that this was true.

As the New Year Carnival grew and expanded, rivalries developed, and then two other groups paraded in addition to the Cowbellions: the Strikers and the T.D.S. ("The Determined Set," some explained, while others called it the "Tea Drinkers' Society"). The celebrations continued to be held at New Year's until soon after the Confederate War, when the Mobilians, following the New Orleans Carnival krewes, adopted Shrove Tuesday, the day before Lent, as the date of their hilarities. From then on, the Carnival was separate from Christmas, although one or two of the organizations continued to hold the events on New Year's Eve.

Mobile was always a social center—a port, a place for plantation people to visit, the most sophisticated section of Alabama. The New Year's Day receptions were a fixed part of the holidays, with hostesses who competed for supremacy by counting the volume and style of their callers. In "leading houses" the shades were drawn about 3 P.M., candles were lighted and string orchestras started to play.

Since most of those who paid calls would be going to a ball that evening, the largest number donned their evening dress fairly early in the day. Even so, the callers often had to work quickly to complete their schedules. The men "made the rounds" four to a carriage, and a kind of ritual refreshment developed— broiled oysters and champagne. And the women, planning also to attend the ball, wore their elaborate evening gowns in the afternoon.

In other parts of Alabama there flourished the "Christmas Riders" or "Fantastic Riders," who went out in the daytime, masked and costumed, from plantation to plantation, for hours of funmaking. On Christmas Day the Riders had a quick breakfast, put on holiday dress, and galloped away on horseback. They donned clowns' garb or "Spanish" costume, wore bandannas or voluminous red trousers, or narrow yellow ones, great hats or tiny hats. So decked out, they followed a full schedule of visits among their friends, although the friends were never supposed to know their identities.

As they appeared, the Fantastics were greeted with applause by adults, excited stares and questions by children, and, according to the tradition, a prompt invitation to enter the plantation or farm residence for a cupful of cheer. The ride lasted for hours, finishing only in time for late-afternoon dinner. And in many parts of Alabama the meal *was* late—4 P.M. By then the Fantastics were feeling either the pinch of hunger or the glow that resulted from those many assemblages around the bowl.

"Once a Fantastic," the saying went, "always a Fantastic"; men had too good a time to drop out.

Nobody else in the South, to the best of my knowledge, had a highly individualized Christmas like that of Grandmamma Shuptrine from the Selma area, whose "Paper Bag Tree" of the days after the Confederate War was described by Erna O. Xan in the Birmingham *News*. Grandmamma was a lady who followed her own inclinations. She was kindly and good humored but also *sui generis*. She was, for example, fond of state names, as she called one of her daughters Louisiana, another Indiana.

Every year, on the great morning, her daughters brought their children—five of each—to the old farm for a Christmas with surprises.

When the buggy rolled up, the family could see Grandmamma Shuptrine, sitting on a chair on her narrow porch, surrounded by a circle of well-tied paper bags of many sizes. The sandy yard was enclosed by a picket fence; within were green cedars and a crepe myrtle bush, which served as the Christmas tree. As Mrs. Louisiana Johnson, her daughter, pictured the day, Grandmamma gave all ten grandchildren a quick greeting, lined them up before the steps, then strode over to the bush and tied ten of the bags to the lower branches.

Next, resuming her perch of honor on the porch, Grandmamma Shuptrine called out: "One. Two. Three. Go!" and the children, scurrying, giggling, elbowing each other, dashed over to the bush. Those who reached for the largest bags were generally disappointed, for these contained least of all—perhaps only a bit of candy. It was usually the smallest one that held the nicest gift, even though it was neither expensive nor elaborate. This was, of course, Grandmamma's way of teaching a lesson. . . .

Then, according to Mrs. Johnson, Grandmamma Shuptrine

attached ten more bags, returned to the porch, and gave a fresh signal. The result was much the same as before, though by now some of the children had learned to pass over the bigger containers. Finally, Grandmamma called a third round, in which the best gifts were to be found, even though these, too, were homemade and simple. There were always a few errors and Grandmamma had to intervene: "No, that's for your sister. This other one goes to you." When everybody was satisfied, the time had come for the treat inside.

Another of the daughters prepared the Christmas dinner, made from the best produce of the farm. Turkey vied with fried chicken, for, as one of the ladies maintained, "children like fried chicken best." There were bowls of chicken gravy, baked sweet potatoes, boiled sweet potatoes, Irish potatoes, and summer snap beans, saved for the occasion.

On the table in front of the children waited three wondrous items, a trio of great pound cakes, iced all over in white and ornamented with "flowers" made out of cotton and egg yolk, with slices of each cake cut like leaves of a book for several servings. Major attention, however, went to the wide bowl in which was a sweet that had become more and more popular in the South—"ambrosia," made from two comparative rarities, oranges and coconuts. They were combined and sugared the previous day and their flavors allowed to mingle overnight. For the young generation the treat was paradisiacal. . . . Not many who attended forgot Grandmamma's Paper Bag Christmas.

Whatever its size, many an Alabama home shared a popular Christmas-time inscription:

> The lintel low enough to keep out pomp and pride,
> The threshold high enough to turn deceit aside,
> The doorband strong enough from robbers to defend,
> This door will open at a touch to welcome every friend.

All of Alabama also shared and still shares one dish on New Year's Day: black-eyed peas and hog jowl, cooked together. This dish came close to an Alabamian's heart and to his inner beliefs as well; he *had* to eat it on New Year's if he hoped for any kind of luck during the year ahead.

Peas and hog jowl have always gone together like porridge and milk, or coffee and doughnuts. Rural cabins, town homes in Montgomery and Birmingham, Mobile and Tuscaloosa, hotels and diners, all have served this combination. "The more peas you eat, the more money you'll get." And if you doubted it, all you had to do was ask somebody, anybody.

Even people who had no special liking for the dish swallowed it, doggedly. Better to feel queasy for a little while, or get indigestion, than have a year of bad fortune. As the Alabama doggerel puts it:

> Those black-eyed peas are lucky
> When et on New Year's Day;
> You'll always have sweet 'taters,
> And possum come your way.

For days before New Year's, grocer supplies and plantation stocks were drawn upon; at times a run on peas would occur. The store owner who had to confess he had none received incredulous looks. New Year's Day without the magic combination . . . that was impossible.

In Montgomery, a few years ago, a number of restaurant operators found themselves short of the peas because *aficionados* were ordering them every day of January, in the belief that the peas did little good unless they were eaten daily. Others insisted that one day was enough, while a third element, keeping an open mind on the question, decided to take no chances, and to have the dish as often as possible during the month.

Peas and hog jowl first became popular before the Confederate War. The dish apparently evolved from the Negroes' humbler version of the Christmas holiday feasts. Gradually it spread to the whites, who learned to appreciate the homey item, even though officially it still remains unpopular in a number of fashionable circles. As an Alabama townsman said, "Certain of the elite would prefer that we common folk didn't know they like peas and hog jowl. But if the deed can be done in the dark, they'll do it every time, and take corn bread with it, too."

Although Alabama seems to be the heart of peas and hog jowl, the dish can be found in many Southern states. In South Carolina the New Year's favorite is "hoppin' John," rice, cow peas, salt pork or ham, heartily flavored with pepper. "Leave out the rice and it don't 'hop,' " an expert cautions.

What would happen to the Alabamian or the South Carolinian if he passed up either of these dishes on New Year's Day? The native is pragmatic. "Mister, I wouldn't take the chance of finding out."

## CHAPTER 12

## Cotton, Steamboats, and Weddings

MEMPHIS, Natchez, Vicksburg. . . . To the Americans of the mid-nineteenth century these cities represented one thing primarily—cotton—the pale, fleecy staple whose overnight development, more than any other single phenomenon, changed the history of the South. And Memphis, standing on its bluffs along the Mississippi, was the capital of the thousands on thousands of surrounding acres of white fields.

The goose (the Christmas one, among others) hung high in the river towns and their tributary lands for thirty years or more, the golden years of cotton in the Deep South. Until Mr. Eli Whtiney produced his epochal cotton gin, the crop was difficult to process. But then swiftly the earth seemed to pour out the bolls.

The change came suddenly. For years the course of American settlement moved ever more westward; in the 1820's Virginians and Carolinians and other Southerners thought of Memphis, if they heard of it at all, as a tiny, muddy outpost on the Mississippi, a rough-and-tumble "Western" landing frequented largely by loud river boatmen. Years afterward an early settler recalled a Memphis Christmas of 1824, notable mainly for a celebration by a band of roaring Indians.

At that time the town was no more than a little trading post, with three general stores, a blacksmith shop, and a scattering of lesser establishments. Joseph J. Rawlings knew a large proportion of the two hundred people in the area, most of whom made their livings by dealing with the red men. The Indians owned a few corn patches in the vicinity but had "no regular pursuits, except hunting," and they loved Memphis, if only because of what they called "fire water"—pure corn whisky which cost twenty-five cents a gallon.

On that Christmas morning fifty to a hundred bleary-eyed red men sat drinking together until, their mood lifting, they staggered to their horses and went galloping around the town. They were "quite harmless" to the whites, and yet, as Mr. Rawlings pointed out, their condition could well make them dangerous to themselves. Mounting their ponies, they spurred them to swift rides down the roads, making daring and reckless turns. There were several fights, but none of them, fortunately, was serious, and somehow the Indians managed to get away without a single broken arm or neck.

Soon afterward, Memphis, squarely in the middle of a vast agricultural boom, was due to become the biggest inland cotton market in the United States. The town lies just above Mississippi which now began to produce more cotton than any other state in the country, a total of nearly a million and a quarter bales a year. Two adjoining states, Alabama and Louisiana, were second and third in cotton. The blooming Yazoo Delta of Mississippi, the White River in Arkansas, the Red River in Louisiana . . . these and others served to make Memphis an ever more thriving center.

Everything, it appeared, went to Memphis, and so did everybody in the region who could afford the ride. The cotton people of Tennessee, of the alluvial Mississippi lands, and of the more remote reaches, all headed there to look after the marketing of their product, to talk about the financing of future crops, and to have a good time. Memphis was still robust and convivial, figuring in a hundred tales of doings hilarious, rambunctious, or merely bright spirited.

It, and the stretch of hundreds of miles along the Mississippi above and below it, was a place of steamboats. For the paddle wheels had also come into their own, rolling along the great "inland sea" of the South. The steamers brought Christmas to the river, carrying luxury products to dozens of scattered points along the Mississippi and to Memphis itself. Whether they stayed in the big town for the holidays, or went back to Natchez or Woodville or Port Gibson, the river people saw Christmas arrive with a jingle of prosperity.

From about 1830 to 1860, the growers were erecting their adaptations of the classic revival along the elevated Mississippi edge or in the long plains that lay beyond. Christmas garlands between the tall pillars of the white-columned mansions . . . they were the symbols of an opulent season, marked by hunts for animals and birds over a terrain which only a short time before had been forest and which was still filled with game "just waitin' to be taken."

Colonel William Falkner of Mississippi (grandfather of the later William Faulkner, with a different spelling) once por-

trayed the region in a novel, *The White Rose of Memphis.*
"Cotton bales and pretty women," Falkner wrote, "seemed to
be a spontaneous product in and around Memphis." However
"spontaneous" those good-looking girls were, they bloomed
most prettily at a somewhat later season than the cotton, in the
December holidays.

The story of Napoleon Hill, cotton broker extraordinary, is
typical of one phase of river country life. In the 1830's Napoleon left a job as a store clerk at Bolivar, Tennessee. Heading
toward Memphis, he took a slight detour by way of California
for the gold rush, then returned to his home state. Although
his pockets were already well filled, he was soon to show that
Memphis could provide another gold mine for him and others
like him. Hill became the town's most lordly cotton dealer, and
remained prosperous even in the dark postwar days. Eventually
he erected an enormous French renaissance home with an interior as opulent as its exterior. As Shields McIlwaine wrote:

"Only the best" was the rule of furnishing the house; magnificence the scale. Mirrors twelve feet tall; a stone vase resting on the
heads of life-sized, gilded herons; Oriental rugs, and paintings—
whatever the Hills liked, they bought. At the Centennial Exposition
of 1876, in Philadelphia, Napoleon and his wife asked if they might
buy the bedroom suite which had won first prize. It was not for
sale; nevertheless they brought it back in triumph . . . its dark wal-
nut inlaid with a variety of oddly grained woods, painted and
stained in many colors from gilt to lamp black, carved and curled
intricately. The bed was the glory of it all: a sofa built into the foot-
piece, a half canopy with red curtain draped against the headpiece,
ten feet high; the upper edge of the side rails was quilted at the
place where one might bark his shins on retiring. Napoleon had to
have that bed. . . . Men who rise to great heights must, it seems, lie
down in splendor. Were not the gorgeous beds of another Napoleon
behind silk ropes in French museums?

Other cotton kings of Natchez, Vicksburg, and sister towns
of the cotton country had marble mantels, Chippendale furniture from England, long galleries of wrought iron, superbly
carved hallways, and fanlighted doors. They lived more quietly
than did Hill; but they, too, are remembered today—and
for things other than canopied beds. One such individual was
Thomas S. G. Dabney, a Virginian who went to Mississippi in
1835 with a band of slaves and purchased, in Hinds County,
not far from Vicksburg, a property of four thousand or more
acres. In many ways Dabney was a remarkable man. He was
strikingly progressive and encouraged his Negroes to earn extra
money through the products of their own small plots. He worked
his people only five and a half days a week instead of the usual
six, and his crops thrived. Thomas Dabney had a theory: "A
laboring man could do more and better work in five and a half
days than in six."

Although Mississippi law forbade the teaching of slaves,
Dabney of Burleigh not only permitted his slaves to be instructed, but trained one of them as a teacher for the rest. He
gave money and other awards to those who did particularly good
work, and organized field operations for efficiency, so that cotton pickers, for instance, were not distracted by having to perform minor side tasks. The planter's daughter, Susan Dabney
Smedes, has told how one of them, Nelly, won a more than
satisfying Christmas bonus.

Nelly, "very tall and lithe," picked two rows at a time, moving down the middle with both hands out "and grasping the
cotton boles with each hand. . . . At Christmas, Nelly's share of
the prize-money was something over seventeen dollars. Her
pride in going up to the master's desk to receive it, in the presence of the assembled Negroes, as the acknowledged leader of
the cotton-pickers, was a matter of as great interest to the white
family as to her own race."

Susan Smedes has also described the Burleigh Christmases. "During the holiday season Thomas and his guests were ready to accept invitations to parties in other houses, but no one in the neighborhood invited company for Christmas-Day, as, for years, everybody was expected at Burleigh on that day." On one night Dabney would ask his overseers and their friends for an eggnog party, and the company watched as the master prepared the drink, beating eggs in a big china bowl, mixing, sampling, mixing again.

At other evenings during the holidays the Dabneys roasted oysters on the coals in the dining room while guests looked on. "Sometimes, not often, there was a Christmas tree—on one occasion one for the colored Sunday school." For another holiday, Susan Smedes said, everybody in the house had to hang up a sock or stocking in a line on the hall staircase. She counted twenty-three, including "white silk stockings, black silk stockings, thread and cotton and woolen socks and stockings." At the end of the line, next to the old-fashioned homespun and home-knit sock of the head of the household, waited the pink one of the new three-months-old baby. In the morning everyone found, in addition to gifts, a variety of Christmas notes in prose and poetry.

The Dabneys were never afraid that their house workers would indulge in "light behavior" before guests. Their attendants were proud of their owners' importance, and a remark that might possibly reflect on "their white people" was considered an affront. One male helper, who had always been of easy disposition, suddenly declined to set foot again on the plantation of a neighbor: one of the maids there "had insulted him by saying that her mistress wore more trimmings on her clothes than his young ladies did"!

Dabney house servants enjoyed privileges. One Christmas, when Susan was about fourteen, Mammy Harriet wished to give a "high tea" in her cabin for the children, and the family agreed. When Arabella Foote, daughter of the Governor, arrived for the holidays, Mammy Harriet was hesitant, "but," wrote Susan, "I took Arabella, and she enjoyed it as much as any of us." They had a good cake, hot biscuits, sweetmeats, nuts, raisins, several fruits—"indeed, a delightful tea." And Mammy Harriet stood there, bright bandanna kerchief towering on her head, and "looking so pleased."

During the holidays "Dabney Negroes" had music, dancing, and hunting like the whites. "The sound of the fiddles and banjoes, and the steady rhythm of their dancing feet, floated on the air by day and night to the Burleigh house."

Now and then sorrow or problems in the family prevented the Dabneys from having more than a subdued Christmas observance. In such cases, "the Negroes felt it." "It 'pears so lonesome; it makes me feel bad not to see no comp'ny comin'," the head maid explained. Even though her work would now be much less heavy, and she would have more time at her own fireside, she regretted that the crowds would not be there.

Then, however, strict religion reached the Negroes at Burleigh, forbidding singing and dancing at Christmas. The whole work force joined the church and "henceforth, not a musical note nor the joyful motion of a Negro's foot was ever again heard on the plantation." In the words of one of the plantation's best musicians: He had busted his fiddle and his banjo, "an done fling 'em 'way."

Yet, though it might be wicked to have music or dancing of their own, the Negroes thought it no sin to enjoy the big house festivities. "They filled the porches and doors, and in serried ranks stood men, women and children, gazing as long as the music and dancing went on. Frequently they stood there till the night was more than half gone."

The feeling against Christmas dancing spread to many Southern sections. Even while the slaves looked on longingly, they stayed apart from the celebrations. Plantation owners did not always approve the prohibitions. U. B. Phillips found a memorandum in a plantation manual: "Church members are privileged to dance on all holyday occasions; and the class-leader or deacon who may report them shall be reprimanded or punished at the discretion of the master."

Sometimes the Negroes themselves figured out ways to reconcile firm everyday religion with Christmas relaxation. As Irwin Russell's "Christmas in the Quarters" has it, Brother Brown went to a heavily thronged dancing place, and asked the Lord to let the gathering "find a blessing" in His sight. God must not judge His people too hard for what they did. "You know it's Chrismus night." All the rest of the year, Brother Brown explained, his people did "as right as they could." If dancing was wrong, he appealed, then "let the time excuse the sin." They labored in the vineyard, working hard and working true, and now surely He would not notice, "ef we eats a grape or two."

In Mississippi, as in other places, religious opposition to Christmas pleasures varied from point to point. In 1859 a schoolteacher from the Middle West spent a holiday at Ridge House, in the vicinity of Vicksburg. A. De Puy Van Buren wrote in some excitement about the slaves' buoyant enjoyment of their dancing.

> To see a group of them on the floor, or on the lawn, beneath the shade of the China-trees, when
>> Hornpipes, jigs, strathspeys and reels
>> Put life and mettle in their heels
> whirling in the giddy mazes of the dance with their buxom dulcenas, each seeming to vie with the other in dancing the most; it is one of the finest specimens of animated nature I ever gazed upon.

No restraint of the etiquettish ball-room, to fetter their actions and motions, but, charged like galvanic batteries, full of music, they dance with a vigorous *vim*.

Restraint! whew! they'd burst like steamers. No. They must dance untrammeled; the action must be suited to the spirit, the spirit to the action—perfect *lusus naturaes!* What luxury of motion, what looks—breathing and sighs! What oglings, exclamations and enjoyment!

This is *dancing*. It knocks the spangles off your light fantastic tripping, and sends it whirling out of the ballroom.

Marriage also flourished with the season; Mr. Van Buren reported that during another evening, in the middle of a plantation party, the younger people mentioned that a Christmas-season wedding was to take place in the Negro quarters, and several of the guests decided to attend the rites. A neighborhood minister rode up to perform the ceremony, and, according to Van Buren, it was warming and dignified.

At Vicksburg, perched high above the Mississippi, a town Christmas thrived with river-country touches. Mrs. B. B. Sterling remembered the 1850's, when the holidays arrived by paddle wheel. The great seasonal event was the coming of boats bearing heavy supplies of holiday products. They had boats all year, Mrs. Sterling said, and oysters in chilly weather, and oranges at other times, but then they lacked that Christmas flavor.

Now "there was 'a feel in the air,' " as the young townspeople of Vicksburg gathered before their houses to see the barrels being rolled into the yard from the water-front landing. The children would peep through the holes in the side to find out what they held. "Oranges were not so plentiful then and came from Florida. California was as far away as Europe and it was her gold and not golden fruit that we knew about."

Oysters were somewhat less exotic, and many families had two or three barrels in the yard, to be opened as the holiday occasion suggested. The youngsters liked to sit on the back steps and watch the opening of the shells. Generally one of the older Negroes performed this task and, Mrs. Sterling said, "I can hear now the 'rap, rap, rap' of old Uncle Bob's oyster knife as that strong flat implement pried open the shells, and the plump oysters dropped into the waiting buckets. (The shells were not wasted, but were placed in muddy places in the streets and on the crossings.)"

The steamboats then carried such luxuries as Malaga grapes packed in sawdust, and green bananas by the bunch, to be hung by hook in the storeroom and permitted slowly to grow yellow. "Also on the wonderful boats came nuts of various kinds, almonds and English walnuts, but our favorites were the cream nuts, which then were always called 'Brazil nuts.' " There might also be pecans, but to river-country children these meant much less; such home-grown products could be obtained any time.

Nobody had heard of grapefruit, but the pineapple had made its debut as a rarity, its aroma filling the air as it sat on the Christmas table. It was not cut in slices, but the top was lifted off by its green tuft, the contents taken out, sweetened, and put back to be served from the shell. And another item arrived on the hoof, the "Christmas beef."

Vicksburg stood four hundred or so miles above New Orleans, and up the winding Mississippi there came a measure of influence from the Creole city. *"Le Grand Boeuf!"* Thus the Vicksburg people of French descent hailed the fine animal that paraded their streets shortly before the holidays. He wore ribbons and colored garlands, or a piece of holly tied to his head, and was led by a bright Negro youth, obviously proud that he had won this role. The children thought the Christmas beef himself tossed his head with a special satisfaction on this day. Whatever his feeling, it did not last long, because he was on his way to slaughter and would soon reappear on Vicksburg tables.

Christmas of the 1850 period was "not the give-and-take system which prevails now, but a bestowal with little thoughts of return," Mrs. Sterling observed. As soon as the children had thrown on their clothes that morning, they ran to their stockings to discover their simple gifts. For the girls there was "the inevitable doll, a long thin one, slim enough for a Directoire gown, with wooden feet and hands, dressed in white tarlatan and red ribbons, and she was always put in head foremost, and we found her with those sharp wooden feet sticking up in the air. Then a little set of dishes, real 'cheeny,' and some little piece of doll furniture, and down in the toe a piece of money, or perchance a tiny, thin gold ring."

For the boys the day produced "a pair of red topped boots, a jumping jack, a Barlow knife and a horn that would blow." Both boys and girls received fireworks or "popping crackers," small ones in bunches, which they exploded at intervals all day long, lighting them from hot coals brought from the house on a shovel. As ever, "Christmas in the South meant noise and plenty of it."

In cornucopias of perforated cardboard or in small handmade bags of white tarlatan, "cut heart-shape and the edges buttonholed around in fancy worsteds," were the candies the children enjoyed so much. Particular pleasure came with the kisses, wrapped in white tissue paper with sentimental mottoes on it, and fringed ends red and blue.

As on the plantations, Christmas Day meant "Christmas gifts," surrendered on demand to the servants. The cook in town, Aunt Diddy, arrived in a costume that seldom varied— purple calico dress, black silk apron, hair tied up in a red-and-yellow bandanna. She gave finishing touches to the house decorations, which had a Deep Southern touch: gray moss and magnolia leaves on the wall or the tablecloth, in addition to the usual holly and mistletoe.

Aunt Diddy's only occupation on this day was the meal itself. The turkey already had a side use; his wing, covered with calico, had become a brush for the hearth, and his tail feathers were being woven into a Sunday fan. . . . The fowl itself was filled with oyster stuffing and placed in front of the master; before the mistress sat a whole roast suckling pig with an apple in its mouth.

First a serving of turkey, then pig, and with them Irish and sweet potatoes, lima beans, hominy and rice, egg bread, biscuit and Sally Lunn, "baked in a Turk's cap pan." At each end of the table were dishes containing a pound of butter in a handsome print; a pair of glass stands held large cakes—fruit, pound, and sponge—the result of days of baking; and the lattice-work fruit stands were full of polished oranges, apples, and grapes. Dessert, like many other things on this day, also came in double style; there were mince pie and boiled custard, "the latter served in tall thin goblets with a little floating island of white of egg on top." As a last touch, the children and adults could select from Canton-blue jars of ginger. Within a half hour after the meal, "portions" of practically everything on the table were on their way to the less well-to-do families of the town.

The day after Christmas had a special meaning in Vicksburg and other river places; it "belonged to the Negroes," whose duties were lightened so that they could leave early for their parties, and for the weddings which took place at Vicksburg as they did at the plantation visited by Van Buren.

All the Negroes of the vicinity were invited to this event and often the white masters as well. If the bride or groom were a member of the household staff, the owner sometimes gave permission for the wedding to be performed on his porch. The supper that followed was usually held in the same place, and if there were not enough tables to seat all the Negro guests there would be additional servings until everyone had eaten his fill.

Such Christmas-time Negro weddings were conducted with high ceremonial and also high order. At the end the minister would lift his hand: "Well, Jim, salute your bride." At that the crowd cried out, the groom would bestow his kiss, and the lighter hours had arrived, with singing and dancing into the night.

## CHAPTER 13

# "Forgive Me...for the New Year"

ALTHOUGH only a short distance up the Mississippi from the
English-speaking South, early Missouri was thousands of
miles away from it in mood and philosophy. And when Christmas season arrived, it had a far different flavor and look and
accent. Many of Missouri's people considered themselves Southern . . . but Anglo-Saxon? Ah, no, *m'sieu!*

For Missouri was French at its birth and remained French
in its heart for most of its first and formative seventy years. Even
after Spain took over the region, the first Missourians and their
descendants, like the good Frenchmen they were, continued de-
terminedly Gallic. To them Christmas and the New Year's were
*Noël* and *le Jour de l'An,* and the Americans of Richmond or

Baltimore or Charleston would have scratched their heads at the scenes which took place on those days.

It was an easygoing society that sprang up along the Mississippi at St. Louis, at Ste. Genevieve, and other original settlements. Starting about 1735, small French groups clustered at a succession of points, with a population as amiable as it was bright spirited. The Creoles, children of those pioneers from the old country or from Canada, had little of the ambition that drove the Scots-Irish-Englishmen along the Atlantic and toward the West.

These Missouri French came in smaller numbers than the Anglo-Saxons; they did not build large towns or spread out in plantations or farms as did the English-speaking elements. Instead, they formed lines of villages in an Old World pattern. Early callers found colonial houses with gabled roofs and friendly galleries suggesting remote, placid areas of the motherland.

These Creoles had no designs for conquest, no plans for domination of their neighbors. They liked visits, festivals, parties. Most were not well to do; they knew the meaning of frugality, practicality, and yet they managed to combine traditional French *économie* with their natural love of life.

Before the beginning of the nineteenth century, the French of Missouri began to feel the effects of a slow Anglo-Saxon engulfment. Long before the Americans bought Louisiana, there were English-speaking adventurers in upper Louisiana. When they first saw the Kentuckians, Carolinians, Georgians, and Virginians who arrived along the Mississippi in search of trade or land or both, the Missouri French could not hide their reaction.

What harsh, determined folk those were, and what dull ones! To the Creoles the *Américains* were money grubbers who knew nothing of the grace that life should provide for any man. . . .

When the American flag eventually flew over them in 1803, many of the Missouri French considered that they had been turned over to barbarians, and old-time St. Louisans went to their graves deploring the alterations around them.

Although they fought a losing battle for control, the earlier Missourians held tenaciously to their own customs. They would not give up the ways of their *grand-pères* and *grand'mères,* and for generations they carried on a French home life, with Gallic festivals, chief among which were those at the year's end.

Not Christmas but New Year's Day was the great holiday. Christmas was a time for restrained family observances, New Year's the occasion for meeting friends—the day for festivity. In St. Louis and other Missouri settlements, as in Paris or Rouen or Marseilles, Noël was primarily a day of peace and contemplation.

In the living room stood the *crèche,* the small box or ornamented scene that represented the story of the Manger, with a candle-lighted Holy Family, the camels, the Wise Men, and other figures. Reverently the children would take their places before it, while Maman and Papa explained the meaning of the evening. This was the extent of the Christmas ornamentation; not for years would there be a Christmas tree or a Santa Claus.

Nor did the Creole children of Missouri expect many presents at Christmas. They would be satisfied with small ones, candies, fruit, nuts, and a tiny trinket or two. Before the fireplace they set, not stockings, but shoes to be filled during the night by the Christ Child, *"le petit Noël."* Before He came, however, there would be another ceremonial for all but the very youngest of the family—Midnight Mass on Christmas Eve.

Before twelve the streets were filled with men and women on their way to the old church, which was decorated with greens, and flowers on the altar, and which shone as at no other time of the year. Flickering lights illuminated earnest faces, glowing with the emotion of the hour. An elderly St. Louisan, thinking back to her childhood, re-created the night: "The good Father Savigne officiating in his priestly robes; stillness pervading the edifice, save when broken by the solemn tones of the Gregorian chant or the word of admonition from the holy man; the consecration of the Host; the multitude, equal in the eyes of God, without distinction of color, thronging to the balustrade to partake of the Sacrament. . . ."

Such scenes, in the early hours of morning, left lasting impressions on the minds of the children, reinforcing their love for this "day upon which a Saviour was born to mankind." Associated with the Midnight Mass was the informal *réveillon*, a late meal that followed immediately after it. This special event combined reunion and thanksgiving, as one observer phrased it. At it, the Creoles duplicated as far as they could the meal they might have enjoyed at this hour in France—a *pâté*, eggs, and meats, much crisp bread in long, narrow loaves, unsalted butter, good coffee, and, of course, wine.

Long before then the children had gone to bed, to sleep until early morning when they arose to find the little gifts *le petit Noël* had left them. Christmas Day itself was a restrained and private day. The evening, however, was a different matter. The Creoles had done their religious duties, fulfilled their obligations to the Church, "and if at night the family . . . indulged in a dance, they felt sure that God would not wax wroth against them on that account."

New Year's meant a heightened excitement, a time of still more pronounced merriment. The eve saw a zesty masquerade, "*La Guignolée.*" About 9 or 9:30 P.M. youths of the town gathered in bands, donning the most grotesque garb they could prepare, dressing as Pierrots, as painted Indians, or in blackface. One or two of the party were fiddlers, and each member carried a basket or a sack to hold the booty they expected to gather.

Briskly the skylarkers started forth, singing a bright carol from earlier French days. Reaching the first house on their route, they pounded, entered, and began:

Good evening, master and mistress,
And everybody in the house.
For the last day of the year
You owe us the Guignolée.

If you have nothing to give us, tell us;
We ask of you only a pork bone;
A pork bone isn't a big thing.
It is only four feet long;
And we'll make a fricassee
Eighty feet long.

If you have nothing to give us, tell us.
We ask only for the eldest daughter
And we'll make her live high.
We'll warm her feet.
We'll make her live high.
We'll warm her feet.

When we were in the middle of the forest,
We were in the shade.
I waited for the cuckoo to sing, and the dove,
And the nightingale from the green cradle.
The ambassador of lovers
Will go tell my mistress
That I always have a happy heart.

And I always have a happy heart, no sadness at all;
But those young girls who have no lovers, what will they do?
It is love that awakens them
And keeps them from sleeping.
Good night, master and mistress,
And everybody in the house.

### Epilogue

In begging the guests
To kindly excuse us
If we have made some foolishness,

It was just to divert ourselves.
Next year we'll take care about this
If we have the honor of coming back.

Good night, master and mistress,
And everybody in the house.
For the last day of the year
You owe us the Guignolée.

As the song went on, the chorus waved their arms and danced about the house, and finally the maskers held out their hands to beg for gifts.

These donations would be used at a ball that was soon to follow; the more there were, the greater would be its success. At one house after another they received such items as meat, chickens, eggs, sugar, lard, coffee, candles. . . . Then it was time to depart, and they did, singing in muted voices, their words dying in the dark.

The serenaders were not always gentle. A few rare families did not enter into the spirit of the evening. But even in such cases they "made a contribution." If they had a henhouse, for example, they would find in the morning that it had lost one or two of its boarders.

Some called the rollicking custom *La Gai-année*, the Gay New Year. The word, however, first meant the beam of a steelyard, the "balance"; and the tradition had a religious beginning. Celebrants would ask help for the Mass box, so that if "poor absent" ones had died, they would not be weighed in the balance and judged wanting "for the lack of a few Masses." But this origin was eventually forgotten.

With dawn of New Year's Day the French Missourians rose to attend early Mass, which was followed by a ceremonial of great meaning. To the house of the family patriarch and matriarch went their children, grandchildren, and great-grandchildren if these had arrived. Each knelt in turn before these "authors of their existence," and asked his and her blessing, saying:

"*Bonne année, bonne santé, et paradis à la fin de vos jours.*"

"Happy New Year, good health, and heaven at the end of your days."

To this the old couple, their voices sometimes shaking with emotion, gave a benediction, with a hope that God, "the Father of us all," would approve. It was an event to which everyone looked forward, and on which everyone would look back in happy recollection.

A few minutes later the various branches of the family had started home for the rest of *le Jour de l'An:* the visits of the day. It was a time of open house and the calls continued hour after hour. The day also provided an occasion for closing rifts and healing disputes; as much as anything else, reconciliation was the meaning of New Year's.

Even if there had not been a break, one St. Louisan would greet another: "I wish you a happy New Year. If I have done you any wrong during the year just passed, I want you to forgive me for the new one." And with that speech men and women would shake hands or embrace.

We are also informed that the more youthful men were known to employ the custom for their own delight, "kissing the rosy lips of some pretty girl, at the same time wishing her a good and happy year, and a great big husband at Easter."

Through most of the day guests appeared at the various houses, and in St. Louis and other French towns each received the standard New Year refreshments—*croquignoles,* small crunchy pastries of a kind popular in the old country, and glasses of cordial. After a dozen or more such visits, only the hardiest individuals could absorb more of the cake and the sweet drink.

Meanwhile for the children the Creole New Year had another significance. It, much more than Christmas, was the day of gifts or *étrennes*. Papa and Maman had dolls and toys for their youngsters and so did others of the family. Each child was expected to make special calls on his godfather, his godmother, and his close relatives, and at every house another *étrenne* awaited him. No matter how much the endless kissings, pettings, and gossiping might bore the children, they always liked such visits.

That evening the old and the young, equally tired, retired early. Yet the good season had not ended. Ahead was January 6, Twelfth Night, and the *Bal du Roi*, which celebrated the adoration of Christ by the Three Kings. In dozens of houses suppers and dances commemorated the evening, and some were served with provisions that had been gathered by masqueraders on New Year's Eve.

As in France, the focus of attention on these evenings was the King cake, a slightly sweetened bread with something of the flavor of brioche. At the proper moment it was carefully cut, and a piece given to everyone in the room. One slice contained a bean, and the young man who found it in his portion was hailed as the King, and given the privilege of choosing a queen. The royal couple were crowned, toasted, and hailed by the others, and they presided over the evening in mock grandeur. When the King lifted a glass to his lips, his court cried out, as it was done on this night in France: "The King drinks!"

The King's parties were sometimes continuing affairs, with a group chosen at one year's ball to plan the next. A man selected by lot for such a role must never refuse; it was an obligation not to be shirked.

In time the Americans took more and more important a role in Missouri affairs, and with them they brought fireworks at Christmas, the hanging of stockings, and, not least, eggnog.

Nevertheless, the French tradition maintained itself in St. Louis, Ste. Genevieve, St. Joseph, and elsewhere in the state, and the New Year's receptions continued to thrive. In 1848 a diarist wrote of St. Louis: "It is the fashion here for the females to stay at home on this day to receive company, and the males to spend the day in making visits and short calls, and to exchange congratulations and mutual refreshments." He described a hostess who received him with "a mingled expression of pleasure and solemnity."

Writing of the 1850's, Captain John Harnois told how men of French descent at St. Joseph, Missouri, followed Christmas Mass with a shooting match. The prize was a turkey or beef, and the competitors took aim in turn, in a manner that resembled the frontier style. The winner named the part of the beef, or the particular turkey, he wished; the man who took second place had next choice, and so on. Celebrity of the day was Uncle Joe Davis, an old man who again and again used his trusty Hawkins rifle to bring home the prize.

The Missourians of the period could still look forward to bear meat for Christmas; it continued plentiful despite prodigal shooting or slaughter by careless people. For Captain John Harnois—a child in those days—the holidays conveyed a particular joy, snowbird (or snow bunting) pie. Horsehair hoops, strung with networks of twine, were the accepted traps. "The ground had to be covered with snow before one of those birds would come to a snare," he wrote, "but with a little skift of snow on the ground and some oats scattered around for a lure," they would soon be entangled. If he went home with enough of the tiny creatures, the cook would bake a pie fit to set before a Twelfth Night, or any other, king.

Over the years St. Louis changed. A letter of 1870 pictures the New Year's Day in quite human style. A young Irish-

American girl advised her mother that it had been "a decided success" as follows:

Katie and I went to Marie's, wore our party dresses and Marie sailed in in black velvet, looking elegant. Zee fled to the country like a barbarian, as some of his friends said. We had ninety calls, enjoyed ourselves wonderfully, had plenty of good things.... These cards enclosed are of gentlemen who called there to see me. ... We received by gaslight, and, besides us, there was with Mrs. Marie, Mrs. Charles Smith and Miss Wilson from Philadelphia, a niece. I never saw so many old Frenchmen in my life. Mrs. W., Mrs. D. and Mrs. Chenie had their visitors in the *pantry*. Fr. Desmet honored us with a visit—Jimmie did not go calling— and what was my astonishment to see Mr. W. Shaw and a Mr. Picton.

The calling was very general, carriages actually blocked the streets. Julia . . . presided at Locust Street with Aunt M., in Russian gray silk trimmed with satin. They too had an agreeable time. Dr. Stiegers had the impudence to call with a friend. Julia was dignity itself, and when the Doctor wished to shake hands today coolly replied, "I don't shake hands on all occasions."

No matter what others did, here was one Missourian who did not believe in French New Year forgiveness!

Others pictured later days when St. Louis men made New Year's calls in "Prince Albert coats, light tan or gray trousers, light spats, silk hats and white gloves." The gloves were considered necessities; the January 1 visitor would almost have preferred to omit his trousers rather than to leave behind these marks of gentility. The women's dresses, as Miss Stella Drumm noted, were of "gay-colored silks covered with ruffles or French muslins trimmed with lace and ribbons."

The tables held pyramids of spun sugar, perhaps a "boned turkey in its original shape," fruit cake, and "a block of ice hollowed out to hold Lynn Haven oysters which were so huge that guests would have to go behind a screen to eat them." In addition there were terrapin, saddles of venison, hot beaten biscuits, chicken bouillon, ornamented ices, and glazed fruits. And a social note: "A New Year's call showed appreciation for past favors and also wiped out any obligations."

The Christmas seasons of the eighties and nineties served as a backdrop for the high elegance of the old Home Circle Club's ball at the Southern Hotel; the Imperial Club's New Year's Week formal at the St. Nicholas Hotel, and the formal events at the St. Louis Club on Lindell Boulevard. There were also cotillions and "Germans" or call-out dances, and Lee Brashear tells us that during the holidays the city's "one excellent hair dresser" started out at eight in the morning and made the rounds of the great houses on Vandeventer Place, Lafayette Avenue, and Lucas Place. "So elaborate were the puffs and curls she achieved that no one of her customers would dare to rest until the ball opened at 8 o'clock in the evening." Then, in lace-trimmed gowns of black or purple velvet, diamond pendants shining in their ears, the ladies went out in glory.

Repeatedly during the last century harassed Missouri officials —like others in other states—tried to curb the holiday fireworks. In December of 1868 the *Boonville Weekly Eagle* reported that the mayor had issued a proclamation banning the shooting of firearms and the burning of firecrackers. The mayor, the editor commented, was "invading the long-established rights of Young America, and we advise them to hold an indignation meeting and 'pass the necessary resolutions.' Why, it is one of the inalienable rights of Young America, for which their 'forefather fought, bled and died,' on Christmas and fourth of July, to burn their firecrackers, frighten horses, put out people's eyes, destroy dwellings, and make themselves generally obnoxious, and we are surprised that the mayor forbids these *harmless* little pleasantries." In spite of the mayor and the newspapers, the pleasantries went right on. . . .

During the nineteenth century another custom was added to the St. Louis and Missouri Christmas. When the Germans arrived in large numbers they introduced the Christmas tree, Santa Claus, and Teutonic family celebrations of the holidays, and in time the Creole and Anglo-Saxon children joined their Teutonic contemporaries around the ornamented firs. One such tree, resurrected in recent years by the Missouri Historical Society, had gingerbread figures, cranberry and popcorn streamers, and candles with bright glass lampshades for protection.

For nearly fifty years St. Louis has given America its—and perhaps the world's—greatest program of carol singing, heard annually today by hundreds of thousands of people. Wearing red capes with peaked hoods, sometimes carrying candles or lanterns, fifty thousand carolers whose ages range from eight to eighty go from house to house to sing of the Christmas season and to bring "tidings of joy" in the older style.

Thousands of St. Louis families respond to the invitation: "Put a light in your window and let the carolers know you'd like to hear them," and this Christmas Eve event, with Christmas music ringing in the air from one end of the town to the other, is one to which countless Missourians look forward through the year.

The observance began almost by accident, when in 1911 nine people went out to sing before the houses of friends. The response was so warm that they continued their caroling calls the following year and the year after that. Soon others asked to be permitted to join the carolers. The first year a number of people, greatly moved by the music, had reached into their pockets and handed money to the nine singers. "Give it to a good cause," the listeners told them. "Use it to help somebody for Christmas."

The carolers contributed the fifty dollars they received that night to a group of St. Louis children's organizations. After all, it was explained by one of the original band, Christmas is a time for the young. . . . In time the red-caped singers took to carrying bright collection cans, but it was emphasized that contributions were to be voluntary. "We do this mainly for spiritual satisfaction—the satisfaction of those who hear the music and those who do the singing."

With the years the movement spread from one section to another, to plain houses on crowded streets, to apartment buildings, to handsome residences. Hundreds of organizations came forward to offer help, including church groups, civic organizations, social clubs, school units. Some carolers were and are skilled singers, whose notes soar into the night; the others, though untrained, have been rehearsed for days or for weeks, so that the level of performance is high.

Today more than three thousand groups cover St. Louis, with Mrs. A. H. Toma, the executive director, working hard from early October to set up detailed and intricate schedules. The singers also go to hospitals, public places, and the homes of invalids who have expressed their hope of hearing the carolers.

In many homes children wait up year after year, to make certain that they do not miss the music. Hundreds call the St. Louis Christmas Carols Association to learn where to go to hear the singers.

Mrs. Toma tells of an incident in which one carol group stopped before a window with a light and started to sing.

A moment later a middle-aged woman darted out, her fingers over her lips. "My daughter's sick and she's sleeping now. But I put the light there because I wanted to be sure to see you, and give you this." Thrusting a five-dollar bill into the leader's hands, she added: "Please come back and sing next year."

In another case the mother and father of a soldier in Korea

asked the singers to enter. They made a recording of the voices and sent the brief program to their boy. He told them later that the record was played so many times that the grooves wore out. It was his "best gift." Hearing the carolers, as he had since childhood, "was the closest thing to being home again."

Today more than $50,000 is gathered annually for welfare agencies of all religions and races. "Christmas carols are for everyone," says the organization, "and Christmas caroling symbolizes a unity among all of us." The program gives milk to children, badly needed special medicines, crutches, day nursery, and a hundred other kinds of care. William H. Danforth of the original group of nine singers was president of the Carols Association for thirty years, and for forty-four years went out with one of the singing units. He died at eighty-five as he was making plans for that year's festivities, and Samuel D. Conant now heads the organization. The year after Mr. Danforth's death, in a tribute to his memory, the family matched, dollar for dollar, the amount gathered by the singers.

One St. Louisan has summed it up: "We've had a candle at the front of my house every year since the carols started, and I'll have one there till I die. It makes this big city feel like a fine little town, the town I knew as a boy. My father put the first candle in our window, to bring the carolers, and I'm sure my sons will carry on after I'm gone. Whatever 'sophisticated people' may say, it gives us that unfashionable thing, a fine glow. Do you know of a better kind of Christmas feeling?"

## CHAPTER 14

# Christmas Days—A Woman's Diary

OVER a sixteen-year period a gentle-hearted young woman of the Mississippi River "coast" went to her desk on Christmas night or shortly thereafter to record the events of these milestones of her existence. What the holidays had meant to her and her family, what the preceding twelve months had brought, how the year ahead appeared . . . Mahala Eggleston Roach reported each in turn, with her fears, her hopes, and her rejoicings.

In particular she wrote of rejoicings, the things which she appreciated. For Mrs. Roach was a happy woman, without reproaches to others or to herself, a woman who accepted calmly what her God gave her. She had a succession of losses—a little child and a warmly loved husband. But she took her misfortunes with good grace and lived her days as they came to her.

Her diary is, in its unpretentious way, one of the most moving Christmas documents I have met, a chronicle of a simple existence, set down with simplicity. Mrs. Roach was a woman who clearly matured in the process of living and between the ages of nineteen, when she started her journal, and thirty-five, when she finished, she became a rather different person.

She was no stylist; she wrote plainly of the everyday happenings she witnessed. In some respects her story is uneventful, and yet she had a full life; she lived through troubled years, through pathos and tragedy and dangers. But always she showed deep feeling for the Christmas season and for the people who surrounded her. In particular, I think, Mahala Eggleston Roach had a rare gift, the gift of gratitude to her Lord, to her family, and to her friends.

Mahala Eggleston was a niece of Jefferson Davis and his brother Joe, who had plantations in the general area of Vicksburg. About three months after Jeff married Varina Howell of Natchez, Mahala exchanged vows with James Roach. Only a year or so separated the two young women, and between the two families there were many ties, many visits.

In her opening entry, written in her country house near Vicksburg, Mahala betrayed a marked uncertainty. The new bride found her first Christmas away from home a somewhat trying period. She wrote:

Wednesday, December 25th, 1844. Clear and mild. ... This is my first Christmas as a married woman, and housekeeper; for one month I have been married, and am very happy; rather lonely today, for no one is here but my good husband and myself; my country home is very quiet; and usually I like it, but today I want to be at home with my dear Mother, my little Brothers, my sweet little Sister, fond Aunts and devoted Uncles—how they all pet and love me!

Last night I received many beautiful presents, by the cars; books from Mr. Peck (our groomsman), Mr. Woodman, and Mrs. Robins and some little things from home. Had a good dinner, then Mr. Roach and I took a long walk on the railroad. I am homesick tonight. Christmas day does not seem like it use to when I was a child! It is so dull now.

This was the only time in the sixteen years of her Christmas journal that Mahala Roach would use the word "dull." The next months were crowded. Shortly after Christmas, she learned she was to have a baby, and by then she had settled into a life that seems, from every indication, to bear out her description of it as "perfectly happy." The next year she wrote:

Christmas, 1845. Have spent a sweet, quiet home day, no time for sadness, or homesick repinings now; my little cottage is the happiest spot on earth to me, it holds my whole heart, my beloved husband and my little three-months old boy, my little Tom Robins. He is a delicate-looking, pretty babe, and all the world to me. My good husband gave me a pretty carriage and a pair of ponies for my Christmas present. We have both been well all this year; everything has prospered with us, and I am perfectly happy. Mother, brothers, sisters are well; and more pretty presents have been given me than I can count. God has showered his blessings on me too.

The year that followed saw meetings with the Jefferson Davises and the Joe Davises and talks with Varina, who had yet to have her own first child. Both the Davises and the Egglestons looked anxiously toward the distant Mexican battlefields, where Colonel Jefferson Davis and Mahala's young brother Richard were fighting:

Christmas, 1846. Mild and damp. Returned last night from a three weeks visit to my friends on the river, and in Vicksburg; went first to "Hurricane" and "Brierfield," where I spent ten days most delightfully; a large party of young folks were there, and several engaged couples among them.... Varina has no children, which is a source of grief to her tho' Uncle Jeff bears it, as he does everything else, stoically. Mrs. Robins came down to meet me, and we went "home" together.

My baby walked across the room, for the first time, while we were at "Hurricane"; he is so sweet, and good. Mr. Patterson baptized him last Thursday while we were in town. Mrs. Robins urged me to spend Christmas with her at the "Castle"; Mother and Aunt wanted me to stay with them, but my dear husband preferred coming to our home; and I was glad to come with him, he is so good and kind to me.

This has been a happy year to us, though a troubled one politically. The Mexican War is still going on, and my dear Brother Dick, tho' so young, is in the army; he is now near Monte Rey, and we hear good accounts of him from Dr. Halsey, and from Col. Davis from whom letters came while I was at "Brierfield." Varina is very anxious about him. Mother has bought a comfortable house on Farmer Street (through my dear husband's kindness), and has gone to housekeeping anticipating Dick's return.

The year of 1847 brought mixed joy and sadness. A second child arrived for Mahala and James Roach, a girl, but with the passing months there came a harsh message from Mexico. Mrs. Eggleston never welcomed back the son for whom she had prepared that "comfortable house on Farmer Street." Mahala wrote:

Christmas, 1847. Cold and rainy. Christmas seems more as it use to in old times, now that I have two little "angels" in my home, my darling Tom, and my six months old Nora, the sweetest, best little thing that ever was. Tom can appreciate Christmas, and had a quantity of pretty toys sent him from our New York relations and my own family; mine are the only grandchildren in the family. Nora came to console us for the loss of my gallant brother who fell at Buena Vista. The sorrow has saddened my life. I have spent much time with Mother and next month we are going to move to Vicksburg, and board with her until we build on my lot on Farmer Street. My husband is, if possible, more devoted than ever, and I am the happiest wife and mother in the world.

For Christmas of 1848, 1849, and 1850 she made no entries. Her role as a mother kept her very busy since two more children had been born to her. When she wrote again she had made history in a fashion; apparently Mahala Roach gave Mississippi and the river region its first Christmas tree.

Christmas, 1851. Thursday, warm and cloudy. Rain after dinner. The cares of a family were too much for even my fondness for writing, so I have not written for several years (four) until now. My husband urges me so strongly to resume my former habit, and has brought me such a pretty book that I will yield to his persuasions and again "keep a journal." My treasures have increased since I last wrote, for beside Tom and Nora, are beautiful little Sophy, and tiny little Mahala Eggleston "the image of her mother," as every one says; she was born on the sixth of this month.

I am not very strong, but am well enough to be up, and have company.... Bishop Greene came up from Natchez last evening, stayed with us until after dinner today; he is such a good man and true friend. The children had such a number of gifts that I made a Christmas tree for them; Mother, Aunt and Liz came down to see it; all said it was something new to them. I never saw one but learned from some of the German stories I had been reading.

All the servants from Mother's came down, and our servants had a regular dinner party. Dear husband gave me a beautiful book; Aunt, a pair of sleeves; Mother a pair of preserve dishes; et. etc. I gave all the servants some presents, and did not scold a single time. Husband says, "I am good and pretty, today." Well, I am old enough to be "good." I am twenty-seven. No, only twenty-six last September. The children are perfectly happy tonight, so is their Mother, Thank God!

As her family grew, the holidays meant more and more to Mrs. Roach. And, though she did not mention it until later, her husband saw Christmas as a time to do good, and to bring a better holiday to a number of poorer families.

Christmas, 1852. Saturday; warm and rainy, no fire. Truly we "live our youth over again in our children." Christmas which was for some five or six years, rather a gloomy time, contrasted with the Merry Christmas of my youth, is now almost as much a season of joy and merriment, as when I was a believer in "Santa Claus," except that I am now at the head of a little family of "believers," and have to provide for their amusement, instead of being amused myself; but after all, the truest pleasure lies in caring for the enjoyment and pleasure of others; so that I have spent a "Merry Christmas" and one of deep, true happiness, and gratitude to God for his goodness.

All are well here and at Mother's, but dear Aunt Sophie is in great trouble; dear kind Uncle died in September, and we all mourned for him. . . . I improved on my Christmas tree and had a nice one today. All the family came to see me, and add their presents. Mr. Jim Gray came with Sister Lizzie; I believe he is in love with the little woman. Had six gentlemen friends of dear husband's to dinner today; three of them were "telegraphers," who have no homes but boarding houses. Little Hala can walk very well, and is very good. Nora is ugly, but good and quiet, while Sophy is a beauty, and good too. Tom is a little fellow. I am content.

During the next year, yellow fever, which repeatedly struck at Memphis and Natchez, Vicksburg, and other river settlements, crept in with a special malignancy, and the Roaches, like those all around them, were seized by it. Mahala Roach declared:

Christmas, 1853. Sunday, cold, icy, everything frozen up. Weak, sick and nervous all day. Spent the greater part of it in bed, my only enjoyment was in seeing our dear little children happy, and through them, living over my youth. The yellow fever left both husband and me very weak, and we have had chills ever since. I spent two weeks in Jackson with Cousin Rosa, hoping the change would benefit me, but it did not . . . our good minister, Mr. Patterson, was taken from us, and many dear friends. I roused myself before dinner and got along nicely. Had Messrs. Cunningham, Tharp, Howe, and Daniels to dine with us, and then the servants had a "dining." Mother, Liz and Fanny Fox are to dine with me tomorrow. Children well, husband better.

Another year brought other troubles and other happinesses. To her journal Mrs. Roach confided:

Christmas, 1854. Monday, warm and rainy; cleared off at night. One sweet name which shown on my pages last year, cannot be there now; another dear one has left the Earth for her Home above; our sweet, precious Lizzie, my only sister, Mother's beautiful idol, died last August, and the poor Mother is almost heartbroken. My dear brother was married a few days ago . . . so poor Mother is alone. She will not come to live with us, though our home is large enough for her.

This has been a "Merry Christmas" indeed to my dear little children, and but for our darling Lizzie's death, would be so to me also. My dear husband has been so good to Mother, and she loves him for it. The yellow fever has visited our little town again this Summer. I had two young men here, friends of Mr. Roach, and we nursed them the fever. Mr. Parker and Mr. Askew both dined with us today, also Mr. Barber (Mr. R's confidential clerk), and Mr. Barney.

Mr. Beaumont came to tea, and all spent the evening. Mr. Parker sent me an exquisite desk filled with everything needful. I am ashamed to receive such a magnificent present. He says "he owes his life to me." Cakes, oranges, oysters, preserves, etc., etc., have poured in on us today and I am tired of laughing, talking and playing with my sweet little children. Hala is my "baby" still, and four better children never lived (we think).

The following holiday season found some of the recent shadows lifted.

Christmas, 1855. Tuesday; bitter cold; ground covered with snow. Real old-fashioned Christmas weather ... snow which fell yesterday and last night. Day before yesterday it was quite warm, and there has been no weather sufficiently cold to injure the flowers. So soon as I felt the weather changing, husband and I gathered all the flowers, so as to keep them for the Presbyterian Ladies who had a supper last night. Every one in town did the same, and I am told the hall looked like a fairy place, with its profusion of flowers and sweet odors; while outside the sleet and snows were falling. . . .

We had a magnificent dinner, and husband declared my pudding was perfect. I am perfectly happy. This is the twelfth Christmas since we were married, and I believe each has been happier than the last. This has been a busy, but very happy year. Thank God.

The next holiday was the most joyful of Mahala Roach's life. Nearly every line of her journal testifies to her deep happiness.

Christmas, 1856. Thursday, clear and warm; one of the mildest and most delightful Christmas days I have ever known, and everyone about me has seemed to enjoy themselves. We had only Mr. Barbour and Mr. Adams to dinner; had a nice dinner, and sent some both cooked and uncooked to our neighbors. The children were up before light to see the contents of their stockings, which were well and tastefully filled. Mr. Adams, Aunt, Mother and Mr. Barbour made them each a pretty present; Mr. Barbour added a beautiful little work case for me, but my gifts bear no comparison with those of anyone else.

The sweet peace, deep happiness, and perfect content are Heaven's own gifts, for which I pray to be made sufficiently grateful. I have never known a happier time, and should add our baby boy to the rest of my Christmas gifts, for he has been given since last Christmas and is truly a blessed gift. Husband went up to see Aunt and Mother this evening; he is very well and unusually cheerful even for his bright, sunny temper; May God bless him.

All the dear ones, my Tom, Nora, Sophy and Hala are good, and like their mother, say they have spent a "Happy Christmas." My life is so full and perfect, that my heart is overflowing with love and thanks to the Giver of my blessings. My beloved husband, five sweet children, loving Mother, many dear friends, health, wealth and this sweet home, what more can a human being wish? Nothing.

But the following year the holidays were far different.

Christmas, 1857. Cool, little cloudy, clear afternoon. The heaviest sorrow of my life has fallen this year. My little Sophy, my bright beautiful child is missing from our little circle. We were all so happy last Christmas. It was hard to bear, but my dearest one, my husband, has been rather unwell all summer, and for his sake, as well as my dear little children, I was forced to bear my loss with composure, and now I am cheerful, yes, happy, contented and grateful; the memory of an angel child has chastened the joy of the day, but not saddened it too much, for we know she is blessed beyond our ideas of happiness; still, I miss that sweet face and joyous prattle; and when I went to hang up the little stockings by the fire for "Santa Claus," and missed hers, Oh, I thought I could not smile today.

No company for dinner; but several friends called. My presents of oysters, oranges, cakes, etc., were as abundant as usual. I have spent most of the day in my room nursing John, who is a pretty, sweet baby, can run about well. Sophy loved him so much. Husband seems well tonight.

With the next year another shadow deepened over the household. Though Mrs. Roach said nothing in her journal, she had begun to be concerned over her husband's health, and the memory of the dead child did not leave her.

Christmas, 1858. Saturday, warm, dark and rainy. This has been a quiet, contented and happy day; the children have been wild with delight over their presents, and this big child has been much pleased with hers, many of which were pretty, others useful. I made several presents, too. Mother, Aunt, Mrs. Mason, Capt. Thomasson, Mr. Barbour, each of the servants, and Mrs. Record sent me some presents, and the house is so full of fruit and candy it seems like a store. I have divided with mother, too.

Had a nice dinner; Lee Daniel and Cousin Harry were our guests. My dear one said all passed off most agreeably. John's delight in his sock full of toys, and in the fire crackers, has amused us all. My heart has turned often today to the memory of my darling little Sophy, and Oh! how I miss her.

In the following year Mahala Roach knew a fresh joy but also a spreading sorrow. Her sixth child was born, another boy; in the same year she learned that her fears for her husband were only too real. Yet when she wrote in her journal she managed for a time to quiet her disturbance.

Christmas, 1859. Sunday, clear, mild and beautiful; cloudy night. A quiet, happy and "good" Christmas; no great gaiety, but much contentment, a tranquil enjoyment; a nice dinner; Mr. Barbour, Eugene Marchant and Lee Daniel, our invited guests; and several families provided with dinners as usual, by my darling's bounty. Dear Husband, Tom and Nora went to church; I stayed at home to take care of little John and Hala.

Husband stayed to Communion; and said he knew it was the last Christmas he would spend with me, for he could not hope to live another year—nor can I flatter myself that he will, for day by day he grows more feeble. We have spent sixteen very happy Christmases together, and it will be a sad, desolate old world to me when my dear kind husband is taken from me.

I cannot say "God's will be done," for it seems too hard to lose him now that we are so prosperous, happy and comfortable, with our dear children growing up in goodness and beauty around us.

How can I live without him? I will not anticipate my loss, or I shall be unfitted for the duties before me; my task is now to make the remainder of his life as happy as possible, and not to sadden his sweet resignation with my bitter murmurings. God help and strengthen me.

Our children are happy; sweet Nora begins to be such a comfort; she is older and wiser than her years, and begins to grow handsome. My baby Jim (Jim Phillips) is a sturdy, manly-looking babe; he is almost seven months old, and looks a year old. Hala is my little gentle darling, May God bless them all. Captain Thommasson sent me a fine piece of beef and some wild ducks; Mr. Riley sent me pineapples, cocoanuts, raisins, beef tongues; New Orleans friends sent me oranges and oysters—I am always in luck.

Some years earlier James Roach had asked her to continue her journal, and she did so for one more Christmas, in many ways the hardest of her life.

Christmas, 1860. Tuesday, cloudy and cold, morning clear and cold ... we have a clear, fine Christmas at last; I am glad of it as good weather adds so much to the pleasures of the children and servants. This is the first Christmas since my bereavement, and the first I have ever spent without some one to whom I could look up for love and protection.

Now, I must think for others, no one will care for me, though it does make my poor children sad to see a cloud on my brow; for their sakes I have tried to be cheerful, and to conceal the utter desolation and sorrow in my heart; they have but me, and I must not let them feel this Christmas to be a gloomy contrast to previous happy ones when their dear, kind father was with us to protect and provide for our happiness.

Nora felt too old to hang up her stockings for "Santa Claus," but the rest did so, even Baby Jim, who is ready for fun. Nora helped me to fill the stockings, which were overflowing; dear, kind friends have tried to make us forget our bereavement, and have showered kind remembrances on us; so we arranged the larger things on the table. My little young lady, Nora, has three devoted admirers—Messrs. Lee, Barbour and Grove; they vie with each other in kind attentions to me of course.

Mr. G. sent me a beautiful basket filled with apples; to Nora a bouquet of violets and geraniums. I found in my stockings (which Tom hung up) a beautiful gold cross; (Ah! am I not bearing my cross now?), a pair of Etruscan sleeve buttons, and two bottles of wine on the table; many costly and elegant toys and books sent the children. Mr. Barbour came to breakfast; had promised to dine at the "Castle"—later. I spent the morning nursing Jimmy, reading to John and Hala, conversing with Nora and Tom. Mr. Lee and Harry Eggleston came to dinner, which was very good; and the servants are having their usual dinner party.

I would not let the poor miss my darling, but provided for the wants of several families, as he would have ordered. After dark, we had some fireworks; then Harry and Mr. Lee went with us to the Episcopal Church to see the Christmas tree for the Sunday School (both white and black). Had a pleasant walk in the moonlight and all the children seemed so happy. I joined Mrs. Robert Crump and we watched the young ones with pleasure....

Got home at 10, found bright fires and a nice supper which I had ordered; after partaking of it the gentlemen left, and thus ended my day which, quite contrary to my expectations, has been very pleasant; thanks to the kind friends who have made it so, and to Him who has given me so many blessings to be grateful for; to Him, I now commit myself and fatherless children, praying for a continuation of His mercies to us.

The shadow continued to hover over Mahala Eggleston Roach. During the months that followed, she saw another darken above her, above the South and the nation. By the time Christmas came again, in 1861, her life and the lives of millions of Americans were changed forever.

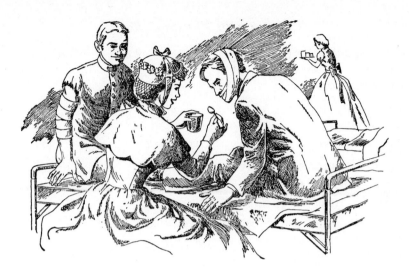

## CHAPTER 15

# Confederate Christmas

For four harsh years most Southerners approached the holidays with mixed feelings. Would the war never end? How would they be living—if, indeed, they were still alive—when Christmas came again? Some met the crisis with sacrifice and sustained courage, others with bitterness and tears. As do all wars, the Confederate conflict brought out the best in one, the worst in another, and although there were those whose speculations made the holocaust a period of huge profit and the display of garish luxuries, most of the people of the South lost steadily, month by month.

Hundreds of thousands greeted the December season with a sense of growing catastrophe, of the impending destruction of the life they had known. Whatever happened, things could never be the same again; whether or not they spoke of it, all of them accepted this fact. And each January 1, between the firing on Fort Sumter in Charleston Harbor in 1861, and the May day of 1865 when Robert E. Lee sat sorrowfully opposite Ulysses S. Grant, Southerners asked themselves: Would the year ahead bring the military success they still hoped for, or would it be the end? The men could only struggle on, and the women could only scrimp and pray and try to "make do" with the meager supplies that remained to them.

Inevitably the war became a spiritual testing. With each Christmas soldiers knelt in prayer at the camps, or with their families and friends—if they had had the good fortune to be able to join them. Their wives and children also fell to their knees to ask God's mercy and His protection. As the hostilities dragged on, a great revival of religion swept the South, and each Christmas saw crowded churches and lines of new converts in the armies.

Yet Christmas was not always a time of prayer. Many, alone and friendless at the "happy season" in Richmond or Atlanta or Mobile, took their fun where they could find it; and shocked Virginians and Marylanders, Georgians and Texans shook their heads at the reeling men who were observing the holidays in the company only of the bottle, or were shouting and fighting in the saloons and dives of the war-crowded cities.

Still others, affecting a cheerfulness they did not feel, went to work to lighten the holidays for those around them. A fortunate few had the gift of laughter, of a smiling composure between interludes of pain. For their wives or husbands or children, such individuals made Christmas seem almost the same joyous fete they had always had—with *ersatz* material.

As a boy I once listened to a white-bearded veteran at New Orleans describe a Christmas late in the war. "Son, *nothing* was what it looked like on the table. It was anything and everything else. But that didn't matter too much. We had ourselves a time, anyhow. You can always manage if you want to." Year after year, many Southerners at Christmas time tried to prove that they could "manage" in a variety of ways.

Few episodes I have heard of give so poignant a picture of innocent victims of the brothers' war as one involving a group of people who settled in Arkansas during the decade before the conflict. A few years ago, W. J. Lemke of the University of Arkansas faculty drew upon the incident for a moving Christmas message to his former students.

In 1850 several German families arrived in the area to establish the settlement of Hermannsburg, known today as Dutch Mills. Frugal, energetic, they fixed the foundations of a good life with farms, a store, and a mill. Their leaders were the brothers John and Karl Hermann, who set their neighbors an example of hard and steady application. The new families got along well with those around them, but as the cloud of war slowly approached Arkansas difficulties arose. These Germans had a slave or two, but they were not members of the traditional planter group, and did not join in the furious talk that went on about them.

Whispers started: the Germans were Yankee lovers, abolitionists. Shaking their heads, the Germans said only that they were neutral, that they had no concern in the clashes between North and South. All they wanted was to be let alone to do their work and look after their families.

But their wish was not to be granted. After the war broke out, the settlers at Hermannsburg spent an uncertain Christmas season, and during the next months the situation grew steadily worse. Rival armies moved about the land, and raiders and "bushwhackers" swept down on scattered sections. The families at Hermannsburg received threats and warnings; every week made it clearer that they and their children could not remain there in safety.

After long thought the Hermanns decided to go to St. Louis, where there were other Germans of whom they knew. As Mr. Lemke noted in his Christmas message, based on an original German volume, they would have to leave almost everything they owned and begin all over again, after twelve years in the place they had chosen and made their home. So be it. . . . Tearfully they made their plans.

General James F. Blount, the Union commander, provided a cavalry escort for them, and they started out just a week before Christmas of 1862. There were nineteen in the band, including eleven children, the youngest one year old, and even for the men the trip would be a hard one. They paused at Prairie Grove, continued on, and on December 24 arrived at Fayetteville, Arkansas. The little group spent the night before Christmas near a spring at one end of the village. As Nanni Hermann, wife of one of the two brothers, wrote in her diary: "Looking up at the star-studded sky on Christmas Eve, we saw once more in memory the lighted Christmas trees of our far-off fatherland." Pathetically she added: "But the Christ child had lost its magic. . . ."

A shadow other than war passed over the party. Nanni Hermann did not survive the trials of the trip. She died before they reached St. Louis, leaving a two-year-old child and another of five, who had been born while she and her husband struggled to establish themselves in Arkansas. "The spot where these nineteen refugees spent their heartsick Christmas in 1862," Mr. Lemke declared in his Christmas message, "is just across the street from the Lemke home." He concluded:

On Christmas Eve I shall walk out in my back yard and look across the ravine. And I shall remember two mothers—Nanni Hermann with her babies, sleeping in a wagon bed in Fayetteville, and Mary with her baby, asleep in a stable in Bethlehem.

Another mother knew a grim Christmas in Virginia during the next year. Mrs. Roger Pryor, daughter of a minister who became a Confederate chaplain, and wife of a brigadier general, had served as a nurse at Richmond during the ominous Seven Days' Battle. Now it was nearly time for her child to be born and she would have to be alone during this difficult period. Mrs. Pryor tried several times to get to her own family in Charlotte County, but the marauders and guerrillas who roamed the area made it impossible for her to reach them.

Therefore, with her two small boys, Mrs. Pryor went to her husband's home town of Petersburg, hunting a place to board. General Pryor's old friends had left, however, and all available quarters were crowded with refugees. For days she "wandered about," until her funds fell so low that she became alarmed. At last she found a former overseer's cabin outside Petersburg. It was in terrible condition—almost a hovel, with an unplastered, windowless kitchen, in which the ground showed through loose planks, and a single other room, curtainless, rugless, bitterly cold. Even so, it was better than nothing; and the officer's wife and her sons started to work, clearing, rearranging the few sticks of furniture, bringing in wood to warm the place. A kindly woman neighbor, who lived some distance away, taught her expedients: "to float tea on the top of a cup of hot water would make it 'go farther' than steeped in the usual way"; "the herb, 'life everlasting,' which grew in the fields, would make excellent yeast, having somewhat the property of hops"; "the best substitute for coffee was not the dried cubes of sweet potatoes" (a source of wartime coffee for many Southerners), "but parched corn or parched meal, making a nourishing drink."

The neighbor taught Mrs. Pryor other, more important things, too, appealing to her to cling to her hopes, stimulating her to "play her part with courage." Daily the older woman sent over "a print of butter as large as a silver dollar, with two or three perfect biscuits, and sometimes a bowl of persimmons or stewed dried peaches. She had a cow, and churned every day, making her biscuits of the buttermilk, which was much too precious to drink."

With Petersburg practically under siege, most foods were almost impossible to obtain. Markets had closed; the lone grocery had a stock that consisted mainly of molasses produced from sorghum cane, "acrid and unwholesome." A grimy closet in the cabin yielded a left-over handful of meal and rice, and a small piece of bacon. Somehow Mrs. Pryor and her sons managed; the boys kindled fires in the open kitchen, roasted chestnuts, and set traps for rabbits and snowbirds, "which never entered them."

Christmas was only a few days off when, after considerable effort, Mrs. Pryor finally found and hired a maid who could give her the woman's care she required. Two days before the holy day a snowstorm swept down; with the time of Mrs. Pryor's delivery very near, she remained in bed while the boys stayed cheerfully near her. "They made no murmur at the bare Christmas; they were loyal little fellows to their mother." She spent the day mending their worn garments, since she lacked materials to make new ones for them. "The rosy cheeks at my fireside consoled me for my privations, and something within me proudly rebelled against weakness or complaining."

At midnight, when the snowflakes were falling heavily, her labor pains began. The doctor lived three miles off; by the time he arrived Mrs. Pryor was suffering badly. "It doesn't matter much for me, Doctor!" she whispered. "But my husband will be grateful if you keep me alive. . . ."

When she wakened, the doctor was standing again at the foot of the bed, where she last remembered seeing him. Putting out her hand, she touched a small, warm form at her side, a girl. Gravely the doctor told her he had to leave and that he would not be able to return. "There are so many, so many sick."

After a while Mrs. Pryor dozed off and woke with a feeling of strength and satisfaction. Then came another blow: on Christmas morning her maid left, because the cabin felt too lonesome.

For the next few weeks Mrs. Pryor cared for the baby herself, "sometimes fainting when the exertion was over." Then one of her boys ran in, his voice showing his alarm: "An old gray soldier is coming!"

The gray man entered. "Is this the reward my country gives me?" he asked in a tightened voice. Only when she heard him did Mrs. Pryor recognize her husband. He had aged so much since their last meeting. . . . Now he called to an attendant: "Take those horses and sell them—sell them for anything. Get a cart and bring butter, eggs, everything you can find. . . ."

All but one of his horses were sold; the money they brought Mrs. Pryor sewed at her waist. General Pryor was able to stay with his family until their situation was materially improved; once the crisis was over, he went back to the fighting. To the Pryors, Christmas of 1862 would long remain a hard memory.

The Christmas season of 1864 found another officer's wife, Mrs. Fannie Beers, nursing the wounded at Lauderdale Springs, Mississippi. Born in the North, she had married young and moved to New Orleans with her husband. At the war's start Mrs. Beers crossed the lines to be with her parents, but soon she returned to the South with her small son. Despite some complaints that she appeared too young, Mrs. Beers served as a hospital matron, working over a four-year period in Alabama, Georgia, and other states.

During the holiday period in '64, hospital supplies fell very low and, she said, articles previously considered necessities had become "priceless luxuries." Whenever eggs, butter, or chickens arrived, hospital workers hoarded them for the very sick, and understanding the situation, most of the other patients accepted it.

Shortly before Christmas Mrs. Beers discovered a newcomer, his head and face in bloody bandages. A fellow soldier, also injured, was breaking up corn bread with a stick in a tin cup of cold water. In reply to her questions the second man explained that his friend had been shot in the mouth and could swallow only soft food.

"I will bring him some mush and milk or chicken soup," Mrs. Beers said firmly. The friend, well used to war shortages, stared with wide eyes. "Yer ga-assin' now, ain't ye?" Assuring him she was not "gassing," the matron sent for broth, got it, and fed it, spoon by spoon, to the wounded man. As the other watched hungrily, Mrs. Beers asked: "Now what would you like?"

After some hesitation he replied: "Well, lady, I've been sort of hankerin' after a sweet-potato pone, but I s'pose ye couldn't noways get that?" She certainly would try; it would be a Christmas treat for all the patients. Granted an ambulance by the surgeon in charge, Mrs. Beers made a foraging expedition among the farmers and came back with potatoes, a few dozen eggs, and butter.

At her temporary home, a rudely constructed cabin, the driver advised her: "Them 'taters has to be taken in out of the cold." His meaning was clear; it would certainly not be best to offer temptation by leaving the sacks outside. That night, after she had gone to sleep, she was suddenly awakened by Tempe, her Negro helper, who ran screaming to her side: an earthquake had struck! Mrs. Beers heard a heavy banging and to her horror saw the floor boards lift and fall. Then one plank fell aside and up came the head of a hog, who, with his brothers, had been drawn to the scent, and had formed a raiding party. Mrs.

Beers had been through bullet fire, she had nursed and tended the wounded and mutilated, she had survived many a hazard. But she had a "mortal fear" of live pork. Luckily Tempe suffered from no such terror, and, seizing a piece of burning wood from the fire, she ran to the intruder. Wedged in the narrow opening, he squealed piercingly as the girl yelled and beat at him. Neighbors knocked and the attack ended. . . . The Christmas treat of potato pone and a cup of sweet milk was a great success, and for most of the patients this was a happier meal than they had known in months.

It was a grim hour for all of the South when William Tecumseh Sherman, after marching relentlessly through Georgia, sent a wire to Abraham Lincoln at the end of that same year. "I beg to present to you as a Christmas gift the City of Savannah with a hundred and fifty heavy guns and plenty of ammunition, also about 25,000 bales of cotton." To many Georgians the words rankled almost as much as had Sherman's fiery progress from the fallen Atlanta to the sea.

A young mother has caught much of the pathos of the hour in several brief entries in her diary. Dolly Sumner Lunt, from Maine, married a planter who lived near Covington, Georgia. Three years before the start of the war her husband died, and as Mrs. Thomas Burge, Dolly continued on the estate with her daughter "Sadai" or Sarah. The Burges were still there when Sherman's men passed, and many of the plantation Negroes, afraid of the soldiers, slipped into the house to be with their mistress.

On Christmas Eve Mrs. Burge described her preparations for a bleak meal, her attempts to provide the plainest of presents for her remaining servants. "Now how changed!" she wrote. "No confectionery, cakes or pies can I have. We are all sad. . . . Christmas Eve, which has ever been gaily celebrated here, which has witnessed the popping of firecrackers and the hanging up of stockings, is an occasion now of sadness and gloom." Worse, she had nothing to put in her Sadai's stocking, "which hangs so invitingly for Santa Claus."

On Christmas night Mrs. Burge penned a sorrowful after-note: "Sadai jumped out of bed very early this morning to feel in her stocking. She could not believe but that there would be something in it. Finding nothing, she crept back into bed, pulled the cover over her face, and I soon heard her sobbing." A moment later the young Negroes had run in: "Christmas gift, Mist'ess! Christmas gift, Mist'ess!" Mrs. Burge drew the cover over her own face and wept beside her daughter.

The next year, Christmas came more happily to the Burge plantation. On December 24 the mother gave thanks to God for His goodness "in preserving my life and so much of my property." And on Christmas Day she added:

Sadai woke very early and crept out of bed to her stocking. Seeing it well-filled, she soon had a light and eight little Negroes around her, gazing upon the treasures. Everything opened that could be divided was shared with them. 'Tis the last Christmas, probably, that we shall be together, freedmen! Now you will, I trust, have your own homes, and be joyful under your own vine and fig tree. . . .

Some, at least, of the freedmen stayed to work on the plantation, which, today, is still in the family's hands.

For hundreds of thousands of Southern children there was tragedy in the non-appearance of Santa Claus during the later war years. Explanations were attempted: the Yankees had captured the old Saint this year. Or perhaps Santa had been caught in the blockade. In the journals were tales and poems designed to make the situation less gloomy for the young:

I'm sorry to write,
Our ports are blockaded, and Santa, tonight,
Will hardly get down here; for if he should start,
The Yankees would get him unless he was "smart,"
They beat all the men in creation to run,
And if they could get him, they'd think it fine fun
To put him in prison, and steal the nice toys
He started to bring to our girls and boys.
But try not to mind it—tell over your jokes —
Be gay and be cheerful, like other good folks;
For if you remember to be good and kind,
Old Santa next Christmas will bear it in mind.

In Richmond a hard-pressed family used ingenuity in providing decorations for its tree. During the cold spell just before Christmas, the few last hogs were killed, even though they were almost "nothing at all but skin and bones." Lacking corn for feed, the family had let the animals shift for themselves in the woods and orchards. When the killing ended and the children looked for the usual ears and tails to roast, they discovered that these choice objects had—oddly enough—disappeared.

On Christmas Day the mystery was solved. Among the greens sat the missing pig tails, "curled up in the most comfortable manner and richly clothed in paper ruffles." Nearby on the tree reappeared the pigs' ears as candle holders, while bits of potatoes and carrots had been put to the same use. Later the vegetable bits were served for dinner, and the children grimaced at the taste of wood that remained in them.

General Lee himself went on one Christmas tree, and—as befitted his station—close to the peak. In January of 1865 Isabel Maury wrote a spirited note:

Saturday before Christmas we were all busy preparing a tree for the Children; it was beautiful. On the top were two flags, our Confederate and our Battle Flag. Gen. Lee, bless his soul, was hung immediately below. My gift from Ma was a pearl pin and earrings—Puss had coral, beautiful, they are. We all united and gave her a point lace collar and cuffs. Of course we had egg-nog Christmas night, but no company.... Last Tuesday night Miss Nanny Dunlop made her debut—we were at her house. About three hundred invitations were circulated (verbal); you know we Confederates cannot afford cards....

Thursday we were invited to Dr. Deane's but did not go. Today being New Year's day, we had numerous calls, tho very unexpected to us.... My only objection is that the Yankees not only do it, but abuse the custom, and I want to do entirely different from them. We are a distinct and separate nation, and I wish our customs to be as distinct as we are.

Many believed as fervently as the writer of this letter that the South would win. Others, more sharply realistic, saw the shape of the future. In Richmond on New Year's Day of 1864, the brisk, influential Mary Boykin Chesnut wrote: "God help my country! I think we are like the sailors who break into the spirits closet when they find out the ship must sink. There seems to be for the first time a resolute determination to enjoy the brief hour, and never look beyond the day.

"I now have no hope. 'Have you any of old Mr. Chesnut's brandy here still? It is a good thing never to look beyond the hour. Lawrence, take this key, look in such a place for the decanter market . . .' etc." As Christmas approached a year later in Columbia, South Carolina, Mrs. Chesnut declared in still greater gloom: "The deep waters are closing over us; and we in this house are like the outsiders at the time of the Flood. We eat, drink, laugh, dance, in lightness of heart!"

Another woman later remembered in clear detail the holiday season in the Confederate White House, in the last year of the war. Varina Howell Davis, Mississippi-born wife of the Southern President, declared: "That Christmas season was ushered in under the thickest clouds; every one felt the cataclysm which impended, but the rosy, expectant faces of our little children were a constant reminder that self-sacrifice must be the personal offering of each member of the family."

Because of the expense involved in keeping them up, Mrs. Davis had recently sold her carriage and horses. A warm-spirited Confederate bought them back and sent them to her. Now she planned to dispose of one of her best satin dresses to obtain funds; with Christmas on the way, the children had high expectations, and she would use all possible makeshifts in an effort to fulfill them.

The Richmond housewives could find no currants, raisins, or other vital ingredients for old Virginia mincemeat pie. But, Mrs. Davis went on, the young considered at least one slice their right, "and the price of indigestion . . . a debt of honor due from them to the season's exactions." Despite the war, apple trees still bore fruit; with these as a base, she and the other women of the city would utilize any other fruit that came to hand. A little cider and some salt were obtained, as was brandy, though its usual price was a hundred dollars a bottle in inflated Confederate money.

As for eggnog, the Negro stable attendant, who brought in "the back log, our substitute for the Yule log," said he did not know how they would "git along without no eggnogg. Ef it's only a little wineglass." After considerable effort, the eggs and other makings were found. Plans progressed for a quiet home Christmas when unexpected word arrived: The orphans at the Episcopal home had been promised a tree and toys, cake and candy, plus a good prize for the best-behaved girl, and something had to be done about that.

Something was done. With Mrs. Davis's help, a committee of women was set up and the members repaired to their children's old toy collections to salvage dolls without eyes, monkeys that had lost their squeak, three-legged and even two-legged horses. They fixed and painted everything, plumping out rag dolls and putting new faces on them, adding fresh tails to feathered chickens and parrots. Robert Brown, one of the house staff, volunteered to build a "sure enough house, with four rooms," for the orphan's prize.

The Davises invited a group of young friends on Christmas Eve to help make candle molds and string popcorn and apples for the tree; Mr. Pizzini, the confectioner, contributed simple candies. For cornucopias and other ornamentation the Davis guests used colored papers, bright pictures from old books, bits of silk foraged out of trunks. All in all, the Christmas Eve of 1864 was far from unsatisfactory. When the small supply of eggnog went around, the eldest Davis boy assured his father: "Now I just know this is Christmas."

The next morning the Davises received their presents. For Mrs. Davis there were, among other things, six valuable cakes of soap, made from grease of a ham boiled for a family, and a pincushion stuffed with wool from the pet sheep of a farm woman. The family walked to St. Paul's Church, to hear a sermon by Dr. Charles Minnegerode, the Christmas-tree pioneer whom we met in an earlier chapter. Dr. Minnegerode had entered the Episcopal church, to win high fame in his region.

After services the Davises had their dinner. For it the cook managed a turkey and roast beef, a spun-sugar hen, life sized, and a nest of eggs of blancmange. The dessert made them all feel, as one of the party said, "like our jackets were buttoned." The children's *pièce de résistance*, however, was still ahead— the great orphans' tree. That night they went to the basement of St. Paul's, where the Davises watched the many gradations of emotion "from joy to ecstasy." To Mrs. Davis the evening was "worth two years of peaceful life," the kind of life she had not known for a long, long time.

About the same time, at Petersburg, the Army of Northern Virginia was to receive, for what would be its final holiday dinner, a meal to which hundreds had contributed. "Lee's Miserables," as many civilians called the soldiers in fond admiration, were tired, weakened. For months they had been subsisting on their usual ration of a pint of corn meal, one or two ounces of bacon, and little or nothing more. In the judgment of Douglas Southall Freeman, this mainstay of the beleaguered South was "starving on its feet." One veteran said simply that he was so hungry he "thanked God he had a backbone for his stomach to lean against."

When the holiday season approached, Virginians planned a feast to let the Army of Northern Virginia know their gratitude and their sympathy for the long-suffering defenders. From all sides came hoarded treasures—hams, chickens, turkeys, ducks, geese, bacon, vegetables. As the *Virginia Cavalcade* declared, "Some gave of their abundance, but most people gave generously of their little."

Provisions became available for an estimated 35,000 men. To cook such supplies called for skill, ingenuity, and perspiration; all of them were available in the big kitchens of Richmond's Ballard House where, under the direction of a caterer, three hundred fowls or meats were baked every four hours. The food was placed in barrels and sent to the front for New Year's Day.

Admittedly some did not get enough, amid confusion and delay. In most cases, however, the food did arrive at the front, where the men reached eagerly for it. They ate and ate and sighed in appreciation. But one group took little of the feast, following the example of their superior. A special barrel had gone to General Lee and his staff; it contained about a dozen turkeys which were placed on a board, the largest in the center.

For a moment the Confederate commander stared down at

the fine display and touched the biggest bird with his sword. "This, then, is my turkey? I don't know, gentlemen, what you are going to do with your turkeys, but I wish mine sent to the hospital at Petersburg. . . ."

So saying, Robert E. Lee went to his horse and rode off. As one of the officers at the scene ended the story: "We looked at one another for a moment, and then without a word replaced the turkeys in the barrel and sent them to the hospital."

For some soldiers there was disappointment. After waiting for many hours, one company received its supply—a sandwich for each man—two slices of bread and a minute sliver of ham. Several hungry soldiers asked: "Is that all?" A moment later, as one reported it, they felt ashamed. Finishing his sandwich, a corporal lighted his pipe and asked God to bless the women responsible for the day's offering. "It was all they could do; it was all they had. . . ."

# CHAPTER 16

# Postwar: Oranges and Cracker Barrels

I N periods of sustained trouble, a people will cling with special tenacity to its relaxations and its times of festivity. During the postwar era, the 1870's, '80's, and '90's, Christmas took a stronger hold than ever upon Southerners. "In the years following the Civil War," Francis Butler Simkins declared, "both blacks and whites remained devoted to Christmas. It was the Southern festival *par excellence*, the only holiday of the year that completely captured the anticipations and desires of the whole people."

Here and there the Christmas of '65, the first after the war, had a happier note than those which followed. For then there was at least a release from tension; the worst had happened.

There would be no more death lists, no more reports of the missing. Economic stress had yet to deepen. There rose, in the South as in the North, a strong note of thanksgiving.

In Baton Rouge, Louisiana, for instance, the 1865 Christmas was "a jolly old day," honored with "eggnog, Tom and Jerry, hot, and other soothing drinkables bountifully indulged in." Many "passed their usual visits," as the homely phrase puts it, and the children made the day and much of the evening bright and loud with their fireworks.

But a new period of restriction and unsettlement was soon upon the South. So many husbands, sons, brothers, and nephews were gone, leaving behind them only debts, with which their families had to struggle. Uncounted thousands lost their support. Much of the land lay barren, many fields were abandoned, with only meager patches of cultivation where once there had been green acres. Men's homes, little and big, had been destroyed; others stood unpainted and crumbling, while their owners, small farmers and once great growers alike, tried to maintain themselves under bleak conditions.

Professional city men took places as day laborers or shoe clerks. Plantation women who had "never worked" sought jobs as teachers or governesses or whatever else came to hand. In the villages the pinch was harder, and the possibilities for success even fewer than they had been before.

Under these difficult conditions and in the face of their uncertain efforts to fit themselves to new ways, the Southerners reached out toward Christmas with an anxious interest. Some were moved only by a simple determination to enjoy themselves, to have two or three days of holiday from care and concern. The devout, on the other hand, found the religious aspects of the good season more meaningful than ever before, and thousands went to church or prayed steadily for guidance.

In the postwar years, the holidays were celebrated on a much smaller scale. Gifts were meager, homemade dolls or ornaments; the meals were only one or two dishes of more or less improvised ingredients. "I think we didn't have a chicken on our table for nearly two years," an elderly Georgian told me as she thought over her childhood days in the 1870 period. As for such things as cake, a former Tennessee schoolteacher explained: "They seemed even more—well, unsweet than those I remembered from the last days of the war. We'd come to expect cakes to taste *plain*. But sometimes . . ." He made a grimace.

Many of the Negro field hands continued in their old places as wage earners or share tenants. The house servants in particular stayed close to their former owners; they had always been connected with the big house and most of them had been given preferred treatment.

The institution of "Christmas gift" survived the 1870's and lived on into the recent past, into the 1920's and 1930's and even, in some cases, beyond. Even after it had died away in the towns, it continued in the country areas; on farms or remnants of plantations, the whites were still waked by the cry and the smiling demand. As late as the mid-1940's, when I spent Christmas at a friend's plantation, I emerged from my room to the accompaniment of four or five simultaneous shouts of "Chris'mus gift!" But on my return, less than ten years later, only one attendant, the elderly cook who was the last of the former helpers, called it in a muted voice and somewhat shamefacedly. Three other house servants, newly arrived from town, appeared hesitant to echo the words.

Finally I broke the ice. "Don't you want a Christmas present?" With smiles that spread from one to the other, they fell in with the spirit as we recalled the old custom. But when I go back the next time I feel certain that this tradition will be gone completely.

The years following the War Between the States witnessed

the rise of the Southern country store, part supply place, part communication center, part sounding post of an area for miles around. In earlier times there had been only a few such stores, for the plantations had imported most of their supplies, and the occasional peddler who came by, a bulging pack on his back or an overstuffed wagon behind him, provided for lesser wants.

After the war's close men of both South and North sensed opportunity in the Southern countryside, and went there to open little frame establishments which promised to cater to practically every need of man, woman, or child. This aim they well fulfilled. About the glowing, potbellied stoves and the famous cracker barrels men gathered to inspect the contents of the shelves, to talk crops and stock, crime and politics. (The last two, then as now, were occasionally related.)

At this center the newer South called for its tobacco, its whittling knives, its shoes and harnesses and women's blouses, and also for many of its staples of nourishment and celebration. By a natural process, Christmas came to the country store and spread out from it as well; without the store there might have been no real holiday for hundreds of thousands in Virginia, Maryland, and North Carolina, Kentucky and Tennessee, Louisiana, Alabama, and Georgia.

An authority on the rural South, H. C. Nixon, in his lively *Possum Trot,* has recaptured the spirit of his father's store in the Alabama Piedmont, a Southern Railway flag station fifty miles southwest of Rome, Georgia. The doughty, enterprising father had the younger Nixon "behind the counter . . . as soon as I could see over it." The store handled snuff, sow-belly meat, Tutt's Pills, Dr. King's New Discovery "for coughs, colds and all throat and lung affections"; it sold corn from its own crib, took in chickens and disposed of them, and provided pine-plank coffins for the tenant families it supported.

During most of the year the Nixons had no call for fresh

stuff, "for every family in the neighborhood either raised vegetables or did without them." But when December approached, Bill Nixon stocked up heavily on fruit which was so closely associated with the holidays in the minds of rural children and their elders. As H. C. Nixon noted years later, "It was in a Christmas season that I first learned there was such a fruit as an orange." Even today, he added, "I still think of Christmas when I smell oranges in the country."

A family that could not afford at least one orange for each child—a shining globe to be dropped into a stocking—was glum indeed. No matter how anxious the mother and father were over finances, their mood improved if their young ones had an orange at Christmas. Even customers who had exceeded the limits of their credit would ask: "Can't you let me have a few oranges for the kids?" And in most cases the store owner, softhearted or hard, would respond to the request, if only to enjoy his own Christmas with a better conscience.

By late fall the store acquired a new air in more than one meaning of the word. From wholesale houses and supply places there arrived heavy boxes, bags, and crates that exuded a dozen aromas of animal, fish, nut, and mineral. As Thomas D. Clark explained in his richly nostalgic *Pills, Petticoats and Plows*, the "holy circle" about the stove might be broken, but the regular supplies stayed where they were while extras were piled around, above, below, and on top of them.

Barrels and boxes of candy were rolled in between the sugar, coffee, meal and flour or put down on the counter tops among the thread and knife cases. Bags of coconuts were ripped open.... Newly opened tubs of corned mackerel sat well back out of range of careless tobacco chewers. ... Toys were suspended from the ceilings among the lanterns, water buckets, horse collars, buggy whips and lard cans, or they were mixed in with everyday merchandise of the glass cases.... On top of the counters were small wooden boxes lined with red paper and filled with sawdust and shavings, and the contents were ruffled into a seductive state of confusion. These contained the firecrackers, torpedoes and Roman candles.

Each Christmas smell held its own story. The burned powder of the fireworks testified to the deep hold 'crackers and other explosives had on the South. Farm boys would save a penny a week, or less, and bring in the hoarded supply with a plaintive appeal: What would this-all buy that made the most noise, mister?

In the corner waited the liquor barrel, and only the most straitlaced held out against the time-tested lure of eggnog with a bit of strengthening. H. C. Nixon explained that "in those days long passed, I knew men who practiced sobriety consistently through all the year. But when Christmas approached, they hit the bottle or the jug." The fumes of Kentucky or Maryland bourbon and of North Carolina corn were unmistakable. The visitor to the store would have found the liquor barrel in the dark.

Only slightly less arresting was the redolence of the cheeses. In the postwar period cheese became an increasingly popular item, Tom Clark notes. After a fair crop year, a customer would splurge on a whole hoop of the stuff. To show how understanding he could be of rural tastes, Santa Claus now and then left a fine yellow wedge by the hearth or even stuck in a stocking. In observations on the mid-Georgia scene, Richard Henry Hutchings in *An Intimate Family History* reported that Christmas bought a succession of other luxuries, "English walnuts, Brazil nuts, Malaga grapes," delicacies available at no other time of the year.

Several weeks before Christmas the country stores began to receive the parade of neighborhood callers who wished to sell, not buy. Meat cured at home, possums, nuts, cowhides, sweet potatoes—anything the farm produced was sent to the cross-roads establishment to be traded for holiday fare. The children watched in eager speculation as the family wagon rolled out for the long trip to the store, then ran up at the first roll of the wheels on its return. But above all, as Mr. Clark declared, farm women saved up their eggs, waiting for prices to rise before offering them for sale. He uncovered one sad note that provides a small essay on the period. A South Carolina mother laboriously scratched out her message:

Willie, I send 5 dozen eggs give just what you can and Sammie will trade it out in something for the children times are very hard that is all I want to give them for Christmas.

Each young one who received an orange shared it with others. Often the farm mother passed it about in sections, a bit to each of her children, and afterward she kept the peelings for sweets, puddings, and cakes. As Mr. Clark noted, apples were similarly divided. "Few members of some families had ever been so profligate as to eat a whole apple at a time. Occasionally pitiful entries in individual accounts show that a dozen apples was the lone recognition which many impoverished customers of country stores could give to Christmas."

An exotic item was the coconut; for a dime it opened a world of unusual taste. The milk was dripped through a hole in the eyes, the meat grated for pies, and the shell saved with care to provide a dipper bowl or an ornament for the house. A cake thickly filled with coconut between the layers, and liberally sprinkled with it on top, would be enough to keep Christmas a happy memory for many years.

But for the young and many of the old, neither oranges nor coconuts, neither apples nor any other edibles, had quite the meaning of fireworks for the holidays. For five cents, a pack of Chinese firecrackers proved a passport to delight. As long as the 'crackers could be obtained, somehow, somewhere, despair was averted. A favorite diversion, Mr. Clark said, was to explode them behind a long-faced deacon, "with the hope of startling him into cussing." Another was to set them off behind a pair of mules, who, as everybody expected (or hoped), would promptly run away. Torpedoes were for throwing beneath girls' feet and Roman candles for lighting the heavens to the screaming delight of the young onlookers.

In these postwar Christmas days "anvil shooting" came into its own. At the country stores, on school grounds, and at various celebrations, intent men packed black powder into the holes of one anvil, put another anvil firmly over it, and lit the powder. The double boom could be heard for many a mile. What if the anvils were badly damaged? Hadn't they all had a right good time?

Christmas also remained the season for hunting. Like George Washington in his day, the simpler countrymen rode out to train their sights on deer, rabbits, or anything else that moved, including, by accident, an occasional neighbor. Others, who enjoyed noise for noise's sake, simply shot at the sky or the horizon, winging a human victim or two at random.

And at Christmas the postwar Southerner often used this day of leisure and holiday spirits to ride off and court the girls. The bachelor was expected to spark his lady or ladies at this time. And when he galloped down the road after a call, blasting his pistol into the air, friends exchanged looks. It was a "sure sign" of something: he had either broken with his girl, or he was going to get married *right* away.

# CHAPTER 17

# Papa Noël of New Orleans

THE Christmas season came to the New Orleans and Louisiana of the 1850's with a French-Southern accent, with humor, and with a happy excitability. Although the celebration derived from France, it underwent a sea change on its way here and also a liberal dipping in the waters of the Mississippi.

To the old-time Louisianan of the plantations and the big, iron-balconied houses of New Orleans' French Quarter, life was meant to be savored, to be appreciated. His December holidays were divided very clearly: Christmas was the day for solemnity, for religion, and for family observance; New Year's the time for conviviality. The holidays reached their climax on New Year's Day, *le Jour de l'An—the* day of the year in more ways than one.

In the middle of the last century the city of New Orleans was unlike any other in America. Its people—Creoles who were descendants of the early French, often with Spanish additions—also had a unique quality. Among them, the Dutch and German Kris Kringle became Papa Noël, a Santa Claus with the regulation bulging stomach and laugh lines around his eyes, but with a sharper Gallic wit, a lifted eyebrow, and a twinkle for the ladies.

Papa Noël's land was the moist-green, alluvial country of the Mississippi and its tributary bayous, twisting as they approached the Gulf. The Greek Revival houses of the rural reaches, with their iron railings, looked strange to Georgians and Marylanders, who were startled by the hint of the West Indies in their deep-sloping roofs and shadowed galleries. When Christmas arrived along the great river or Bayou Teche, Bayou Plaquemine, or False River, it might be enjoyed beside banana plants and camellia bushes.

In New Orleans the holiday festivities took place in buildings more Spanish than French in style. The oldest part of town, the French Quarter, covered about twelve square blocks within a curve of the Mississippi. Founded in 1718 by the French, the Quarter remained Gallic at heart, although the Spaniards ruled it for about forty years before the Americans finally acquired it in the early 1800's. A series of fires had wiped out most of the city, and the new structures that rose had stuccoed walls and patios and used decorative ironwork in a definitely Spanish style. The houses stood flush with the brick sidewalks or *banquettes*—the New Orleans word—and the family lived with its back to the street, its face to the building's inner court. Among the New Orleans Creoles the family was a vivid group, warmly loyal, its members tending generally to accept the foibles of their fellow men. New Orleanians have always been a people who think of life not as a struggle but as a realization. The Louisiana

Creoles had a more "Southern" manner than did the Creoles of Missouri, maintaining a well-defined identity and close ties to the mother country. They had their French opera, their French newspapers, and their French cuisine, with pungent Spanish additions, and extra zest added by their Negro cooks. English was an alien tongue to them. To a suggestion that he learn it, any of the older Creoles would have shrugged. Why, *monsieur?* There was no need. . . .

In the words of one of my Royal Street friends at a recent Christmas party, "My family fought for this country in the War of 1812, the Mexican War, and most of the later ones. Still"—he smiled—"that didn't mean they stopped talking French or behaved like Yankees on New Year's Day. Even now, I don't quite do that myself."

By 1850 the Creoles were losing to the Americans in the competition for rule of Louisiana. Nevertheless, French customs held sway in much of the state. At New Orleans newcomers reigned in the swiftly prospering "American section" above Canal Street, the dividing line, while the Creoles held to themselves in their original area. Intermarriages took place, but most of the *grandes dames* shook their heads when they heard of it. Poor Amélie, so she's going to marry *un Américain.* I always did think there was something flighty about that girl!

And to the Creoles, whatever was best at Christmas, as at any other time, came from France, and that went for dolls and mechanical toys, wines and preserved foods. As for the American dish of turkey and cranberries for the holidays, most Creole women admitted that they had heard of it. But, one asked, why experiment when people had so many other fine items on hand, things they *knew* were good?

In many respects the Creole-American town was a free-living place, roaring, flamboyant, to some the most wicked city in America. At the same time it was a city of vivid religious beliefs, and of many demonstrations of faith. In the Christmas season, while some of the raffish river elements looked on in wonder, the Creoles thronged the streets on their way to church, knelt and took communion with a warm devotion.

In both the sugar-cane country, where the thick green stalks grew close to the houses, and the narrow streets of French New Orleans, the family was the rule, the dominant consideration, and its importance was never clearer than in the December holidays. To be a Livaudais, a Villere, a De la Houssaye signified a great deal. To belong to such a group was to be one of a strong, tight clan.

Sisters, brothers, uncles, aunts, grandparents, cousins close or distant—all had a right to recognition. When *la famille* assembled during the Christmas season, neither age nor interest isolated one member from another. The generations jostled amicably for space—the Creoles never believed in small families —the old in comfortable chairs, the young at their feet, the rest wherever they could find a place.

Many Louisiana French families celebrated Christmas on their country property, moving between double parlors with tall folding doors and the parish church along the river "coast" or the bayou. Whenever it was possible, however, the country dwellers joined their relatives in New Orleans, taking the steamboat or the carriage for the ride up- or down-river to the heart of Creoledom.

*Le Jour de Noël.* . . . Christmas Day and its eve were a time for one's immediate relatives—and nobody else. In New Orleans and upriver Baton Rouge, Donaldsonville, Thibodaux, Houma, and other towns the night before Christmas brought the *messe de minuit,* Midnight Mass. A man might miss almost any other service during the year, but he would feel deep regret if he did not join the women for the solemnities of the holy night.

Many returned from trips and rearranged all their affairs to make certain of attendance on this occasion.

The hours after dark on Christmas Eve saw the Creoles gathering in house after house. In would come a family branch from St. Martinville or New Iberia in the Teche country, the women's high-pitched cries mingling with the calmer greetings of their husbands. From the carriage would pile out an unbelievable mass of LeBretons or Duquesnays or De la Villebeuvres, with news and questions and gossip: Had the city family heard the good news about the sugar predictions? Was it true the opera had only one good tenor this year, and that one soprano hit the other over the head with a bouquet when the curtain fell? And who would sing at tonight's Mass?

Most families had relatives staying with them, perhaps an old maiden aunt or a bachelor uncle. Yet even if these lone wolves happened to live elsewhere, they made it a point to be with their families on Christmas Eve. When one did not appear, it was cause for deep concern. Clearly, he or she was seriously ill or mortally offended.

For several hours the clan talked at length, *oncles* and *tantes*, *cousins* and *cousines*, *grand'mères* and *grand-pères*, sometimes all at the same time. With the conversation went small glasses of wine or a cup of coffee to help the sleepy keep awake for the midnight ceremony. The younger children, full of the season's excitement, stayed up as long as their eyes, and Maman and Papa, allowed. Then they stumbled upstairs or were carried to bed by a Negro servant. The older ones remained below, proud that they were now considered adult enough to attend the Mass.

It was a good-humored assembly, though usually not a hilarious one; the service soon to come cast a reflective shadow over its members. At about 10:30 or 11 P.M. the first church bells rang and the family reached for their hats and coats to walk along the brick *banquettes* toward the Cathedral. The Creole woman would feel "all but naked," as one assured me, unless she carried her prayer beads, her prayer book, and her purse with her contribution, and she checked all three before she left the house. She also checked her several shawls and wrappings. In such a bland climate, these might seem quite unnecessary, but Creoles *tantes* were famous for their coverings. *Chère,* everybody knows that the night air is bad for you!

Crossing the corners of the cobblestoned streets at Dumaine or St. Phillip, Bourbon, Chartres or Royal, they became part of a throng approaching the old *Place d'Armes,* the early parade grounds. Here stood the three-spired St. Louis Cathedral, occupying a site which had had a church ever since the city was established. This was New Orleans' heart; here were the heavy Spanish government buildings of older days, and the new redbrick, magnificently galleried Pontalba buildings, just erected by the Baroness of France and Louisiana. And one could see the Mississippi flowing beyond the half-open levee.

For Creole New Orleans this was the only place to be tonight. At the tall gray cathedral doors a subdued festivity showed itself as friends hailed friends, then hurried through the portals. On Christmas Eve the Cathedral glowed as it did at no other time; its altars were a shining white and silver, with dots of flame from red tapers and greenery at the great central one.

Crowds filled the pews in the wide lower floor and the narrow upper balcony as well; scores would stand in the back from the beginning of the services to their end. As midnight neared, whispers stopped abruptly with the first clang of bells in the central tower. These bells had rung over New Orleans for generations, "with a sound I could hear and recognize in my sleep," a neighbor told me.

As the echo of the twelve strokes ended, the organ opened the processional with thunderous chords, and the voices of the choir rose over the nave and aisles. Before the throng moved the priests in gold-and-white vestments, assisted by acolytes carrying lighted tapers and incense. When the smoke sent its fragrance through the church, making the figures behind the altar rail appear far away, the Orleanians were stirred, as always at this high Mass, by the solemnity of the hour.

Now a voice rang out in a hymn that the Creoles knew from its very first note. Frequently the singer was a member of the opera troupe, chosen not only for his artistry, but also because he was respected in a community that could be sharply critical. Often the hymn would be *"Minuit, Chrétien,"* the "Midnight, O Christian"; practically every member of the congregation hoped to hear this favorite. No matter how beautiful the Mass, the historian Roger Baudier observed, if this traditional number were omitted, there would be disappointment. The words soared:

> *Minuit! Chrétien, c'est l'heure solennelle*
> *Où l'homme Dieu descendit jusqu'à nous....*

> Midnight, O Christian, 'tis the hour so solemn,
> When God as man descended from heav'n....

The last note of the Mass died away, and after a moment's pause the devout throng arose. Few lingered for any length of time on the flagstoned walk outside the church. Most families were going home for the *réveillon,* the Christmas breakfast that followed the service. There spirits lifted swiftly at a meal as far removed from the American style as were the Creoles themselves from the uptown Americans.

Some of the ingredients came from supplies in the family kitchen, which faced the patio in an attached wing at the back: herbs, preserved fruits, the soup stock on which the Creoles drew as do Gallic experts in matters gastronomical. The others were from the French market, located a few squares from any house in the Quarter. In the market, only a short distance from the levee, with its long sheds and stalls, were succulent vegetables—"Creole tomatoes" or "Creole corn" meant the highest possible grade; crabs and shrimp and oysters from the lakes, bayous, and river; meats brought in from farms in the neighboring parishes (the Louisiana word for counties); and game shot in the half-salt, half-fresh water marshes below the city.

Choctaw Indians had long sold sassafras leaves and wild herbs to the French and Spanish at this market center. Everybody went there—natives to buy, outsiders to gape at the strange sights and people, staggering river boatmen, steamboat dandies, water-front hangers-on. Here the French housewives had called the day before, each with her cook behind her, holding an enormous basket. And tonight, after hours of steaming, pounding, broiling, marinating, seasoning, tasting and retasting, the repast was ready.

By Creole food standards, the meal was a comparatively small one, but its ingredients were rich: eggs in one or two styles, several different kinds of wines; sweet breads, raisin breads, and platters of the long crisp loaves which New Orleanians believe to be the equal of those of France. And always there was a Creole *spécialité* of *spécialités*, the imaginatively flavored *daube glacé*, jellied meat "taken on a trip to heaven," as a New Iberia Creole has said, with bay leaf, pepper, cloves, and other ingredients transforming the dish into a dark delight. There were seldom leftovers of *daube glacé*, and nobody in New Orleans has been known to refuse the offer of a second or even a third slice.

The meal ended with a cake filled with jelly, dripping with wine or rum, and topped with a hill of whipped cream, or a molded dessert from one of the several noted confectioners who flourished in the French Quarter. As a postscript came the New Orleans coffee—blacker, stronger, and more pungent than in practically any other part of America. In many cases the *café* served as a test for a stranger; if he appreciated it, he had passed. A refusal, and the Creole might wonder about him.

At the *réveillon* the talk was long and buoyant. Centers of interest were the *grand'mères* and *grand-pères*, heads of the clan who, as the French New Orleanian put it, "deserve our respect and our thanks—and our attention." The Creole elders were enveloped in endless regard and deference: the best chairs, the finest view, the first cake, the first kiss, the first bow from Jean and Jeanne. At a word from Grand'mère all conversation stopped, and throughout the evening she was brought into the debates for her opinion, her approval. An American woman, connected years later by marriage with one of the Quarter families, shook her head as she said: "At my first meeting with them, I saw the old mother, and found out what it was like to be a queen."

The *réveillon* might go on for hours, and although the men would sleep late the next morning, the women could not. There was the matter of the children, restless soon after dawn, and anxious for Christmas to start. They needed no stimulant to make them stir; the adult, who did, received it with a small, bedside cup of black coffee. (For the *réveillon* it might have been either dark or *café au lait*, coffee mixed with equal parts of steaming hot milk; in the morning it came straight—with chicory as always.) "When you taste that, you know you got coffee in you," say the natives.

Today's breakfast was probably a hasty meal in *petit déjeuner* style, with delicate brioche, pats of butter, and more *café au lait*. Even so the children were anxious. "Maman, when will things start?" "Papa Noël, he is on his way?" The young knew that today's gifts would be mere tokens of the generosity to follow at the New Year. But a present is a present, and children are children.

The last cup was filled from the coffee urn, the gentlemen had a cigar or two, and Papa got up. *"Eh, bien."* Maman signaled, and the servants threw open the folding doors. There stood a small, sparkling tree, and the children ran to it to exclaim at the tiny *crèche* with its manger scene beneath it. The stockings held hard candies, toy trumpets, and similar small gifts.

As the children cried out over the tree, the adults looked on, sometimes in amusement, sometimes in surprise, especially if they were of the oldest generation. For the Christmas tree had arrived only lately in New Orleans, and a number of the elders considered it—well, a bit odd. In France the families always had the *crèche*, but this innovation . . .

And the New Orleans Christmas tree of the period, and for years to come, was hardly the formalized, ornamented fir that the Germans favored. One account of several years later in the *Daily Picayune* told of a well-to-do Orleanian who used a Mespilus or Japan plum as a Christmas tree: this was surely one of the most curious substitutes for a fir that the New World has seen.

By now the children were craning their necks and inquiring again about Papa Noël. Papa glanced at Maman, who made a motion to an aunt, who signaled to someone in the hall. At last the chain of communication reached the second floor, and down the stairs, with a clump of feet and a rumble of laughter, advanced the Creole St. Nicholas.

He was a jovial, well-padded gentleman in red and white, not unlike his Anglo-Saxon relative, except that his banter was in French and he had an excitability that would have puzzled his Rhineland and American counterpart. "And how were Térence and Sosthène, Alita and little Dieudonné?" Papa Noël was everywhere, asking everything, offering lively advice—and giving everybody his attention, including the good-looking *cousine* from New Roads and the young widow from Breaux Bridge or Lafayette. Laughter and roars of approval greeted whatever he did; the smallest members of the family shrieked, and the more sophisticated older children pretended that they did not recognize Cousin Théodule from Bayou St. John.

A final bon mot, a rub of his stomach, and Papa Noël pounded out. The day was well launched. The children had another event before them, a visit to the Cathedral during which they would behold the handsome *crèche,* with its softly lighted manger scene. With them went several members of the household, including a dark maid or two to manage the lot. Today the old church was crowded again, with hundreds of children, and few left without a long pause before the manger.

"Now we will kneel," Maman or Tante Burdette would whisper, and the children took their places before the *crèche* and prayed to *"le p'tit Jésus."* If time permitted, they might also go to one or two of the smaller churches in the French Quarter, to admire the manger there and also to send up petitions for the Christ Child. Christmas without a series of visits to the *crèches* . . . for the Creole young that would be unthinkable.

The rest of the day passed quietly for the family, and then everyone settled down to await the truly great day. There was a steady hum of work in the kitchen and in the rest of the house; carpets, curtains, stairs, cut glass, and dishes, all had to be specially clean; everyone would be inspecting, and who could notice more than a relative?

New Year's Eve might or might not bring another *réveillon;* if one took place it had singing and dancing, a more festive air than the *réveillon* of Christmas. Even then, however, all interests turned toward the next day, that time of times. As the New Year dawned the household stirred behind the galleries and in the courtyards with their arched windows.

*"Bonne année, bonne année!"* A good New Year. . . . The words would be heard over and over, whenever one Creole first

saw another, and sometimes several times if he met him later in the day. Maman arose ahead of the rest, to supervise the garnishing of the jellied dishes, to sniff the gumbo pot, examine the pralines. Half grave, half smiling, the family finished the first cup of coffee and went out to greet one another, and to wish one another good luck, good health, a fine New Year. Nobody must be absentminded or abrupt, because, the saying went, the way one acted today was the way he would act all through the year.

The children performed without fail a rite which they had rehearsed for days with an aunt. In their hands they held decorated verses, written with the help of several adults. In carefully fashioned if awkward letters the poem declared:

> My dear Maman, my dear Papa,
> A good New Year. . . .
> I salute and love you
> With a love everlasting.

With this *"compliment du jour de l'an,"* a Mr. Baudier notes, went a bow or a curtsy, and an earnest greeting, and the elders would catch up the child for a kiss. Without this ceremony both young and old would have thought New Year's poorly launched. A pause, and Papa and Maman, *tantes, oncles,* and others took out the holiday gifts, *les étrennes.*

These were the real presents of the season: sets of soldiers in Napoleonic dress, an embroidered dress over which Tante Margot had labored for weeks, and beyond everything else for the Creole girl, a doll from France. *"Une poupée parisienne!"* The little one's cry of delight was her parents' reward for the negotiations with the French relative who had made the selection, and the worries that it might not arrive in time.

Next, duty for old and young. In the Creole tradition of tribute to age and authority, Maman, Papa, and the children must pay a visit to each of the boys' and girls' godparents, his *marraines* and *parrains*. After that, a call on favorite aunts and uncles (to be realistic, the richer ones in particular) and also, and especially, to Grand'mère and Grand-père in their own quarters. Salutations, formal greetings, kisses—formality and informality combined—a few tears were shed and then, without being too obvious about it, the parents hurried the children away, to be home for the first of their callers, in a procession that would go on for the rest of the day.

Before they had settled themselves, and while Maman was making a final check in the hall or kitchen, the bell would ring and Papa would groan in mock despair. Especially if the host and hostess were among the older members of the family, everyone within riding distance was expected to call. An aunt might confide to a cousin: "I have a fever, but I came anyway. It's easier than to try to explain afterward."

A circle formed in the big living rooms or, if the day were bright, in the green courtyard with its sun-flecked iron furniture. The gathering altered, enlarged, and grew smaller, but the circle was there for the whole day. "Everybody talked, and some listened," as a smiling Creole described it. Everyone wanted news of the family, but wanted even more to tell his own.

Some were meeting today for the first time since last New Year's; and so many momentous events had passed in the interim: a child had been born, a brother had died, a marriage had been arranged. While the women "gossiped," as the men put it —although they themselves did much the same thing—the latter gravitated toward a sideboard from which Papa dispensed a choice wine or brandy and also a joke or story, usually about a character in the remote bayou country.

A silver bowl of eggnog stood ready, and a sister or aunt made certain that it was replenished from time to time. Around the bowl were plates of fruit cakes both light and dark, each heavy with spirits, and also the Creole specialties of *dragées,* sugar-coated almonds; *bonbons* or sugar candies; *petits gâteaux*, little cakes; and pralines. Every New Orleanian was an authority on pralines. "Angèle, this is even better than last year's. You have added something new this time? . . ." If she had, Angèle probably would not tell. A true innovation in praline making, as in any other dish, need not be shared with even a sister or a mother.

Occasionally a new face appeared, and one of the guests tightened his lips with sudden constraint. There had been a quarrel; everybody had heard of it. Then one of the disputants would come forward; a man would offer his hand, a woman an embrace. Tension relaxed; the old rule had been followed: all differences must be reconciled on *le Jour de l'An*. The two talked together more easily as the moments passed, and the Creoles reminded one another of the saying that the New Year often marked the beginning of the warmest and most lasting friendships.

The women sipped the liqueurs that were the favorite social drink of the distaff side in New Orleans. Anisette, cherry cordials, orgeat, home-concocted sweet syrups were considered ladylike drinks, and mild enough, though occasionally not so mild as they might have been. Everybody knew that Tante Clarice, for instance, became rosy cheeked and talkative after only three or four tiny glasses. But, as someone usually explained: "That Clarice, she is so unused to drink that she gets dizzy when she smells the cork."

So went New Year's in the Quarter. As the day wore on, and visiting gathered momentum, new arrivals took the place of departing guests. Few left without first sipping a cup of the restorative coffee; this was an integral part of the ritual.

Finally the last one had gone, and the family had its New Year meal, at 6 P.M. or later, with several rich main dishes, including a gumbo made with shrimp and crabmeat or chicken, and a dozen other ingredients; with salad and wines from

France. And often it ended with the Creoles' beverage supreme for a ceremonial close to any occasion—*café brûlot*.

This was coffee glorified with brandy, cinnamon, and other spices, orange and lemon peel, and set afire. Some called and still call it *café diabolique;* to most of us it comes, instead, from the place above. . . . As all watched, the transcendent mixture simmered and sent its fragrance over the room. Papa motioned, lights were lowered; the concoction was touched so that it blazed. As he dipped the ladle, lifted it, lowered it, the flames sent dancing shadows on the walls and the circle at the table, and the assembled family heaved a collective sigh. *Oui,* the year had begun well. . . .

In the French Quarter of today, in the uptown and other American sections as well, New Year's Day has a suggestion of the same flavor that it had in the older era. With the Americanization of the past century, the giving of presents has shifted to Christmas rather than New Year's, and Papa Noël has been replaced by Santa Claus. But the *crèches* still shine about New Orleans; people still come in from outlying sections, pay calls on the oldest members of the family, enjoy *daube glacé* and *gumbo,* and take black coffee at the final moment. And the Creoles' *café brûlot* has never died; the Americans adopted it, and now it blazes brightly over holiday New Orleans.

## CHAPTER 18

# No French Minuets for Kentucky

A NEW Country Called Kentucky," declared a Virginian of the late 1700's, "is reckon'd the finest Country in the World, affording almost all the necessities of life Spontaneously. . . ." Others agreed with this estimate of the rich land to the west, and the movement toward Kentucky had begun. Tobacco, an ever-hungry crop, was devouring thousands of acres of Virginia soil; from that area, from Maryland, and from Pennsylvania, scattered bands of men started for the fresh green frontier.

In 1777, however, two dangers stood in the way—Indians and English soldiers. But unfrightened by this double threat, a hearty, adventurous young colonel embarked on an expedition that was to have important consequences for the country.

He was George Rogers Clark, a Virginian who had hunted and found excitement in the Kentucky wilds. Returning to Williamsburg, he conferred with Patrick Henry and Thomas Jefferson about a bold project. The plan, as announced, was simply to "defend" Kentucky, but instead, the expedition, after reaching that region, was to push up to the Illinois country in a swift attack on both the red men and the English.

The secret was magnificently kept; for most of the trip, even the expedition's members did not guess its full purpose. Although Clark had hopes of a much larger band, only 150 men followed him. Still, they were enough. And with them went a party of twenty families who were to figure in the tale of the first Christmas in their new part of the South.

The young Colonel took the families with him in spite of many misgivings, his own and those of his men. These civilians were anxious to test their fortunes in Kentucky, but a long trip without protection through the Indian-infested region would have been an ordeal for the women. After considerable persuasion, however, Colonel Clark gave in to their petitions, and permitted them to join his group. The expedition set out by boat from Redstone settlement on the Monongahela River (known today as Brownsville, Pennsylvania) and in late May approached the Falls of the Ohio.

There the settlers established themselves while Clark and his men pressed on toward the Illinois territory. The party halted at the river's edge, at a spot that was later to be the future site of Louisville. Recognizing, however, that their position in this exposed place might be precarious—they could be wiped out in an afternoon or even an hour—they decided that, for greater safety, they should establish themselves for the time being on an island in the river, and to it they gave the name Corn Island, in honor of the rich green stalks that rose over it. If affairs went well with Colonel Clark's foray against the enemy, they might then transfer back to the shore. Hastily, with the help of the militia, the men started to work to build small, plain cabins to serve as temporary dwellings, and a month later the pioneers bade a nervous good-by to the military.

As the soldiers moved down the dangerous rapids, the sun went into eclipse, and both the superstitious and the devout crossed themselves. Was the sudden darkness a forewarning of disaster? They tried not to dwell on the "sign," or what it might signify. . . .

With the settlers was a Negro, a wrinkled helper named Cato, who played a masterful fiddle. In the months that lay ahead they were to rely on Cato's art in more ways than they had expected.

Waiting for whatever fate would bring, the party labored during the day and retired to their grim huts at dark. Repeatedly they turned to Cato, enjoying their only solace in listening and dancing to his lively music. One day a messenger appeared. He was exhausted after the long trip but he brought with him happy word. The revolutionists had defeated the British forces, and the newcomers would be safe from at least one of their enemies.

At once the band made ready to transfer to the shore, selecting for settlement a well-watered stretch of rich soil. Jim Chenoweth, a skillful builder who was the natural leader of the party, took over the task of supervising construction of sturdy log cabins, connected one to another around a central court, with blockhouses at the corners.

A new goal before them, these first Louisvillians cleared the ground and selected the best trees in the forests. Through late summer and autumn they struggled, sweating, laying foundations, piling up logs for walls. With Chenoweth in the lead, the men of the Pope, Clark, Bullitt, Meriwether, Helm, Kincheloe, Boone, Linn and other families labored to create this region.

Although the men worked until they were ready to drop from

exhaustion, the settlers gathered every week or so for an evening of happy relaxation. At such times Cato would again take out his fiddle and play as the young men and women—and the older ones as well—circled and swung in the Virginia reel and other light-spirited, light-footed dances of the colonials. One chronicler declared: "In truth it may be doubted if the families could have kept together on Corn Island during the summer and fall of 1778, if Cato's fiddle had not been there to cheer them with its stirring music."

Cold weather had come to the river edge. Although by that time the work was not completed and some walls and roofs were still open to the air, the settlers decided to move at once to the mainland so that they could celebrate their first Christmas holiday there. In the words of the *Southern Bivouac*, it would be "a housewarming on Christmas day," combining two meaningful events in one. And since Jim Chenoweth had borne the major brunt of the labor, he was given an additional honor, that of managing the event.

To the new Kentuckians, Christmas meant two things, each equally important: a feast and a dance. The first came easily. During the last week before the holidays, the best marksmen went out with their muskets and returned with deer, rabbits, and turkeys, and—happily for most of the group—a possum or two. But the second. . . . Old Cato was oddly mute. He pointed to his ancient fiddle; he had been using it so much that he had broken all except one string. He struggled for hours over various substitutes. He tried the hair of a horse's tail, the sinews of a deer. The first produced a wild screech and the other a low groan. What could be done? The answer was—nothing, and sadly the colony accepted the verdict. Perhaps they could sing a little and clap hands. . . .

It would be a poor holiday without music. Still they would have that rich meal of theirs, and the women hoarded corn and pumpkins, fruits and vegetables, for their pone and pies and heaping dishes. The meats were hung in the coolest places; the men worked over the skinning, salting, and other preparations; and suddenly Christmas Eve had arrived.

And with it, a surprise. A small boat appeared in the river and tied up near the embryo city. The settlers thronged about it, asking a dozen questions, pressing invitations on the strangers. Wouldn't they stay? One day wouldn't throw them off their schedule, the company-hungry Kentuckians insisted. They had plenty of everything, they assured the travelers, and they would "count it an honor." The strangers announced that they would remain.

Quietly Cato went about the boat, putting his own questions. One of the party, a handsome, trim little man, with odd speech and manner, proved to be a Frenchman—Monsieur Jean Nikel, here to see the New World and also to help the Americans in their fight against England. To Cato's discreet query, he gave a prompt reply. Ah, *oui,* he had several fiddle strings; he was a musician himself. But what would he get in return for these scarce and valuable objects?

Cato and M. Nikel bargained, and Monsieur ended with three raccoon skins in return for three fiddle strings. With a gleam of delight Cato left; he would say nothing, his music would be a surprise.

Christmas Day brought a magnificent meal. In the morning the men set up a long wooden table in the biggest chamber at the fort, a double apartment which would later be a storeroom. The women worked for hours over the pots and pans, basting and sampling, adding salt and corn, making gravy and testing pies. At last they carried their marvels to the table.

The floor was made of earth, the table not quite firm. Dishes were primitive, mainly wooden bowls and trays. The settlers had a few forks with horn handles, a few pewter spoons—far from enough to go around. Nevertheless:

There was venison, and bear, and rabbit, and turkey, and raccoon, and buffalo meat, prepared in different ways. There was cornbread in pone, in hoe-cake and in batter-cake form; there was hominy, boiled and fried; there was milk and butter and home-made cheese. But the great dish of the occasion was an opossum baked whole. It hung by its tail on a stick of wood in the center of the table, and every one present had a piece of it.

The young Frenchman, Jean Nikel, drew considerable interest from all the settlers, and was the object of admiring glances from the girls. As Isabel McMeekin described him, he wore satin and his wig was well powdered; this study in Gallic elegance made the other men rub their bearded cheeks and feel like awkward backwoodsmen. Monsieur spoke a fair English, and the ladies were eager to teach him more about the language and all things American.

The company ate with gusto. This was the best meal the settlers had had since reaching the site of Louisville, and the finest the travelers had had in many months. At last one man after another sighed, patted his chest or stomach, shook his head at the extra platefuls pressed upon him, and a lull fell upon the crowd.

A youth sighed; what a pity there would be no music today. A moment later, during a pause, the French guest was heard to make casual mention of his fiddle. At that word, one of the younger women "gave a joyous shout," and the others gathered about Monsieur. Did he have the fiddle with him? Yes, the caller said, he did. Cries rose all about him: Couldn't he get it? Wouldn't he play?

Several times Monsieur Nikel declined, and then "the girls hugged and kissed him and patted his face until he yielded." As

Monsieur walked over to the boat to get the instrument, the women removed the dishes and the men dismantled the improvised table. The older people and a few women with very young children took places along the wall. Few noticed poor Cato, who sat gloomily near the door.

So he was going to lose his chance, and also the extra coins on which he had counted today; he had given up those raccoon skins for nothing. . . . Cato continued silent as the powdered visitor returned, assumed a position in the center of the room, and announced that they would do—the minuet.

At the last word the Kentuckians blinked in wonder, and Monsieur explained. It was the most beautiful of all dances, the dance that the best people of France would be doing on this glorious Christmas. First, he said, he would teach them the long, graceful bow, the way to balance themselves, then glide forward. *Comme ça.* . . . Would the young lady try it, and the gentleman next to her?

Although the performances were not entirely satisfactory, Monsieur decided that the Americans could learn. *Eh, bien,* they would improve with practice. One of the girls, who had been especially taken with the good-looking newcomer, murmured that they should all be happy to do something original and fashionable—

A brand new dance
Just come from France!

*"Commencez,"* the fashionable guest called out as he applied his bow. Awkwardly the young men and women started forward, halted, started again. In a moment they were entirely out of time; the figures were mixed, then lost. Instead of gliding, as directed, the dancers hopped. They did not bow slowly and delicately, but bobbed their heads "like geese dodging a shower of stone."

Monsieur Nikel groaned. Clearly the minuet was not for *les Américains*. Very well, they would try another dance, the pavan. The main point, he said slowly, was to promenade proudly, like peacocks, as ladies and gentlemen of the court did at Versailles. *Allons!* He demonstrated while the audience watched with widening eyes, and once again the soft violin notes rose over the room.

Several boys came forth, strutting as directed. At the sight, first one girl giggled, then another, and as the ladies caught their skirts with both hands and went forward in high pride, a young settler snickered and cried like a peacock. In a few minutes pavan became pandemonium.

Monsieur's English left him. Furiously he cried out, bemoaning their behavior, lifting his arms to the sky as he deplored the insanity in which he had become involved. He asked the heavens to be his witness if he had not done his best to. . . . Understanding no word of what he said, the settlers gaped and laughed. Retiring to the wall, Monsieur stood there, his violin in his trembling hand, looking over in mingled fury and despair.

Through it all Cato had been sitting impassively to the side. At the first moment's confusion, he had nodded to himself; he had only to wait. . . . A pause followed, and the Kentuckians looked at one another. Was the day over, then? Cato approached the Frenchman. Would his honor mind if Cato played while he took his rest?

The stranger turned a hard stare upon the dark fiddler and nodded briefly. The crowd cried in surprise when Cato drew forth his fiddle with its new strings. "All right, ladies and gent'men. . . ." As he bowed the first few notes of the good old Virginia reel, the cry became a shout of joyful recognition.

Swiftly the men lined up on one side, the women on the other; with hardly a pause they chose partners. Through the middle the first couple dashed, "cutting all sorts of capers, interspersed with jigs, hoe-downs, shuffles and pigeon-wings." The audience shouted its approval until, exhausted, the pair went to the foot of the line and another took their place.

A second couple stepped forward, trying to outdo their predecessors, and the yells rose even higher. Then a third and a fourth. The dance continued for hours; participants rested, ran forward again, rested, began anew. This, everybody agreed, was worth all the hardship they had gone through. The only limitation was Cato's capacity; but, with a brief pause and a drink now and then, the fiddler seemed indefatigable. Neither he nor they stopped until midnight, and only then, reluctantly, wearily, did they all go home.

Only a few noticed that, in the middle of the zestful doings, Monsieur Nikel had put away his violin and slipped off to his boat. Several expressed their regret. He had been a real nice fellow, that one, but somehow, they all agreed, the minuet and the pavan were not the things for Kentucky.

From such hearty beginnings came Kentucky's major city of today, home of the great Derby, a center which combines a Southern air of good living with, as a Louisville friend phrased it, "more plain busy-ness than you'll see in most places below the Mason-Dixon line"; and many more opulent, more urbane Christmas celebrations have occurred since that original event to the twang of Cato's fiddle.

In later years the settlement at the Falls became a crossroads center and a market town for planters and farmers. Many growers built Greek Revival houses outside Louisville. Behind the columned porches the Kentuckians enjoyed holiday parties that were, like sections of the state itself, westerly extensions of Virginia ways and customs. One account pictures the arrival of a servant in the "big room" of the planter's house early on Christmas morning, with a steaming bowl of spiced apple toddy and, of course, a companion one of eggnog.

"As the master's special old bottle is taken from the ponderous mahogany sideboard, the Negroes burst in." They received small presents, and also drams of the spirits poured by the master into the glasses held before him. They drank his health and he drank theirs, and soon afterward the mistress distributed clothing, dolls, and toys, and, not least, a highly prized Christmas present—store-bought candy.

At Christmas dinner the planter entertained the minister, the schoolmaster, the doctor, and their wives. "Roast pig and baked ham shared honors with wild turkey and pumpkin pies, and those of mince meat flavored vigorously enough to make one's head swim." After the meal a barrel of golden pippins was opened and distributed among members of the family and their guests. The Negroes received a boon of another kind. With the holidays the slate was wiped clean: "no one was disciplined after Christmas for sins committed before Christmas."

In late December of 1857 a quick-eyed visitor to Kentucky, W. H. Venable of Ohio, told of Negroes who thronged the holiday streets of Mt. Sterling "dressed in their Sunday apparel and bent on pleasure." It had long been the custom, Venable learned, to grant slaves freedom from all duty at this time "and, indeed, to allow them large liberty during the entire holiday week."

The liveliest of all, it seemed, was a squad of "hands" who came into Mt. Sterling from the nearby "Iron Works," where many were employed. Their leader headed the march, laughing and singing in a rousing voice, improvising as he went:

> Oh, Lord, have mercy on my soul.
> The hens and chickens I have stole!

As he reached the end of each couplet, the rest of the smiling group joined him in a jubilant chorus. The Ohio visitor watched them until they disappeared down the street. A week later he beheld them on their way back. This time they moved far more slowly, faces downcast, eyes and voices mournful. The leader still directed them, but in lugubrious style.

> Fare ye well, yer white folks all ...

Behind him, as if from some deep musical instrument, rose a low, sad chorus:

> Woo—oo—oo—

While the squad advanced down the street, one member walked to a gate. A girl raced out, caught his hand, and they kissed. A moment or two later the dark man left her to rejoin the other slaves, and she turned away, her apron to her face. The file continued on, disappearing down the road, the strange words fading into the distance. For the blacks, Kentucky's season had ended.

Yet the slave-holding area was only one part of Kentucky. The state was and is several subregions combined: the rolling bluegrass country about Lexington, home of superb horseflesh; the eastern mountains; the western section. Land holdings in Kentucky were generally not so large as in Virginia's Tidewater, and most of the Kentucky Christmases were on a smaller scale.

Then, as now, Kentucky remained largely a rural state. Whatever the section, as James Lane Allen remarked: "the people are out in the country with a perennial appetite and passion for the soil. Like Englishmen they are by nature no dwellers in cities." Even if they had moved to other places, they always tried to return to the rural scenes for Christmas, for they agreed with the early observer who had called their land "the finest Country in the world." (One preacher informed his congregation, in praising Heaven, that it was "a Kentucky of a place.")

Rural Kentuckians observed Christmas by holding open house. In the words of W. S. Kaltenbacker, "In many Kentucky com-

munities not to drop in during Christmas week would be regarded as a breach of good fellowship and Yuletide traditions."
If those who had gone away to live came back to see relatives or
family, they must "visit around" with friends, or disapproval
was prompt.

Generations ago there began the still flourishing Kentucky
tradition of the "Christmas social," the rural gathering with
music, singing, and other neighborhood festivities. As Mr. Kaltenbacker observed, "Many Kentucky customs have radically
changed, but the old-fashioned Christmas social still continues
to hold its own . . . with a strong sentimental appeal."

Whenever Christmas-time Kentucky "turns her face toward
the North," the people wade, usually happily, through a snow
that covers paths and fields, hills and valleys. They form sleigh-
ing parties of a kind unknown to more southerly Southerners. In
the evenings their assemblies around the piano, with a warming
drink in hand, have an additional zest.

Today, as in other days, people of the larger houses go se-
dately through dignified dances, the waltz and those of later vintage. But in thousands of other places the Christmas nights ring
with the merriment of the old-time breakdown, or hoedown, or
square dance. And fiddlers and banjo players apply themselves
far into the evening, much as old Cato did for the pioneer Christmas at Louisville.

## CHAPTER 19

# One Play-Pretty Would Be Fine

THE highlanders of the South . . . for generations they were a "lost" people, cut away from the rest of the country. Only in comparatively recent years have other Americans grown curious about them, and gradually the mountain people have emerged. What the outsiders have found is a people who in the present have the habits and speech of an earlier era, the America and England of earlier centuries. The world has changed, but thousands still live much as their grandfathers did.

By and large, such highland folk have known only a narrow existence, a gaunt one, eroded by want. Yet they were in a place of rich loveliness, a scene of rushing waters, craggy heights, and gentle valleys; of white and pink laurel, carpeting ridges that disappear into the gray of the high horizon. And in spite of the loneliness and suspicion of the outer world in which so many of them live, these people have always had a beauty of belief and tender faith.

In the mountain Christmas of the South there is a quality of earnest conviction that cannot always be found among the more sophisticated, among those accustomed to greater wealth and easier opportunities. The guests who have been permitted to join the highlanders in the holy season have seldom forgotten what they have seen and learned.

Here is an area larger than England, Scotland, and Wales combined, an irregular rectangle which begins close to Pennsylvania and thrusts downward across parts of Maryland, West Virginia, Virginia, Kentucky, Tennessee, Alabama, South Carolina, and Georgia and includes the Appalachians, the Cumberlands, the Blue Ridge, the Alleghenies, the Shenandoah, and the Great Smokies. Then beyond the Mississippi stretches a further highland region—the Ozarks of Arkansas and Missouri, about half the size of the others.

Many years ago the ancestors of today's highlanders went to the mountains in search of hunting and farming land. In origin, they were people much like the others who occupied America: Scotch-Irish, English, Welsh, French Protestants, Germans, all of them were inclined toward the stricter creeds; they were not given to easy pleasures. They made their homesteads in stretches of fair land and stretches not so good—in basins or plains beneath the gorges, on the sides of gentle hills. Some of them lived in spots only a short distance, at least as the crow flew, from the well-settled lands.

In the beginning the highlanders met occasional outsiders traveling over their winding roads. Then, however, America changed; as it advanced westward, river travel improved, new routes opened through the plains, and the mountain folk were "left behind." Their lives were dull; their diversions meager; and their monotonous diet, mostly fried meat and corn pone, had its effect on their health.

Distances in the Highlands could be deceiving and the isolation was more severe than it seemed at first. One man noted that to advance four miles he had to go up and down eight ridges; to reach a point forty miles away, he had to travel over no fewer than ten mountain chains. Descendants of the early settlers worked fields tilted at angles that made city dwellers gape and bring back unlikely tales about farmers who "kept falling out of their acres" and rolling down the incline.

But the weathered cabins of log or plank remained on the mountainsides through the years, growing more worn, and the pattern of living remained as it was in the old frontier days. Here and there families did well by their own standards, plowing the better land, keeping themselves supplied with game. For others, however, life was reduced to a fight for sheer existence. The names of neighborhoods and coves tell the story: Long Hungry, Need More, Poor Fork, Torn Breeches Ridge.

The highlander said "hit" for "it," "yit" for "yet," "ax" for "ask," "perk up," "afeared," "fotch" and "holp," "tetchy," and "agin" and "sich-like." While the city man may smile, these highland words were those of Milton and Chaucer, of the Elizabethans and Shakespeare and of ancient church songs. The mountaineer's pronunciation of certain vowels was better than the average townsmen's; he said "dew" and not "doo," "new" rather than "noo." He also used the language with vigor and clarity: That neighbor woman was the sittin'est one he ever seen. . . . He beat a rattlesnake over its head till he had "mashed it to a poultice."

Despite their deprivations the mountain people maintained their dignity and their native shrewdness, and were generously hospitable to one another and to outsiders whom they came to know. On their guard with strangers, they held aloof at first; once they came to trust a city or town man, however, they gave him an openhanded welcome. Occasionally they would gather for a special event—the rebuilding of a neighbor's house after it had burned, a revival service, or a dance. To the highlanders their music, played on the fiddle, banjo, harmonica, and *guit*-tar, meant a great deal. They favored swift, zestful rhythms, hearty old tunes, ancient ballads in a moving minor vein, and carols of a touching simplicity. All their interests crystallized for the mountain Christmas season.

The "real day," the highlanders let town guests understand at once, was not "that new-brought-on Christmas" of December 25, but the Old Christmas of January 5. "Don't care what some folks call that December time," the older people always said. "With we'uns the day is January 5." And January 5 it remained for a long time. As communication and transportation became easier, however, the mountain people began to give attention to December 25 as the starting date of the holidays. Even then everything led up to January 5 and culminated on that day; it was the occasion for the solemn festivities.

Christmas against the upland background might be bleak by some standards, but it was heart-warming by others. In earlier years, of course, Santa Claus and the German Christmas tree were unknown. Asked to hang up stockings, the children would have blinked at "the idy." And had they given "the idy" a chance, very few of them would have found anything in their stockings in the morning.

For the highland girls Christmas meant, if they were fortunate, a "play-pretty," a small, homemade doll fashioned out of wood or cloth or corn shucks. To a boy happiness came in the shape of a plaything whittled by his father or older brother, or a rifle passed down after many promises. A store-bought gift?

Few children of the ridges or mountain coves even considered that possibility.

Soon after her marriage the mountain woman became a drudge, rising at four in the morning, carrying water long distances several times a day, looking old before she reached thirty. In most things she was Pa's submissive servant; at Christmas, however, she frequently exercised ingenuity, thrift, and long effort, putting things aside and hoarding them in the corner of the cellar or in a side building to which only she had access. Even in times of special difficulty, during months barren of fortune, she tried to manage "something extry" for the Christmas meal.

She accumulated extra sorghum, a few apples, dried fruit, and other "makings" for a pie or cake. She put Pa and the older boys on the lookout for rabbits or winged game. Or there might be a good bit of salted meat, or a hen in a pot with big, soft dumplings. I can testify, from visits in Tennessee and Georgia, that mountain cooking—at Christmas or at any other time—can be memorable. Home-cured ham with dark gravy, or pork ribs covered with their own fine drippings, or a simple cake still warm from the open fireplace . . . each has its own particular quality.

On Christmas Pa would ask a special blessing, and there would follow talk of God and of the Good Book which lay on a nearby shelf. Although none could read the volume, everyone agreed that the pictures were real fine to look on, and many who could not make out a word had memorized Bible passages at length after hearing them at church. Their great-grandfathers had been able to read the Bible words; and each family's fondest hope was always that one of the children would go to school and come back to read the Book from beginning to end.

The mountain Christmas season has always had its lighter moments and its louder ones as well. Pa and the boys did not have firecrackers or other such effete items; they shared the old American colonial taste for the firing of arms. Celebrants in the lowland sections might use blank cartridges for the ceremonial days, but the highlanders scoffed at the notion. Gathering all their ammunition, they went forth exuberantly to blast at game, at trees, or at the skies, to "shoot up the woods."

Christmas was a day of powerful liquoring. The boys tried to make certain of an ample supply, usually from a still over the ridge, and they drank early and often. Some of the young men celebrated in a way reminiscent of the low-country people; they made up singing, laughing bands and went from cabin to cabin. If they could, the inhabitants of each place visited were supposed to offer something to their "unexpected" guests—sweets, dried fruit, or a handful of nuts. If their luck was specially good, the callers might get a prize—strong cider that would give the night a glow.

During the holiday season, dances were held for all who could attend. They were informal affairs; word of them was "norated 'round" and folks would come from many miles away, by wagon or horseback or on foot. The dances themselves were simple country figures, antique in style, similar to those popular in rural England or the American colonies of generations earlier.

The mountain boys and girls "promenaded," formed circles, and "went right and left" at the orders of a caller whose reputation depended on his ability to produce ringing cries. The one-room cabin, the biggest available, would be cleared of furniture in advance and the members of the family who owned it would get to bed very late that evening. Often the cabin did not have space for all who arrived, and politely some of the menfolk would wait outside, watching for a chance to get in, leaving after a while to make place for others.

At times the stern highland religion made dancing "flat forbidden" as a device of the devil. Whole families would stay away from the Christmas celebration, but others found a way to solve the dilemma—to go to the dances and yet not "dance."

One solution was "twistification," a formal rhythmic movement back and forth, without music. And there was the "play party," at which people sang, clapped hands, or stamped their feet.

The mood changed with January 5, Old Christmas. On that day the mountain people would gather in an old church for morning service in a setting of soaring mountains and green meadows. Services were held at night, too, with pine torches or lamps for lighting, the congregation listening earnestly to the minister, joining in fervent songs and hymns. Although they could not read, they knew all the words, because they had been singing these songs since childhood and had brought them to their own children. A reverent calm fell upon the hollows and ridges; Christmas had come to the mountains.

Although most Americans of the past century paid little attention to the mountain folk, a German observer made a long trip to the more remote parts of America, including the Ozarks, in the mid-1850's. Frederick Gerstaecker has left a graphic picture of the scene he found. With a dog, "Bearsgrease," and a frontier American, "Slow Trap," as a guide, he moved slowly through the steep hills, deep ravines, and irregular plateaus. Late December, at the end of a hard day's riding, as Gerstaecker and Slow Trap were following a narrow, little-used path, they were caught in a penetrating rain.

It was dark, the rain became heavier, and the travelers risked precipices, which appeared "where least suspected." They went down a slippery incline, passing so close to several ravines that they could hear the stones fall to the bottom as their horses' hoofs kicked them up. About 11 P.M. they heard the barking of dogs, and tracing the sound they came at last to a hut that stood before a mountain stream at the foot of the hill.

The owner grudgingly gave them shelter. It was clear that he did not care for them, and they returned his sentiments.

Pushing on after some hours, Gerstaecker and Slow Trap met a second farmer much more friendly and hospitable, who pressed them to dry out and remain until the next day. Then the travelers pushed on in the hope of reaching the home of Slow Trap's father-in-law, a Mr. Conwell.

"It was Christmas Eve," Gerstaecker wrote, "and growing dark. My heart sank as I remembered former joys of this season, and thought of my present loneliness. Strange! That recollections should be so sweet and yet so bitter." Finally they spied a blockhouse along the White River, in the middle of a range heavily covered with trees, and Gerstaecker learned about a true mountain welcome.

The family, gathered around the fire, promptly opened its heart to him. The mistress of the house rose to greet him; her two bright sons, lads of eleven and eight, and her daughter Sophy, a graceful girl who "at first kept modestly in the background," then came forward. "I who, a few moments before, had felt so deserted and miserable, now experienced a silent joy. . . ." Never had a first meeting made Gerstaecker feel so much at home.

Now the mountaineer Conwell appeared. In spite of his white hair, he had the look of a young man. He was dressed in an open-throated hunting shirt, trousers, leggings, and moccasins. He had a spring in his step, and "if ever uprightedness was stamped upon any countenance, it was upon his." Christmas Eve passed with "incredible swiftness." Christmas Day started with a sharp cold, and the family and the guests were "delighting in a glorious fire" when one of the boys dashed in. "A large gang of turkeys in the corn!"

Seizing his rifle, Gerstaecker called his dog Bearsgrease, ran outside, and returned soon afterward with a magnificent wild prize. Slow Trap had to leave that day, but the German remained for days of happy hunting with the older man. He and Conwell spent New Year's Eve together, wrapped in blankets on a high plateau. On that ceremonial night the newcomer's thoughts saddened:

In my native land, many a happy pair were forgetting past pains and sorrows in the tumult of the dance in lighted halls; while I was stretched under the starry skies . . . for seven months I had not heard from home . . . the world closed behind me . . . nothing left but to advance; and yet the future offered no inviting picture.

His American friend began to speak, describing the life of a mountaineer. Conwell had reached his sixty-second birthday that day; he had the frontier and highland spirit, and he had "continually preceded civilization, first in Carolina, then in Kentucky, Tennessee, Missouri and now in the Ozark mountains." Now he was a trifle sad; "people were gathering too thick about him, and he said he felt a strong inclination to make another move. He mentioned how fortunate and happy he was in his family. He spoke of his children, and as I listened to him my own troubled thoughts were soothed. . . ." Here was one visitor who found the mountaineers an admirable folk.

As time passed, roads were cut into the mountains, and eventually the most distant settlements opened to the world through the establishment of such institutions as the Berry Schools of Georgia, Berea College of Kentucky, the Pine Mountain School of Kentucky and others. The teachers at these schools were dedicated people, who were particularly moved when young mountain charges told them they had never received more than a single tiny Christmas gift at a time. In the words of a girl of ten, "One little old play-pretty would be fine."

An acute student of the Southern mountaineers has left an interesting account of a later Christmas. Not the least admirable of the highland people's traits, John C. Campbell decided, was the deep affection each new child received. Brothers and sisters of all ages turned with love to the "least one," helping the bone-tired mother care for the infant. He described a holiday party at a school high in the mountains:

Here were scores of children who came from homes of poverty. Most of them were poor in the most common possessions of childhood elsewhere. Christmas was the one day when they might expect gifts because of the large generosity of the school's friends. A little daughter had been born to one of the faculty a few weeks before and made her first public appearance on Christmas morning. As the doors were opened the room lighted with holiday cheer, and the bulging stockings hung by the fireplace caught the expectant eyes of the children, their faces lighted with anticipation; at the sight of the cradle, however, they turned and crowded about it to welcome the little stranger—forgetful for the time of ball, trumpet, drum and doll.

Their eager interest satisfied, the children went over to examine their Christmas gifts.

With the passing years the Christmas tree made its entry into the mountains, first in the schools and churches and then in the cabins. Boys and girls returning from school read the Bible to their elders, as the latter had so long hoped they would; they decorated the rooms with greens and brought gifts more satisfying than the old-time play-pretties. Little ceremonies developed, like the lighting of the small family tree, an occasion on which the oldest child had the place of honor.

From the fireplace the mountain father took a candle or a brand, handed it to his son and, as the family watched solemnly, the boy touched it to the flame and went to the tree. There Pa lifted him to the star at the top, and now it shone there, the highland people's symbol of good will and hope for the days ahead. Then, perhaps more than once that evening, the highlanders would lift their voices in the Christmas carol which they have preserved from the older English tradition: the "Cherry Tree Carol," sometimes called "Joseph and Mary." The mountain people preserved it when it was lost in most other parts of America. After a brief introduction, the carol went:

Then Mary spoke to Joseph so meek and so mild,
    "Joseph, gather me some cherries, for I am with child."
Then Joseph flew in anger, in anger flew he,
    "Let the Father of the baby gather cherries for thee."

Then Jesus spoke a few words, a few words spoke he,
    "Let my mother have some cherries, bow down low,
        cherry tree."
The cherry tree bowed low down, bowed low down to ground,
    And Mary gathered cherries while he stood around.

Then Joseph took Mary on his right knee,
    "What have I done? Lord, have mercy on me."
Then Joseph took Mary on his left knee,
    "Oh, tell me, little baby, when thy birthday shall be."

"On the sixth of January my birthday will be,
    When the stars in the elements shall tremble with glee."

Hearing such songs, even those whose lives have taught them to keep a close check on their feelings have wept quietly, and the little girls have clung to their mothers . . .

In Little Rock, not far from the Ozarks, a town-style New Year's and Mardi Gras in combination was long a lively custom. Fireworks were an indispensable part of the Little Rock celebration, tossed before the more staid natives by youths and adults. Christmas visiting, complete with eggnog, was a general rule. But a specialty was the group of young men called the "Callithumpians."

These were bachelors or young husbands who put on costumes and rode about the streets in the evening, engaging in horseplay and also a sort of polite bribery. They went out to "serenade" the homes of good friends—or of pompous individuals who could do with a bit of comeuppance. The Callithumpians would sing in screeching voices, play on washboards, hot-water bottles, or chamber pots, blow horns and whistles which made eardrums tingle, and shout out the names of those within.

Those who were serenaded usually expected the Callithumpians and invited them in for food and drink or at least drink. It was unwise to ignore them, or even to try to; even if the householder extinguished the lights and attempted to sit out the experience, left town for the night to escape the Callithumpians, they would find him out. The best advised gave in and accepted the situation. The Callithumpians were offshoots of the old English or German mummers and they appeared in several Southern states. But these other groups seldom had quite the Arkansas flavor or vigor. . . .

# CHAPTER 20

# The Cowboys' Christmas Ball

BACK in 1901 Captain Dick Ware, of Cross C Ranch near Big Spring, and formerly of the Texas Rangers, had a mind to give Christmas presents to his two brothers, one at Fort Worth and the other out at Amarillo. What the Captain did, as J. Frank Dobie tells it, is a bit of instruction in Texas ranch-style bounty.

First he had his ranch hands prepare four hogs. Two of them were "large, weighing between 250 and 300 pounds each," while the others, practically runts, weighed only 150 pounds apiece. Next the Captain himself went hunting with a friend, bringing back from his excursion some excellent blue quail.

As a final step, Captain Dick had each "little hog," "absolutely stuffed with quail," placed inside one of the bigger ones. The weather had a nice bite, and the enormous packages of meat stayed fresh during their trip by buckboard to Big Spring and their later trip by express to Amarillo and Fort Worth. Just a little thing, Texans might say, but it showed a man you were thinking of him.

Such was the Lone Star holiday spirit, a thing of size and scope, and, as we shall also see, of soul-filling zest. . . . As has often been remarked, Texas is a world in itself, and it has enjoyed a variety of Christmases. In its eastern section could be found observances similar to those held on the plantations. In and about cotton-growing areas, the settlers had replicas of the festivities they had originally known in Louisiana and Virginia, Tennessee and the Carolinas. Texas has had, too, an occasional lively French Yule. It has also known the touching Spanish Christmas brought to this land by the Europeans and fostered by devout Latin-Americans. But for many the Texas season has meant above all the bouncy cowboy holiday which is like nothing in America, or for that matter anywhere else on earth.

Although the Spaniards pioneered in exploring the Gulf from Texas to Florida, it was the French who wrote the earliest Christmas history of the Lone Star state. In 1685 La Salle landed off Matagorda Bay while exploring in the area. The newcomers moved inland and established their Fort St. Louis. When the Christmas season arrived, even though they had a dozen harassing problems to face, they did not forget the holiday or its meaning. Monsieur de la Salle having "recover'd from his indisposition," wrote a chronicler, "preparations went forward for the next journey. But we first kept the Christmas *Holy-Days*. The Midnight Mass was sung, and on *Twelve-Day* we cry'd 'The King drinks' . . . though we had only water."

As Walter Prescott Webb said in a survey of the holiday in Texas, this was probably the first Christmas observance ever held in the region. At subsequent celebrations at least some of the people tried to find a substitute for water as a holiday beverage.

The French effort to colonize Texas failed, but it prodded the Spaniards into action and soon there was established the first of many scattered outposts and missions north of the Rio Grande, under the direction of officials in distant Mexico City. In the adobe quarters at San Antonio de Bexar, at Nacogdoches, and the present-day Goliad, dark-robed monks observed the holy period with Masses and other rituals: veneration of the Christ Child, processions, and festivals which dramatized the meaning of Christmas to both the Indians and the Spaniards.

From this era dates the tale, told many times in Texas, of the original Christmas plant at the Alamo. About 1720 Padre Antonio Margil, first *padre presidente* of Texas missions, was placed in charge of the Mission San Antonio de Valero. Padre Margil became a beloved figure, and his mission assumed an important role. One day, as Christmas approached, plans culminated for the usual pageant. To the shining altar the Indians brought gifts: buffalo horns, animal furs, blankets, handiwork of many varieties. Shavano, one of the young boys, cried as he watched the presents mount; he wanted to give something, too, but his family was so poor that he had nothing to offer. The gentle Padre Margil chanced upon the child, and after considerable urging persuaded Shavano to explain his tears.

Padre Margil smiled and shook his head. A present to the Christ Child, he said, need not be elaborate; any simple sign of love and faith was enough. Together the older man and the boy searched for a suitable gift and finally saw along the mission walls a small vine with green berries, which hundreds had passed without notice. Padre Margil and Shavano uprooted it and placed it in an *olla,* an old pottery jar from the boy's home. Then the child went to the altar, where he set the vine alongside the many brightly colored objects that surrounded the manger scene.

Looking at the crib and its surroundings, Shavano lowered his head in sorrow. His plant was so little, hardly more than a weed. . . . He was still subdued next day as he walked slowly toward the chapel where Padre Margil waited. Suddenly he heard a cry, *"Milagro!"*—a miracle! The boy pressed forward through the crowd around the altar and his eyes widened at the sight he beheld. Everyone was pointing to his vine. In the night it had twined over the crib itself; its leaves spread everywhere, and its berries had brightened to a shining, flaming red.

Today the plant is recognized as the Margil vine, and to the Latins of San Antonio, Corpus Christi, Brownsville, and the Rio Grande valley and other places of Texas, it is an ever-present part of the Christmas. Many say that, until the incident at the mission over two hundred years ago, the vine has never been known to blossom; since then it has burst into radiant bloom every year at the holy time.

The following decades witnessed the coming of the Anglo-Saxons, first gradual, then more rapid; first the filibusters who risked, and sometimes met, death in crossing the vague line between Louisiana and the Spanish province of Mexico; then other Americans who, at considerable hazard, joined the log-cabin colony Stephen Austin managed to establish after much effort in the fertile soil near the Brazos River.

Those who made the long trip by water or land or both met harsh suffering on the way and also after they arrived. A Texas immigrant of 1823 counted himself fortunate in receiving the gift of a Christmas meal from strangers; it consisted of "hominy beat in a wooden mortar, and fresh milk." Many greeted Christmas with far less.

By this time Mexico had won its independence from Spain, and Texas became one of the states of the new republic. More Americans thronged in, overcoming deprivations of all sorts to build up one settlement after another. Soon they became restless, demanding more freedom than the Mexicans allowed, and making aggressive protests that stirred angry friction.

Christmas of 1833 dawned bleakly for Stephen F. Austin, "Father of Texas," who had gone down to Mexico City to present a resolution asking for greater rights. The Mexicans answered his request promptly: they thrust him into a prison cell. But on Christmas Day friends succeeded in obtaining Austin's freedom on bond, thus giving him an unexpected holiday present. Yet he could still not leave, and he was to spend nearly two years there, under Mexican control, before he returned to Texas.

Four years later Christmas approached to the growing threat of war between Mexico and the Texans. A picture of this tense holiday season has been given by Mrs. Mary Austin Holly, a perceptive woman who arrived at that time in the embryonic Houston, capital of the newly born Republic of Texas. The town on Buffalo Bayou had a row of one- and two-storied buildings, and practically nothing else; streets had been laid out, but they were "chiefly designated by stakes."

Mrs. Holly spent Christmas week as the guest of a wealthy landowner and his wife, "very genteel people" who had mahogany furniture and red-velvet rocking chairs—true luxuries in a muddy, water-soaked semi-waste. The new Houstonians prepared to celebrate, though the observance would be very expensive. Eggs for the eggnog were "worth 50 cents each, $6 per dozen in Houston. Heard of one doz. sold for $13 . . . candles 50 cents each. Sugar—none."

And even this hard-bought Christmas could not be enjoyed in quiet. The Eve brought a breathless message: the Mexicans were prepared for war on the border! Houston burst into action; meetings were called and six hundred soldiers were enrolled in a day. Money was subscribed. "All was business and bustle" as the Texans planned, prepared, and rushed in and out of the residence of President Sam Houston. Texas destiny was in the making.

By January 1 Mrs. Holly had reached Brazoria and comparative peace. "We had a gay supper last night," she wrote, "and danced in the New Year, though, being Sunday, we did not dance out the old. A few young persons were in, among them two young gentlemen, excellent singers and musicians on guitar, flute, violin and accordion. . . . After retiring they serenaded us with those instruments combined—and vocal soloes. Very sweet musick. It lasted till near the time the birds commenced their morning concert." Never let it be said that even a war would unhinge Texas gallantry!

When Texas gained its independence, a roaring new boom broke over the vast area. From all parts of the United States and Europe, thousands raced toward the accessible Gulf edges, the plains and the more distant reaches. The civilization thus created was made up of many elements, many combinations— rawboned, sandy, and rasping in some places, in others as stable and "genteel" as the lady with her red-velvet rocking chairs along Buffalo Bayou. Wherever they were, no matter how many miles apart—even if a "fur piece" by Texas standards—the people managed to gather for the holidays and to have their parties and dances.

An easy democracy was the rule, perhaps the necessity. It was best to offend nobody by failing to bid him to a Christmas "sworray." In his compilation of holiday data, Walter Prescott Webb has noted a typical invitation extended through the *Telegraph and Texas Register* of December 26, 1838. "We have been requested to mention that a ball will be given in this city on New Year's day at the Houston House. The subscription list is now open for those who may wish to participate in the recreation." A year later Charles F. Taylor offered a picture of the good-time season at Nacogdoches:

Fiddles groan under a heavy weight of oppression, and heel-taps suffer to the tune of "We Won't Go Home 'Till Morning," and now and then the discharge of firearms at a distance, remind me that merriment now despotic rules to utter discomforture of dull care, while I, O Jeminy! have nothing stronger wherewith to lash my cold sluggish blood than Water.

In that same year Adolphus Stern wrote from Nacogdoches:

W. K. English gave a Ball in the Evening—*quite a Business* transaction—The Ladies God Bless Them, looked as lovely as ever but it requires the pencil of a Hogarth to give a description of the heterogenous set of men, who were there congregated.

Also heterogeneous in its make-up was a Christmas Day festivity of 1841, held in Austin and attended by members of the free-wheeling, free-dealing legislature. The *Daily Bulletin* enthusiastically described a gathering of the "Rounders of the Republic," including members from "Screamersville, Slizzlejig County, Screw-Auger Creek, Toe Nail, Epidemic, Hyena Hollow and Raccoon's Ford."

The gentlemen fixed rules: If any gentleman were too far gone to rise for a speech, the chair "shall appoint a committee of three to hold him up." If, however, the member be "unable to speak, the chair shall appoint an additional committee of two to speak for him; provided, however, that if the member is able to hold up by tables, chairs, etc., then, and in that case, one of the committee shall gesticulate for him."

The Congress of Vienna, over in that other place called Europe, had not been more magniloquent or more jovial, the newspaper asserted. The Christmas Rounders of the Republic voted quickly to abolish the Texas government *in toto* and substitute a new one, its own. According to the regulations, no member need speak with any relevance to a subject, and immediately bills were passed for "gulling the world" with measures whose general tendency would be to "benefit the people a great deal" and the Rounders "much more, a course for which there is plenty of precedent." In a word, a happy time was had by all. . . .

Two years later at Huntsville a British visitor, William Bollaert, encountered an older Southern Christmas holiday. The slaves enjoyed the week as, "bedecked out in their best, they visited each other, the evenings ending in singing and dancing." Bollaert approved the white people's visits to their neighbors, their dinners and their merrymakings. As for the eggnog, "the favourite beverage this morning," his verdict was equivocal: "somewhat pleasant, but of a bilious nature."

On December 26 Mr. Bollaert attended a Texas festivity which, unlike the others he had seen, reminded him of Christmas at home, a "candy pulling." About fifty young men and women gathered to cook molasses until it thickened, to pour it out, and then to pull or work at it until it grew cold and took on a yellow look. The great sport at a candy pulling was to "approach slyly those persons whose candy appears to be well pulled and snatch it from them."

The daring new dance known as the waltz had not yet reached Texas Christmas balls, but the Englishman enjoyed the reels and figure dancing. Whenever the mood hit him, a Texan would announce such an event, at any place that was available, whether the room for it be large or small. Among the dances "called out" were Roaring River, Piney Woods, Killicrankie, Harper's Creek, My Wife's Dead, and I'm a Widower. The visiting Britisher considered the next year's Christmas far less exhilarating, for personal reasons. The little females of Texas, it seems, had done him in. "I believe," he wrote, "that it is a very general observation that small and thin women are without exception very capricious and devilish, at least I have found them so, and they have made me suffer because I have not been sufficiently independent of them." (Whether he found any bigger, plumper Texas ladies we do not know.)

A year later Dallas was still mainly a small collection of families living in tents with mud floors near the Trinity River. "Hord's Ridge" was a cluster of pioneers whose first Christmas was described by Thomas A. Hord.

It was a bitter, bleak day. The wind cut over the prairie. The children received no toys or playthings; there was no Christmas tree, no Santa Claus. Tom, then about six, got two very practical presents, a pair of Indian moccasins and a "calico slip." Like the other boys of the area, Tom wore neither pantaloons nor stockings; shoes and a single garment, "cut very high," were his entire costume. But with these two articles, Tom Hord felt "as big as a lord."

Even this restricted Christmas had its fireworks. The boys drilled a deep hole in the earth, filched all the powder they could from their fathers' supplies, filled the cavity, and set it off. Some of them were slightly burned, but their worst injuries, as Tom Hord recalled, were inflicted by their parents, when they lifted the calico slips and applied a "stout limb" to the juvenile backsides.

An early Dallas Christmas brought Tom and his family close to real trouble. The Delaware Indians who camped nearby in the Trinity River bottom lands were a good-natured people who frequently visited the whites for friendly trading. One day during the holidays, Tom looked out and saw the red men approaching the Hords' quarters. He acted swiftly. "Taking down a small rifle, I leveled it at them and was on the point of firing when my mother snatched the gun from me." A hundred or so years later any young, TV-conscious Texan might have done the same thing. Again, however, Christmas or no Christmas, the calico slip was lifted. . . .

By the mid-1840's, Texas had received a striking group of newcomers—the largest band of Germans to reach any state of the Lower South or Southwest. Most of the new immigrants were hard-working people who saw little hope for themselves in the Rhine region or the Palatinate or Bavaria in which they had been born; others were liberals seeking escape from tyranny. Colonization societies formed, and whole families arrived to start a bountiful life in this land, which other Germans were hailing as a "new paradise."

Some were tricked in transportation, while others were sold land with clouded titles. In one case thousands landed at Indianola to wait helplessly for directions; hundreds died of fever, exposure, and lack of adequate food. There were grim scenes of want and disease. A number of the wealthy sponsors of the colonies were completely unsuited for life in the New World; the Prince of Solms-Braunfels, for example, tried to conjure up in Texas a castle life with aides and retainers in velvet and plumes.

Yet hundreds of the new Texans were not to be discouraged, and in time they built neat Old World villages at New Braunfels, Fredericksburg, and other places, or settled in the older towns. A German visitor, Ferdinand Roemer, arrived in the thriving Gulf port of Galveston in 1845, to discover a place in which, "next to the Anglo-Americans, the Germans form a large part of the population," as artisans, hotelkeepers, small merchants. But, thus far at least, they had not brought the German Christmas tree with them. During the Christmas holidays, Roemer heard the music of the Negro balls "resounding late into the night." At the leading hotel, the Tremont House, he joined others for whisky punch, "the national drink here with which Christmas is celebrated." The sky and air reminded Roemer of May and at his hostess's home he found roses blooming and a tree laden with oranges. "A feeling of joy and contentment crept involuntarily over me." How different this was from Germany's holy season, and yet how pleasant! . . . On New Year's night, however, a true norther howled over Galveston, and Roemer began to learn about the changeability of Texas climate.

A year later the same visitor observed the holidays in the Teutonic settlement of New Braunfels, and discovered that the traditional Christmas of his native land had reached the Lone Star State. Members of the German colony gathered in "jolly companionship . . . around a richly decorated and illuminated Christmas tree," a young cedar brought in from the woods. And in this area Comanche campfires had burned only two years earlier.

Another man met another side of Texas Christmas when he came upon a German children's country home for survivors of one of the colonization fiascos of a few years earlier, which had struck down their fathers and mothers. A teacher, Louis Ervendberg, had encountered a weeping, hopeless party of orphans, "starving upon the river bank." For sixty of the haggard children he built a farm in the New Braunfels vicinity, and he, his wife, and the youngsters labored together in the fields. The professor had become a tiller of the fields, with well-callused hands, but he appeared to be happy among the young ones, who called him Papa.

The visitor first saw the children outside the comfortable building in a grove of live oaks. The boys ran to open the gate, the girls, in neat dresses and new Christmas caps, smiled at him from the porch. In the schoolroom stood a white-covered table; on it were a glittering tree and holiday gifts for each child. There was a manger scene with stones representing the mountains on which the shepherds tended their flocks. Excitedly the young German-Texans described the way the Christmas presents had been made; for eight weeks the girls had knitted socks and sewed clothes for the boys, all managing to keep secret the nature of the gift each was working on. Now they sang and told stories, and the caller found a fine air of *Gemütlichkeit* strengthened by a warming sense of new family ties. For the once-sad orphans, Texas had become indeed a place of hope, and also of a happy Christmas.

As they did to other Southern states, the Germans popularized the goose in Texas as a Christmas bird, and thousands of Texans consider the holiday unsatisfactory unless they have that fowl for their main meal. A Galvestonian once recalled a frugal German who luxuriated in goose gizzards, "stuffed with pecans and spices and parboiled, then roasted." Fredericksburg and New Braunfels still have something of the air of Teutonic settlements, and this atmosphere is especially noticeable at Christmas, with the tree and the nativity scene, the cakes made from Old World recipes, the turkey, the goose, and the carols and family songs.

In 1872 in West Texas Captain Jack Elgin, a member of a party which was surveying unsettled land, had a Christmas meal which, even by the ever-growing Lone Star State standards, ranked as a spreading banquet. One section of the group had an Anglo-Saxon helper, said to be the state's best camp cook; the other had a superb Latin-American chef; and the two competed with each other in providing an overflowing bounty. Captain Elgin counted fourteen varieties of meat, prepared in almost as many different styles.

We had buffalo, antelope, deer, bear, rabbit, prairie-dog, possum and possibly other animals that I do not recall; turkey, goose, brant, ducks, prairie-chicken, curlew, quail and other birds. The most expensive meat which we had upon the table was bacon, which we had had to haul 500 miles. Of course I had a small supply of bacon to use in a contingency and we took a little of it to fill up the menu. . . . Two of my men had killed a young bear on Christmas Eve. The bear had climbed a tree, and after the man killed him, he discovered it was a bee tree, so for our Christmas feast we also had honey.

The Texans could have had sixteen instead of a mere fourteen meat dishes, for one of the hunters offered "a mess of rattlesnakes and polecats, which he assured us were a most excellent delicacy." At this, however, the line was drawn.

One last item might have seemed to the gourmet a desecration of all this superb food, but Captain Elgin recounted proudly that he added to the meal a "delicacy of civilization." By diluting with warm water the supply of condensed milk he carried with him he produced "a large amount of excellent milk."

An Englishwoman has left perhaps the liveliest recollection of all with her impressions of a ranch holiday of 1890 at Junction City. The weather was somewhat warmer than that to which Mary Jacques had been accustomed at the Christmas season— 90 degrees. Because of the heat, she and her aides delayed the stoning of plums, chopping of suet, and all the other activities necessary for the production of her mincemeat, plum puddings, and cakes until the hours after dark during Christmas week.

In the middle of the preparations an announcement arrived: deer and wild turkeys had been sighted nearby. Quickly the men formed a hunting party; with their return Christmas supplies multiplied further. The day brought a beaming sun. There were fireworks from Kerrville, including Roman candles, rockets, and "fire balloons," and the Englishwoman thought of her relatives across the sea on a "cold, raw, frosty morning" and then of the "glorious sunshine" of Texas. At 2 P.M. the ranch people held "the races," also glorious in a highly casual fashion: "horses, ponies of all ages and sizes, carrying any weight, and ridden with or without saddle as the case might be."

The men competed in tournament style, "lifting the rings" with every bit of horsemanship at their command. "Our champion," Mary Jacques reported, had "drunk not wisely, but too well, and, actually seeing double, remained under the impression that he had all the rings on his pole when there was but one." To the protests about his condition, he retorted that he was "not quite gone, only seven-eighths." In other competitions men at full gallop picked up hats, handkerchiefs, and dollars from the ground, until the riders felt tired.

Now the time arrived for a rest that would last until the evening meal. And with that, Mary made a discovery which added to the Christmas excitement: the roof of the gallery had caught fire. . . . Surely nothing in London had ever been like Texas!

Long before then, the Texas cowboy had come into his own as a great American figure, the wry, slit-eyed, tight-lipped hero of countless tales told in admiration, in resentment, and in simple good humor. During most of the year the cowman was far from the towns, keeping watch over the herds that moved under the Southwestern skies. As he and his buddies sat around the chuck wagon and the bunkhouse, they took their troubles with a shrug. The job war'nt easy, and who said it was?

Few cowpunchers would have been reconciled to their work, however, had they missed whatever Christmas dance was held within miles of them. As soon as the good season arrived, the cowboy headed to town, where the fun waited, inside or outside the several kinds of establishments that catered to him. Before the night ended some of the band would be skylarking on the streets, riding with a fury that made townsmen mutter, and shooting briskly at the stars, or at least in their general direction.

Then there were the more formal types of Christmas fun, the dances to which the cowpunchers invited friends or were invited by friends, to which they took ranch girls whom they courted. Such balls, according to J. R. Craddock, were announced in a simple way; several men went out to "ride it up," making a tour of the locality and bidding everyone they met to join in the frolicking. The message was simple, and avoided bad feeling from any source: "Everybody invited and nobody slighted."

Hours in advance, the boys put on their Sunday best and got under way. Mr. Craddock has cited one who arranged to hire a buggy, call for his girl, and take her home after the "swowray." To settle the subject with her in advance, he rode twelve miles to her place and twelve back; to get the buggy he rode sixteen miles each way. On the great day he covered twelve miles to fetch her, eight to the dance, eight back to her home, twelve to his ranch, and a thirty-two-mile round trip to return the buggy —128 miles in all! But clearly the night was worth it.

Few have pictured such an event as well as did a mere Easterner, Larry Chittenden of New Jersey. Larry went to Texas, liked what he saw, and eventually bought his uncle's ranch. Several years after his arrival, in 1891, he published his ballad, "The Cowboys' Christmas Ball." He was far from a remarkable poet, but in this composition he had struck a more than responsive chord. He had watched, he had listened, and he had caught the swing and feeling of a teeming scene. He had, in fact, produced a Texas classic, which is today repeated in place after place, dramatized, laughed over, and wept over.

Way out in Western Texas, where the Clear Fork's waters flow,
Where the cattle are a-browsin', and the Spanish ponies grow;
Where the northers come a-whistlin', from beyond the neutral strip

Way out in Western Texas, where the Clear Fork's waters flow, where the

cat-tle are a-brow-sin' and the Span-ish ponies grow; where the

northers come a-whistlin' from be-yond the neutral strip     and the

prairie dogs are sneez-in' as if they had the grip;

And the prairie dogs are sneezin', as if they had The Grip;
Where the cayotes come a-howlin' 'round the ranches after dark,
And the mocking-birds are singin' to the lovely "medder lark";
Where the 'possum and the badger and rattlesnakes abound,
And the monstrous stars are winkin' o'er a wilderness profound;
Where lonesome, tawny prairies melt into airy streams,
While the Double Mountains slumber, in heavenly kinds of
    dreams;
Where the antelope is grazin' and the lonely plovers call—
It was there that I attended The Cowboys' Christmas Ball.

The town was Anson City, old Jones' county seat,
Where they raised Polled Angus cattle, and waving whiskered
    wheat;
Where the air is soft and bammy, an' dry an' full of health,
And the prairies is explodin' with agricultural wealth;
Where they print the Texas Western, that Hee McCann
    supplies,
With news and yarns and stories, uv most amazin' size;
Where Frank Smith pulls the badger on knowin' tenderfeet,
And Democracy's triumphant, and mighty hard to beat;
Where lives that good old hunter, John Milsap from Lamar,
Who used to be the Sheriff back East, in Paris, Sah.
'Twas there, I say, at Anson, with the lively Widder Wall
That I went to that reception, The Cowboys' Christmas Ball.

The boys had left the ranches and come to town in piles;
The ladies—kinder scatterin', had gathered in for miles
And yet the place was crowded, as I remember well,
'Twas got for the occasion, at The Morning Star Hotel.
The music was fiddle an' a lively tambourine,
And a viol come imported, by the stage from Abilene.
The room was togged out gorgeous—with mistletoe and shawls,
And candles flickered frescoes, around the airy walls,
And wimmin folks looked lovely—the boys looked kinder
    treed,

Till their leader commenced yellin': "Woah! fellers, let's
    stampeed."
And the music singin', an' a-wailin' through the hall,
As a kind of introduction to The Cowboys' Christmas Ball.

The leader was a feller that came from Swenson's Ranch,
They called him Windy Billy, from little Deadman's Branch.
His rig was kinder keerless, big spurs and high-heeled boots;
He had the reputation that comes when fellers shoots,
His voice was like a bugle upon the mountain's heights;
His feet were animated an' a mighty movin' sight,
When he commenced to holler, "Neow, fellers, stake yer pen!
Lock horns ter all them heifers, an' russel 'em like men.
Saloot yer lovely critter; neow swing an' let 'em go,
Climb the grape vine 'round 'em—all hands do-ce-do!
You mavericks, jine the round-up—jest skip her waterfall."
Huh. Hit was gittin' happy, The Cowboys' Christmas Ball.

The dust riz fast an' furious, we all just galloped 'round,
Till the scenery got so giddy that Z Bar Dick was downed;
We buckled on our partners, an' tole 'em to hold on,
Then shook our hoofs like lightning, until the early dawn.
Don't tell me 'bout cotillions, or Germans. No sir'ree!
That whirl at Anson City just takes the cake with me.
I'm sick of lazy shufflin's, of them I've had my fill,
Give me a frontier break-down, backed up by Windy Bill.
McAllister ain't nowhar! when Windy leads the show,
I've seen 'em both in harness, and so I sorter know—
Oh, Bill, I shan't forget yer, and I'll oftentimes recall
That lively gaited sworray—The Cowboys' Christmas Ball.

## CHAPTER 21

# A Lodging for Mary and Joseph

In heaven's name, I beg shelter.
My wife can go no further tonight....

BEFORE a plain adobe house in the Latin section of San Antonio a man chants these ceremonial words as have thousands of others before him through many generations. This is the ninth night before Christmas, and he is playing the role of Joseph, the husband of Mary. She has grown faint and must have a place to lie down. And so he knocks repeatedly.

But the owner of the home, unmoved by the plea, replies: "This is no inn. Go away from here—you may be thieves. We do not trust you." Sadly Joseph and the woman who will be the mother of the Christ Child turn away, to continue their search as they re-enact the long journey between Nazareth and Bethlehem. They are not alone; with them are others, who sing as they walk and who stand about with Joseph and Mary as they stop at the other houses on their route. At each house the couple's petition is rejected. But at the last the door is opened, and words of comfort reach them:

> Enter, holy pilgrims,
> And receive as a mansion,
> Not our humble dwelling place
> But our humble hearts. . . .

For every one of the nine nights before Christmas many groups will follow the same observance, telling the central story of the Christian faith. On their march they are guided by the *luminarios*, lanterns set in the trees, or in the doorways and galleries, to light the way. The custom dates back to the time when the *conquistadores* came to Mexico and Texas, and even further back, to older times when devout Christians hung out lamps to guide Joseph and the Blessed Virgin should they pass in the evening.

*Las posadas*, "the inns." . . . This is the term which the Spanish-speaking people of San Antonio, of Brownsville, of Laredo, of Corpus Christi, and the Rio Grande give to the Holy Family's hunt for quarters. Originally the ceremony took place in the churches; today it is held at private homes. Groups of families join for the season to take part in the nine nights' observance, and each evening the wanderers are granted admission to one of the homes, where they find a room in which a richly colored manger, the *nacimiento*, shines beneath many lights. The callers gather around it to sing sacred songs and to recite prayers of the season. The *nacimientos* are of a dozen kinds: there are cardboard ones, wax ones, simple ones and ornate ones, small ones and large ones; some take up nearly all the floor, and in them are handsomely carved figures brought here from Mexico or from Spain itself. Before Christmas the shops in the Texas cities with Latin populations are filled with figures of the Virgin and Child, of St. Joseph, the Three Wise Men, the angels, and with miniature models of sheep and cows.

With the prayers before the *nacimiento* the serious part of the evening ends, and now the celebration becomes festive, a happy party with lots of food—*enchiladas, tamales, bunuelos* (the sweet cakes like fritters, fried in deep fat and served with sugar and cinnamon). All is bright spirited, and all leads up to the climax, the *piñata*. Above a doorway or from the ceiling hangs a light pottery jar, covered with colored paper in the shape of a man, an elephant, a bird, an airplane—almost any figure—and filled with small presents: candy, nuts, fruit. One of the guests is blindfolded and given a long stick. Then he is whirled around three times and the others watch as he tries to hit the *piñata* and break it.

The feat is more difficult than it might appear to be. Repeatedly, while the others laugh and shout, a man or woman or child reaches out, bangs—and misses the *piñata* entirely or touches only its edge. After three trials, it is the next guest's turn. Eventually someone smashes the *piñata*, its contents pour to the floor, everyone scrambles for a present, and the party ends merrily. Here is a lesson for children, too; rewards come through faith, and the blindfold is a "symbol of such faith."

This Christmas observance is a touching demonstration of a simple and profound religious feeling. It is also eloquent in drama, and its emotion is part of the deepest nature of the people.

Traditionally the children of Mexico and Spanish Texas received their Christmas gifts on January 6, the day when the Three Kings took their presents to the young Christ, and they wrote to the Kings much as other children write to Santa Claus. In recent years, however, the date of December 25 has reached the Latins, as has the Christmas tree, with the result that some of the Latin youngsters get gifts on both days! And meanwhile the Texas Latins continue the heart of their old-time holiday observances.

The people will remind you, as they have me, that a plant that has become a major Christmas favorite in the United States came originally from the country south of our border, and was brought here by a Southerner. In 1825 Joel R. Poinsett of Charleston was appointed the first American Minister to Mexico, where he was drawn to a graceful flower with a crest of burning red leaves and a center of yellow pods, which the natives called "Flower of the Holy Night."

When he returned to the Untied States, Poinsett brought the flower with him. To many the poinsettia seems a floral star of Bethlehem.

To San Antonio, Corpus Christi, the Rio Grande, and other Latin parts of Texas, Christmas brings the sound of guitars, the slap-slap of the *tortilla* makers, and the calls of candy vendors. Along the streets are men selling herbs, red peppers, lines of pottery, and paper flowers for altars or living rooms. Elderly women in black *rebozas* move slowly down the streets. Dark-haired, placid-eyed girls call out their pralines and work over open fires at which chili and other concoctions simmer in pots, and the air is heavy with tantalizing aromas, piercing or subtle.

Against this background, each Christmas season witnesses the strange, highly colored *Los Pastores*, "The Shepherds." This is Latin Texas' miracle play, a combination of medieval drama and Spanish and Indian elements, with modern insertions—a demonstration which has great meaning for the thousands who sit or stand for four hours or more to see it.

Centuries ago the Spanish church, like the church in other European countries, sponsored vivid plays as a method of teaching its followers the life of Christ and the events of the Bible. These dramas came to Spanish America with the *padres* who accompanied the explorers and early settlers, and *Los Pastores* has been passed down in Mexico and Texas from grandfather to father to son. In San Antonio and other places the performance depended largely on the players' memories; there were no scripts or written versions. From year to year, and from place to place, changes were made, and although various curious anachronisms were injected into the work, the basic story remained the same—the efforts of the shepherds to reach Bethlehem at the time of Christ's birth.

*Los Pastores* is presented nightly from Christmas Eve to the end of January or early February, and many go over and over again to witness it. Frequently the members of the audience know nearly every one of the five thousand or so lines and all of the parts, yet none of them want to miss a single moment of action, or any one of the many songs and long speeches. On both sides, among the players and the people who watch them, *Los Pastores* is a matter of faith, of spiritual satisfaction. No admission is charged, and not only are the actors unpaid, they are expected to provide their own costumes and effects. And they will move untiringly—sometimes with bright humor, again in deep piety—through the sequences of speeches, songs in minor key, plaintive solos, and sonorous choruses for all the hours that the play goes on.

Originally *Los Pastores* was given in the churches, and here and there it still is. But most often the drama is presented in a back yard with a "stage" that holds only a few props. On one side stands a table with the statue of Mary and Joseph and the baby Jesus, perhaps a large doll; this represents Bethlehem. On the other is a canvas booth with a monstrous painted face—Hell, from which evil beings will emerge.

There are twenty-four characters in the play and all of them have long roles and a great deal to do and say. First there appears a young boy in white dress, with long wings—the Angel Gabriel, here to tell the shepherds that Christ has been born. There are fourteen herdsmen, each a well-defined character and each wearing a costume over which he has worked long and ingeniously. Since their means are meager, the men have to take whatever comes to hand and refashion it—sashes, bright shirts, improvised headgear, and always tall staffs, the special pride of the actors, which are topped with paper flowers and bells, sometimes holding birds that flap their wings when properly manipulated. The audience knows most of the players, and often they are greeted with applause and cries of amusement. At the same time, the listeners are deeply reverent and understanding of the religious significance of the occasion.

With the shepherds is the *Hermitano* or Hermit, dressed in a Franciscan habit with cowl and beads. (The Franciscans, of course, were not organized until centuries later, but that does not matter. The originators of *Los Pastores* wanted a Franciscan, so they put him there.)

One of the shepherds, a lazy comic called Bartolo, who sleeps as often as he can, and rests if he does not sleep, is an invariable favorite of the audience. When the others wake him with the word that the Saviour has been born, and ask if he does not want to go and see the Glory, Bartolo is unmoved. "If the Glory wishes to see me, let the Glory come here." Finally he agrees to go, but suggests that his friends carry him on a mattress. And as a gift for the Christ Child, the big-stomached Bartolo suggests—a tamale.

After a time the shepherds start on their way, but, as the

audience expects, they remember that they have had no supper. Therefore, logically, they eat a good meal, which is always provided by the owner of the residence in whose yard the drama takes place. That over, they go back to the play. . . . But now there is a disturbance in Hell; the intentions of the shepherds have been learned there and have caused consternation among the evil spirits.

Suddenly the devils spring out of Hell. In the audience the children scream and the women cover their faces at the sight. The main devil and his assistants are horrendous sights, in black and red capes, with hideous faces, the horns of antlers, bits of mirror sewed into their garb. They talk in sepulchral tones, and they sometimes wear Christmas sparklers on their heads to add a final touch of infernal detail. The devils confer, take an oath to thwart the shepherds, and then begin to tempt them by appealing to their all-too-human instincts.

The shepherds falter and lose their way. Good battles with evil in a long series of skirmishes. First one wins, then the other. At one point, into the biblical scene there bursts an American Indian in buckskin jacket and feathered headdress—another wicked force who must be downed before the shepherds finally win out.

The audience takes an eager part in every moment of the play. When the shepherds suffer, it groans; when they triumph, it exults. The drama rises to a point of true excitement when, toward the end, the main devil encounters St. Michael, the little boy, who, even though he is much smaller and weaker, is the victor in the battle, striking down the evil one with a powerful blow.

And then, singing of their joy, the *pastores* finally reach the table on which rest the holy figures. They bow in adoration and place their gifts before the Christ Child. The conclusion is particularly touching: the shepherds pause before the manger and sing their farewell:

> Good-by, Joseph. Good-by, Mary.
> Good-by, my very little Baby....
> Give us life and health to return another year.

"*Adiós, niño chiquitito ... adiós, adiós, adiós, Jesúsito....*"
Afterward the members of the audience file forward and kneel before the holy figures on the improvised stage. For them the play has had a vast significance as a thing of love and faith and reverence. For the outsider, too, despite its great length and its often puzzling anachronisms, it can be a stirring evening—a survival of a long-past age, presented in earnestness and conviction by a people of humble spirit. As Father Carmelo Tranchese, S.J., of the Guadalupe parish at San Antonio, said, it is "in the blood of my people."

The crowd files slowly away, and outside the lanterns shine in the trees and over the doors and windows, still ready to light the way should the Holy Family or the shepherds indeed pass through Texas. For in this place Christmas and Christ come very close to the people....

## CHAPTER 22

# *Christmas in the Spring, and Others...*

A CHRISTMAS that arrives in March; a St. Nicholas who slides in by boat and another who flies low, dropping gifts to children by parachute; the "world's biggest living Yule tree" in the shape of a towering live oak more than seventy-five feet high. . . . During the past few decades the Southern Christmas has taken a turn that would surprise the original seaboard dwellers of two centuries and a half ago.

Christmas several months late is better than no Christmas at all. . . . For years it has come in February or March or even later to a band of several hundred Louisianians along the narrow, curving Bayou du Large in the yellow-green marsh at the Gulf fringes. On December 25 these people are far from home, making a hard living about the *prairie tremblante*, the quaking earth beyond New Orleans. They are muskrat trappers, who run their lines among the small, moundlike dwellings of the fur-bearing animals.

Although the muskrat season lasts only a limited period, a man with energy and luck can manage to support his family for some months with what he may earn during its ninety or so days. One told me: "I'd feel guilty-like if I took all that time to ride home for Christmas, bringing in the children and the wife by boat and car, and then have to take them back the same way. We wouldn't enjoy it, neither; we'd be thinking of all the fine skins somebody else would be getting for *his* family."

And so when the happy occasion arrives, the trappers of Terrebonne, parish of the Good Earth, spend it as they do any other day during this period when they live in tightly packed houseboats or one-room huts like matchboxes on stilts. With dawn Pa and the older boys go to the grassy wastes to tend and mend their traps, while Mama and the girls help skin the catches and dry the pelts to "make the most" of the short season.

On December 25, some of them may think now and then of the meaning of the day, of the scenes at Houma, the nearest town and center of a thriving shrimp, oyster, oil, and sugar-cane economy. But usually they have no time for such ponderings. "For us it's just a day on the calendar—somebody else's Christmas," a mother explained.

The residents of Bayou du Large are a people without records, a so-called "lost colony" of mysterious origin, different in appearance and speech from the French all around them. For the most part they are Anglo-Saxons, whose cheeks are pink rather than olive, whose hair is often blond instead of black or brown, whose eyes—gray-blue and bland—are unlike the snapping jet orbs of the Gallic Louisianians.

Their names are Lovell and Adams rather than Bourgeois and Boudreux; and their language has a faint British or an older Southern sound; their archaic words are like the highlanders'. They talk of going a "fur piece up the road"; a man says of his son: "a rale swimmer, that 'un"; a neighbor describes a fellow trapper as "a solid man," meaning he is sturdy, dependable; and one woman remarks about another: "Mary is a fine, common person," indicating that she is simple and unaffected.

Some of the Du Large folk think their ancestors were a party of Englishmen shipwrecked many years ago on the Louisiana coast. Others believe that their great-great-grandfathers came from "way up North, maybe Kentucky or Tennessee," and moved down by flatboat. A few claim a connection with the near-legendary pirate, Jean Lafitte, who plundered ships in this area early in the last century; and some suggest that their ancestors were the victims of one of Lafitte's raids, held prisoners for a time and then released. In any event, the Du Largers learned long ago how to cast nets, tong up oysters, trap muskrats, and otherwise fit themselves to the area.

Only in comparatively recent years has even the existence of the colony been generally known. About forty years ago the Episcopal rector at Houma heard a knock; at his door stood a family, hesitant, confused. Could you get a baby baptized here? During the rite the minister found these strangers did not give the ceremonial responses; "all we know is, our people was Prot'stant."

Once they lost their timidity, however, the Du Largers responded eagerly to the Episcopal church. Land was given for a mission house, and among those who attended its Christmas services for years was the man who had been brought to town for baptism. . . . When the trapping season ended, in February or March, members of the colony returned home to prepare for their deferred celebration of the Nativity.

Usually the services take place in springlike weather, on a day of light breezes, when the heavy foliage presses against the windows of the plain white mission building. Once I attended the service; that Sunday is still vivid in my memory. For days the church staff had prepared for the occasion. As the Reverend Mr. George Pardington, the rector, said: "The girls in the Houma store looked at me strangely when I asked for Christmas wrapping paper and tree lights in March."

The young Du Largers gathered in a setting of palmettos, mangroves, and vines, and no children in a setting of snow and other conventional Christmas surroundings could have been more excited. A bell rang and they went quickly forward, to stand about the bayou version of the holiday tree, a wax myrtle from the marsh edge decorated with popcorn and handfuls of trailing gray Spanish moss.

The benches that filled the room were crowded with people of all ages, from great-grandmothers to infants in arms. This year brought a special event, a christening. A simple wooden stand, without ornament of any kind, held a bowl of water, and at a signal the family presented the little one, wrapped in a pink blanket. Mr. Pardington reminded his listeners of another day when another child was born—one who came to earth to redeem mankind. Devoutly the bayou people listened and echoed "Amen."

As the children's tension heightened, the mission teachers stepped forward and called the names one by one. Each child hurried up to receive the doll, set of trinkets, or toy train that was given him, and then the youngsters joined with their elders in singing "Silent Night, Holy Night" and "Little Town of Bethlehem." And though the time was March and the birds sang at the windows, there was in this plain, unadorned room the solemnity of Christmas, of a holy day, and the joy that it brings to the eyes of the young.

That night, at Bayou du Large, the marsh dwellers had their own combination of Christmas tree and fireworks. The men and older boys built a sort of Indian tepee of long poles, wide apart at the base and joined at the top, with a taller pole above the whole. At dusk a torch was set to masses of dry "roseau reeds" piled around the wood. As the reeds burned, their joints cracked, popping like firecrackers and sending sparks to the sky while the children danced and cried their delight.

In one-man observances of recent years, an easygoing former Coast Guardsman has brought a white-bearded, red-and-white Santa Claus to the marsh children of another section. At Hopedale, below New Orleans, Roger Le Breton, bachelor operator of a fishing camp, has become an amphibious St. Nicholas who arrives and leaves by motorboat.

One day while on a fishing trip, Le Breton noticed the lonely youths of the isolated area racing to their doors to call and wave as he passed. Suppose, he asked himself, they were to look out one day and find Santa Claus?

The next Christmas found a disguised Le Breton chugging through the wind and uncertain weather, a merry figure with a big unwieldy sack at his side. He tooted a siren, hailed the children, and climbed up at the narrow wooden landings for calls at the one-room houses. The little boys were sometimes so exuberant they could barely speak, and the little girls wept with happiness. Some had never beheld a true Santa Claus in their lives.

To each of them Roger Le Breton gave candy, toys, fruit, and nuts. The day went so well for them and for him that he has repeated it year after year. For weeks before Christmas he builds wooden toys, tiny chairs, and tanks that shoot fireworks into the air. The children have come to expect him, and often they wait for hours for the first sign of his boat, the first sound of his siren. They know nothing of his identity, and Le Breton has tried to make certain that they get no clue. "I want them to keep right on thinking only about that waterborne St. Nicholas."

In New Orleans, another passing thought has led to the establishment of a large-scaled modern organization which makes a better Christmas possible every year for twelve thousand or so children. It all began back in 1896, when a newspaperman sat at one of the new typewriter machines and tapped out a story: "The *Times-Democrat* wants dolls for the tots. Who will help? Who will be the first to come forward with a doll? No matter what the doll is, it will be welcome. Poor though it may be, that of last year or that of this year, big or little, so long as it is a doll, it will do."

Immediately after the story appeared two small girls, Alma and Amelia Heim, called at the *Times-Democrat* with a pair of neatly wrapped packages containing their own dolls. Gravely they handed them over. Others brought rubber jumping jacks, trains, toy soldiers, even a few silver spoons. Within a short time the sponsors counted three thousand dolls, twenty-five hundred toys, and a thousand packages of candy and fruit. Five thousand boys and girls received tickets to the party at which the toys were to be distributed and after the merrymaking, as each left, he received a nickel for streetcar fare back home— "a pure profit," because many had walked or had been taken by neighbors.

Since then the institution has grown steadily, continuing without letup in spite of hard times, the Spanish-American War, two world wars, influenza epidemics, and bubonic plague. The *Times Picayune*, successor to the *Times-Democrat*, carries on the event largely as it began, and thousands make contributions year after year and offer services to assist in the distribution. Many men and women provide funds in the names of their own children, sometimes in the memory of one who died while still a little boy or girl. And the first contributors, Alma and Amelia Heim, lived to watch the movement thrive as they had never expected. The two dolls which they handed over to others meant more to them, they said, than any they ever received or gave.

Virginia's Holly Ball Christmas began because a native of the "deep country" area of Lancaster County admired a certain handsome tree. In 1895 John Palmer and James Carter farmed neighboring properties in the Northern Neck area. The fine round branches of the holly trees on Carter's property, with their shiny green leaves, seemed to have the first and best red berries of the region and to keep them longest.

John Palmer, a somewhat original man, frequently visited James Carter and nearly always spoke of his liking for the beautiful holly beside the road. Then one day Palmer said: "I wish I had something you wanted as much as I want your tree." He had, Carter replied—that Jersey calf of his. No sooner said than done, and Palmer drew up a deed for the holly and the ground around it, and also arranged to honor the handsome women of the Northern Neck.

James Wharton, telling of the incident in *Virginia Cavalcade*, quoted the document:

This deed, made and entered into this 20th day of December, 1895, by and between James Carter, party of the first part, and John A. Palmer, trustee, party of the second part, witnesseth:

That for and consideration of a certain sound yearling calf this day delivered by John A. Palmer to James Carter, the receipt whereof is hereby acknowledged, the said James Carter doth hereby give, grant and convey unto the said John A. Palmer, in trust, for the use and benefit of the "Queen of the Holly," and her duly appointed successors in office, for all time, that certain large and fruitful Holly Tree, standing and growing in the front field of the home place of James Carter, located near Kilmarnock, Lancaster County, Virginia, together with the land shaded by its boughs, and all rights and privileges thereunto belonging or in any wise appertaining.

The said John A. Palmer to have and to hold said Holly Tree, in trust, for the sole use and benefit of the "Queen of the Holly," and her duly appointed successors in office forever, as an emblem of the "Holly Ball."

Meanwhile John Palmer announced a full-scale Christmas supper and dance at Eubank's Hotel, with holly as the motif. From the girls who attended the men would pick a queen, and escort her to the tree, where the "queen's minister," whom she would designate, would cut her name on the trunk.

That night, as Mr. Wharton recounted the tale, all the young women of the neighborhood sallied forth in flowing white dresses, trimmed in holly leaves, with holly berries for necklaces. While the Virginia reel, two-step, and waltz went on, the men held a series of consultations and without much argument chose the queen, Cora Brent. In the ballroom a circle formed under a kerosene-lamp chandelier, and Mr. Palmer drew out the beautiful, brunette Miss Brent and placed a sprig in her hair, crowning her Empress of the Holly Realm.

The annual Christmas ball of the Kilmarnock area has never been abandoned. At first the event was small; with the passing Christmases word spread and more and more people attended from farther and farther away. Chaperones brought girls from many miles about, to stay with friends for the occasion. Original rules are still in force, and even now the invitation gives tribute to the first beauty, its wording identical with that of '95:

*Her Royal Highness*
*Queen Cora*
*Empress of the Holly Realm*
*requests the presence of her loyal subjects*
*at the*
*Holly Festival to be held in*
*the Castle of Kilmarnock.*

Queen Cora later married—not, in storybook fashion, the innovator, Mr. Palmer, but Albert Noblett of Kilmarnock; and she lived to watch fifty or more young women follow her as Empress. But today the queen's name is no longer carved on the tree trunk; the people of Northern Neck want the handsome growth to continue healthy. And in any case, there is little room left.

The Atlantic coastal city of Wilmington, North Carolina, is the home of a thirty-year-old tradition—the "largest living Christmas tree in the world." A giant water oak, said to be three hundred years old, it stands more than seventy-five feet high, and has a diameter of one hundred feet—a shining hill of green leaves and moss in Hilton Park above the Cape Fear River.

In 1929 it was decided to make the great tree a symbol of Christmas. That first year Wilmington workers installed 750 lights, which sent dancing reflections to the water below. Thousands went to look and talk of the spectacle, and since then the decorations have increased with each season. Today four thousand lights and many ornaments shine over the live oak, with a high Star of the East and tons of Spanish moss at the top.

Most of Wilmington's Christmas centers around the town's great tree. The lights are turned on during the week before December 25, and the tree remains illuminated until January 1.

Bands play, choral groups sing carols, and night after night there are musical programs. Ninety to 100,000 people visit the live oak every year.

For some time another North Carolina city, Charlotte, has had a "singing Christmas tree," a striking musical program in which about eighty members of the Charlotte Choral Singers' Society appear on a wide stage. Dressed in green capes, the members stand in rows of diminishing width in the shape of a towering tree which is decorated with glittering tinsel and silvered magnolia leaves. Basses are at the bottom, sopranos at the top, and the musicians take their places in an "enchanted forest" of wintry-white tree branches, pines, stars, and a wide blue sky. The funds raised at this concert go to those in want.

The Good Fellows Club in Charlotte has also helped end grim Christmases and dreary New Years for many families by bringing together opera singers, businessmen, and newspaper writers. During a recent season 500 people were helped through contributions made in that one evening by 450 Good Fellows.

At that year's program the newspapermen got up to tell of people who, from their knowledge, needed assistance. Harry L. Golden, editor of the *Carolina Israelite,* stirred his audience when he pictured a hard-beset young couple with eight children. There were, said Mr. Golden, many things the family did not have that Christmas. "But two things they do have; they have humiliation and they have despair with them all their waking hours."

With that Mr. Golden quoted a Hebrew legend: There are always thirty-six men on earth who do God's work. Any man, he added, can decide he is one of the thirty-six and "help remove humiliation and despair." Like many other groups in the South and in America as a whole, Charlotte's Good Fellows

Club joined the thirty-six and gave its time and its means at Christmas to help remove want and misery.

Through much of the Lower South, a Flying Santa Claus drops gifts to thousands of children. Nearly ten years ago, Stanford Downey, safety director of the Southern Natural Gas Company, was on a trip with a company pilot when he noticed that hundreds of children in isolated rural homes stopped to look up and wave to the planes. The pilots fly regularly over nearly three thousand miles of territory at low altitudes, trying to locate line breaks or other troubles, in an area that stretches from the marshes near New Orleans through parts of Mississippi, Alabama, Georgia, and South Carolina.

Mr. Downey's observation on that trip led to "Operation Toy Drop" or "Candy from Heaven." Two thousand pounds of candy and two thousand toys of various kinds are placed in long plastic stockings, attached to surplus parachutes, and lowered at the proper moment, as the light plane, bobbing and weaving, is jockeyed into position over the boys and girls along the route.

The hardest task is to make deliveries to those living in houseboats and stilt homes in the bayou areas. But the pilots do it. And one of them, George Guthrie of Birmingham, has a special drop for a dog who waits on a pipeline right-of-way just north of Meridian, Mississippi. His stocking carries a meaty bone and assorted tidbits for a dog at Christmas.

Across the South, in Baltimore, recent decades have witnessed a surge of new interest in the city's "Christmas Gardens," the indoor manger scenes around German-style Christmas trees which Baltimore has not only continued but also enlarged in number and variety.

Although the Christmas Gardens have a central religious scene, they are highly diversified. In some there are movable Ferris wheels, doors that revolve, engines that put out flames. One offers a waterfall and a town at a mountain base, another a summer landscape with a swimming pool and miniature bathers who have been cast by a silversmith. Others present vistas of Baltimore itself, with miniatures of famous buildings, trains crossing well-constructed trestles, and cathedrals which swing open to show the nave and the congregation worshiping to the sound of chimes and organs. And one Baltimorean has constructed a volcano which sends up curling smoke.

Some people work for months to carve and fashion the displays; one man keeps his Christmas Garden in place the year round. Old Swiss or Bavarian villages settle near complete railroad systems with signal towers, water towers, and safety gates; there are tennis courts, baseball diamonds, and, in one instance, a theater with an electric-lighted marquee whose lights go on one letter at a time, then in a complete sentence, then back to the single letters. Yet the religious theme is still there, and the Baltimore Christmas thrives in a bright new coloring.

Understandably, Texas may claim one of the biggest of all free-standing Santa Clauses. In the South Texas city of Luling an eighteen-foot, three-dimensional figure, a large man "even for Texas," in the words of his admirers, appears annually in the center of town. Built of wood and specially treated canvas, he stands shining in red and white through storm, sun, and rain.

In Anson, Texas, that Lone Star favorite, "The Cowboys' Christmas Ball," goes on today much as it did in the days when the Easterner, Larry Chittenden, first put it on paper. The men still "come to town in piles," as officials say, for "great doings" on the Saturday night before Christmas. They wear high-topped, polished boots, bright-colored, checkered shirts, and cowboy handkerchiefs, and the women often don the flowing skirts of the earlier years.

The music, too, is much the same, with a fiddle, tambourine, and banjo to provide accompaniment for the square dance, Virginia reel, schottische, heel-and-toe polka, and other stand-bys. In these days, however, the cowmen "ride a gasoline steed," and there are other changes. Larry Chittenden's old ranch, like those of many another Texan, spouts oil into storage tanks that stand at the side. And to keep things "going just as they should," modern organization has entered into the shape of a Texas Cowboys' Christmas Ball Association.

Nevertheless, affairs move with the lively tempo of the 1880's and '90's. A grand march opens the evening, and then follow sights which, it is guaranteed, most city critters have never seen. Again there sounds "that wailin', frisky fiddle," and "feet are animated" as the caller gives directions: "Lock horns ter all them heifers, an' russel 'em like men!"

Among the women who attended the ball in past years were Mrs. Hattie Morgan of Anson and Mrs. Mary L. Roberts of Paducah, who had been at the original dance in 1885. Mrs. Edna Best has traveled to Anson from Phoenix yearly to relive some of the earlier times, and a particular notable was W. W. Wilkinson of Stanton, Texas, who figured in Chittenden's poem as the mighty "Windy Bill." Ignoring the years, Windy Bill said he enjoyed the later balls even more than the frolicsome one that started everything. And this year men and women from many parts of the South and Southwest will head to Anson for "that lively gaited sworray, the Cowboys' Christmas Ball."

At Louisville in recent years a "Birds' Christmas Tree" has been created, with baskets of grain, popcorn, and cranberries for the Kentucky birds, and thousands of children have attended ceremonies accompanying the custom.

In St. Petersburg, which its officials note is in "the identical latitude of Bethlehem," the Holy Family is shown in life-size statuary and garbed in dress of the precise period. The statues, surrounded by palms and lighted by sunlight or artificial illumination, stand on the long Municipal Pier, at the sea end of the two-block-long Christmas Tree Lane, made up of Australian pines.

Also in St. Petersburg, to which thousands of older people go each winter, hundreds of holiday parties occur for travelers, and in the center of town the people who sit on the city's famous "green benches," which line the main streets, watch a large-scale children's party around a municipal tree. Here, too, as in other Southern cities, more and more townsmen place candles and other lights in their windows, before which bands of singers chant carols.

At another Florida point, West Palm Beach, two brothers have made community history with a family pageant prompted by what they believe was a miraculous cure. Twenty-five years ago Conrad and Bernard Hetzel planned to set up a *crèche*. The time was one of deep financial depression and they hoped to fashion a simple manger scene, to be enjoyed without cost by their friends and others of the town.

They began work in the summer, laboring over papier-mâché figures in a hot attic room. One brother, who had been pronounced incurable, had a full recovery, and in thanksgiving the Hetzels promised to make the event an annual one. For their first display they completed three camels, the three Magi, and a crib, with the scene softly lighted against a background of trees. Thousands at West Palm Beach asked the Hetzels to extend the presentation, and they gave it nightly for a week. The following year and the next and the next the scene was repeated and extended; annually the brothers added figures in the garden that they used, then outgrew that. The Hetzels changed locations several times until the display took up nearly a whole block and the city of West Palm Beach provided a place of permanent exhibition on the shores of Lake Worth.

Through the years the Hetzel brothers' presentation has steadily enlarged as its earnest, pious note brought more and more viewers. Today it is a pageant which goes on for seven days, its scenes changing nightly as they offer the full story of the Nativity. Opening at dusk, it has music and a narrator, Robert F. Hetzel, son of Bernard, and each scene is presented for a half hour. Given under the skies, it remains open to all who wish to attend.

During the episode centering upon the birth of the Saviour, many take off their hats and bow their heads in deep respect. And thousands return night after night to study the panoramic holy city of Jerusalem, built to scale, and to inspect the market place which shows vendors shouting their wares, and traveling merchants, wayfarers, shepherds, and sheep as they advance about the lanes of Jerusalem. . . .

For me a warming high note in latter-day individual Christmas customs comes from the Lone Star State, where the fifty-year-old Rip McKenzie of Mexia has pioneered in his own fashion. Not rich, though a Texan, Mr. McKenzie annually has a telephone installed in his home from December 7 to December 25, in the name of Santa Claus, with an address of "North Pole No. 1, Mexia."

Children from many parts of the Southwest telephone Rip McKenzie and his wife, and as the calls arrive the answer is "Santa Claus speaking" or "This is Mrs. Santa Claus." In each case the McKenzies write full information on the children's wishes, trying to sidetrack requests for too many gifts, or too expensive or impossible ones. Soon afterward a letter goes to each home, signed by "Santa Claus." To make things simpler for the parents, Mr. McKenzie includes the lists.

## CHAPTER 23

# The Night the Animals Talk

ALL over the South various people believe that on one night of the year, Christmas Eve, the animals can speak, and that in the barns the cows and sometimes the horses talk of many matters, including the good season and its meaning. There is, you are told, a very good reason these gentle creatures should have received this temporary gift. After all, the cattle breathed upon the Christ Child to keep him warm on the evening in the manger, and they have their reward. . . .

As midnight strikes on Christmas Eve, the animals, as on that other night two thousand years ago, are believed to sink to their knees and turn their heads in the direction of Bethlehem in adoration of the Christ. This is, of course, an evening of miracles, when evil is held at bay and only good prevails, as William Shakespeare wrote in *Hamlet:*

> Some say that ever 'gainst that season comes
> Wherein our Saviour's birth is celebrated,
> The bird of dawning sings all night long;
> And then, they say, no spirit dare stir abroad. . . .

On this eve, too, the bees in their hives are supposed to hum the melody of an old carol from dark to dawn. In the mountains of Kentucky and North Carolina, in the Ozarks and Alabama and Georgia, older people say that they have heard the music of the bees, have seen the cows kneel and heard them speak. "I was shook hard when it happened," one told me. "My breath came fast and I just stood there a-quivering. Then I got so scairt I lit out."

Most people, however, advise their friends against making any attempt to eavesdrop on the creatures. To do so may mean death. In four or five states I have heard—in slightly varying form—the story of a man who once concealed himself near the horses and whose flesh tingled as midnight tolled; they knelt and they *were* speaking!

A moment later their words sent another kind of chill through him. They were talking of his boldness, and his mistake. The man weighed a lot, didn't he? And the cemetery was a long way off—a good distance for them to have to carry him. . . . Soon after Christmas a hearse made its slow way to his grave.

During the sacred night, it is also said, the plants will bloom as they did on that earlier evening. The ground may be covered with snow and the vegetation withered, but on this night soft tendrils will appear. All you have to do is push aside the white carpet and you will discover the green shoots sprouting from the chill earth.

Back in 1821, writing of upper Canada, John Howison gave

a touching account of the traditions of the magic night in the Western World. One Christmas at midnight, he wrote, he was strolling at the edge of a wood, enjoying a "delicious reverie," when all at once he observed a dark object moving cautiously among the trees. He continued:

At first I fancied it was a bear, but a nearer inspection discovered an Indian on all fours. For a moment I felt unwilling to throw myself in his way, lest he should be meditating some sinister design against me; however, on his waving his hand, and putting his finger on his lips, I approached him, and notwithstanding the injunction to silence, inquired what he did there. "Me watch to see the deer kneel," replied he; "This is Christmas night, and all the deer fall upon their knees to the Great Spirit, and look up." The solemnity of the scene, and the grandeur of the idea, alike contributed to fill me with awe.

Old Christmas, or January 5, is also surrounded with mystic beliefs. On its eve, legend tells us, day breaks twice. The first dawn comes about an hour earlier than usual, and the skies brighten until sunlight seems close. The pokeweed thrusts up its sprouts, "big and clear for everybody to see that wants to see." Then slowly dark returns, and the sprouts wither, and after a while the true dawn arrives.... During the week or so before Christmas you may hear the rooster in the middle of the night "crowing for Christmas," trying to make the day arrive earlier.

Such beliefs are held by thousands of Southerners; although they are most common among the rural people, many who dwell in villages and towns subscribe to them. Often they have a gentle beauty and a compelling imagery, and all of them are held with deep conviction. There are also more earthy superstitions, direct and menacing, which make up a firm series of do's and don'ts. Over a period of years I have gathered them in the Lower South and the Upper, the Southeast and Southwest.

Dozens are shared with other Americans, with Europeans of the nations from which the earliest Southerners emigrated. Some are English and Scottish, Irish and Welsh in origin; others Teutonic and Middle European, French and Mediterranean; certain of them are held primarily by the Negroes, others by the whites, although frequently both races believe in them. The superstitions are manyfold, manynatured; nobody could follow all these injunctions even if he wished. For what they may be worth, here are some of them:

Wear something fresh and new on Christmas Day—your luck will improve. But don't wear new shoes. At best they will hurt like fury; at worst they will walk you into a catastrophe.

If you wish to avoid trouble, don't wash clothes on the Friday before Christmas. And don't wash and press a Christmas present before you give it; you will only wash out the good luck and press in the bad.

If you would like to hear angels sing you can, provided you are willing to pay the price. If you sit under a pine tree on Christmas Eve, their voices will rise all around you—but then you will die.

Don't let a fire go out on Christmas morning. If you do, spirits will come to you, then and later in the season. And be careful not to give anybody, even your best friend and neighbor, a match or a warm coal, or even a light, to be taken out of the house. If you do, you'll be "giving out" your hope of future well-being.

If you leave a loaf of bread on the table after Christmas Eve supper, you will be sure to have a full supply until the next Christmas.

Eat apples as the clock strikes midnight on Christmas Eve. This will guarantee perfect health for the year ahead.

Be sure you make some start on your year's work between the New Christmas and the Old. Just a bit of ditching, the beginning of plowing, enough to "show your intentions." But never fix your roof between Christmas and New Year's, or the holes will come right back.

It is bad luck to eat certain fruits, preserved out of season by unusual methods, on Christmas. A watermelon, kept out of the weather in a haystack, may taste fine, but it is "just too unnatural." Only harm can follow.

At any time it is bad enough to let a black cat go across your path. If it happens on New Year's Day it will eventually bring ruin. And if you look down and see your shadow without your head showing, you may lose the head to a hangman, a man with a knife, or some other agent of doom.

What may be done to avoid that tragedy is uncertain. But you may help the situation by slipping money—silver—under your door on New Year's morning. That may improve your fortunes.

If you have no money in your pocket on New Year's, you'll have nothing for the rest of the year. Have at least a few coins to jingle, and you will be in the money, or at least some money, from then on.

The general principle underlying New Year's beliefs is simple: Whatever you do on January 1, you will keep on doing all year. If you hang out your wash on New Year's Day, you will have washing to do every day for the following twelve months. Worse, if you wash clothes on New Year's Day—even one sock or handkerchief—you can be sure that before long you will be washing the garments of a dead member of your household.

And don't sweep out the house on New Year's morning, lest one of your family not be with you when the next January 1 comes around.

Trip or fall on that day, and you will be doing the same thing for the rest of the year.

Clean out your well on New Year's, and you will have to clean it over and over again from then on.

Don't quarrel on New Year's, or you will be quarreling the year round. Here is a corollary, of course, to the custom of making up with your enemies on January 1.

Don't take anything out of the house on New Year's—mop, valise, chair. If you do, you will watch your possessions removed from you, one by one, as the year goes by.

By similar reasoning it is a good idea to have every caller bring in a token gift, which may be practically anything: the end of a branch, a few pecans from your yard, your garden shears. Some people have been known to meet guests outside and hand them a little item to bring in, "just to make sure we have luck in this place."

Don't pour out even dirty water; save it for the next day. Never carry ashes from your home on New Year's Day. It can mean assorted bad luck for all the year, or death for you or one of your family.

Don't cut your nails, and certainly don't trim your hair on January 1. When you do, you cut your good fortune.

In Alabama, South Carolina, and other states, black-eyed peas and hog jowl are to be eaten on this day to assure good fortune for the year. In other places, such as New Orleans, the necessary food is boiled cabbage. Even if these precautions are taken, however, you would do well to put a shiny dime under your plate, to guarantee a supply of money.

On New Year's Eve, a few minutes before midnight, throw open every door and window, no matter what the weather—rain, snow, sleet or wind. The good results will justify any exposure short of fatal pneumonia.

No matter how pretty your calendar, never put it up or refer to it before dawn on New Year's Day. If you do, you will regret it.

The first letter you get in the New Year will be no ordinary one. It will bring either deep trouble or extreme happiness.

If a child is born on New Year's, give him extreme care and attention, or he will depart the earth before the next January 1.

Do not sew between Christmas and New Year's; whatever you sew between those dates won't wear well.

Don't leave the house before 7 A.M. on New Year's, or you will meet up with early trouble.

If your left eye quivers on this day, someone close to you will be gone within two months.

If you want your apple or other fruit trees to bear better, be certain to pass them on January 1 and wish each a Happy New Year. And be sure to speak clearly; mumbling will get you nowhere with the trees.

Don't wear a clean shirt on New Year's Day, or you will suffer from boils. Here is one of the few mild penalties to result from mistakes of the season.

If the first caller of the year is a man, you'll have luck, especially if he has dark eyes or hair or a dark complexion. But if it is a woman, you had best look out. And if she be a widow, may the Lord have mercy on you.

Only quick action will save you from the harm a woman can bring under these conditions. Take her arm and leave with her through the front door, then return with her through the back door. You'll never regret the step.

Redheads are nice, but not for an exclusive diet, and not on New Year's Day. If you see one coming toward you then, turn and run. Otherwise you might have nothing but redheaded dates for the rest of the year, which might be a little too much of a good thing.

In some parts of Maryland, I have been told, careful husbands used to keep the womenfolk out of the dining room on New Year's. The kitchen, of course, was not out of bounds. Understandably this tradition has withered.

During slavery, people arranged for a Negro man to become

the "first footer" on New Year's. The darker he was, the finer fortune he brought. Later, especially in Baltimore and on the eastern shore of Maryland, a householder went to his door as the New Year's Eve bells clanged, whistles blew, and gunfire blasted. The first man who passed, no matter who he was, received a pressing invitation to enter.

When he did, he received a standard fare—pickled herring, bread, and coffee. Natives generally understood the custom, and accepted the invitation. This custom, alas, is almost dead, pickled herring, coffee, and all.

The Christmas weather always "predicts" the climate for the rest of the year, and it also determines the number of corpses to be expected during the months to follow.

A warm Christmas, and many will die; as the phrase has it, a green holiday brings a fat churchyard. As for January 1:

> If New Year's night wind blow south
> It betokenth warmth and growth;
> If west, much milk, and fish in the sea;
> If north, much cold and storms there be;
> If east, the trees will bear much fruit;
> If northeast, flee it man and brute.

To many, the first twelve days of January tell the predominant weather for the twelve months ahead. A rainy January 1 means wet days for the rest of the month. A bright January 2, and February will be sunshiny. An overcast January 3, and March will be dark, and so on. . . . Others differ: The determining days are the twelve days between New Christmas and Old. December 26 settles the matter for January, December 27 fixes it for February, and so on.

# CHAPTER 24

## Sauces, Aromas,
## and the Inner Man (and Woman)

For most of us, Christmas would not be Christmas without a large supply (sometimes too large a supply for comfort) of foods associated with the season of good eating and good cheer.

From a variety of places and individuals I have assembled the following collection of dishes with Southern Christmas connotations. The December holidays are hardly a time for calorie computation; most of these "receipts" are probably not for those who are haunted by visions of the bathroom scales.

## MARTHA WASHINGTON'S "GREAT CAKE"

The first First Lady served this frequently at Christmas. Copied laboriously by one of her grandchildren, the recipe is still preserved at Mount Vernon by the Mount Vernon Ladies Association. It reads:

Take 40 eggs & divide the whites from the youlks & beat them to a froth. Start working 4 pounds of butter to a cream & put the whites of eggs to it a spoon full at a time until it is well work'd. Then put 4 pounds sugar finely powder'd to it in the same manner. Then put in the youlks of the eggs & 5 pounds of flower & five pounds of fruit. 2 hours will bake it. Add one half ounce of mace, one nutmeg, half a pint of wine & some frensh brandy.

My friend Helen Duprey Bullock, historian of the National Trust for Historic Preservation, has scaled down the recipe for a present-day Great Cake, as follows, using only fruits known to have been available at that period:

| | |
|---|---|
| 1 pound butter | ⅓ cup sherry |
| 10 eggs (separated) | 2 teaspoons lemon juice |
| 2 cups white sugar | 1 pound white raisins |
| 4½ cups flour, | 15 ounces currants |
|    sifted with | 8 ounces orange peel |
| 1 teaspoon mace | 6 ounces lemon peel |
| ½ teaspoon nutmeg | 8 ounces citron |
| ½ cup brandy, or more depend- | 3 ounces candied angelica |
|    ing on dryness of fruit | 2 teaspoons lemon juice |

Figs, cherries, or candied pineapple may be substituted for any of the above fruits if wished. Pick over the raisins and currants and cut up fruits. Put in a tightly covered bowl to stand overnight in brandy. Stir occasionally. If fruit is dry, more brandy should be added. Soften butter to room temperature; slowly beat in one cup sugar. Beat yolks until very light, and slowly add sugar, beating

constantly. Add lemon juice slowly. Combine. Sift in dry ingredients alternately with sherry. Add fruit. Fold in lightly beaten
whites. Bake in an earthen ten-inch Turk's Head mold (filled
within 1½ inches of top), an aluminum mold, 8½ inches in size
(filled within ¾ inch of top), or two large loaf pans. Grease and
flour molds. Put a pan of water on oven bottom. Start at 350° F.
for about 20 minutes. Reduce heat 300°-325° for 40 minutes for
small cake; 1 hour and 40 minutes, approximately, for large cake.
Test with straw. Cool on racks. Wrap well and store in crocks or
tins. This keeps several weeks and makes at least 11 pounds of cake.

## GEORGE WASHINGTON EGGNOG

| | |
|---|---|
| 1 quart cream | 1 pint brandy |
| 1 quart milk | ½ pint rye whisky |
| 1 dozen eggs | ¼ pint sherry |
| 1 dozen tablespoons sugar | ¼ pint Jamaica or New England rum |

Combine the liquors, then separate the eggs into yolks and whites.
To the yolks, when beaten, add the sugar and mix. To this slowly
add the combined liquors, very lightly while you beat very slowly.
Then add the milk and cream, again working slowly. Beat the egg
whites until they are stiff and fold into the mixture, then set for
several days in a cool place until ready to serve.

## MARYLAND ROAST TURKEY
### from Frederick Stieff

Select a plump turkey and clean well. Make a stuffing of three
cups of stale bread, crumbled fine and moistened. Add the liver
and a slice of boiled ham, minced fine, a hash of onion and parsley,
salt and pepper to taste. Mix well, adding if desired two well-
beaten eggs, and fill the turkey. Season the fowl with lard, salt,
and pepper. Put in roasting oven with small quantity of water, just
enough to prevent the pan from burning at the start. Baste frequently with essence from the pan. Roast, not too fast, until well

done and a golden brown. (Recipe originally from Edwina Booth Crossman, daughter of Edward Booth of Tudor Hall.) With this serve sauerkraut, a recipe for which follows.

## MARYLAND SAUERKRAUT
### to be served with Turkey, also from Frederick Stieff

A year's supply of kraut should be made in the fall from fall cabbage. A twenty-gallon crock jar will hold about 125 pounds of cabbage shavings, cut coarser than for coleslaw.

Put a layer—about two gallons—of slaw in the bottom. Pound with a wooden mallet until juice forms on the top. Then put a layer of cabbage leaves, about an inch thick, on top. Take a circular board so cut to fit freely inside the crock and weigh it down with a clean smooth stone, and put in a warm place until fermentation ceases. It should be ready to use in about five or six weeks. (Recipe originally of Miss Zaidee Browning of Oakdale in West Maryland.)

## DAUBE GLACÉ
### from Miss Dolly Veters

Cut ¼ pound salt fat pork into larding strips and season the strips well with salt, pepper, and cayenne. Chop together one sprig thyme, two bay leaves, two sprigs parsley, one onion, and two cloves garlic. Cut a number of incisions in a four-pound piece of beef round and fill the incisions with the herb mixture and the larding strips. In a Dutch oven in one tablespoon lard brown lightly two onions, cut in quarters. Add the meat and brown it well. Add five carrots, cut into thick slices, and one onion, finely chopped. Cover the pot and cook gently for ten minutes. Turn the meat over, cover the pot, and simmer for ten minutes. Add one quarter-cup sherry and enough boiling stock or water to cover the meat. Cover the pot very tightly and let the meat simmer slowly for about three hours. The meat should be very tender.

In the meanwhile, season three pounds veal and two pig's feet well with salt, pepper, and cayenne; and simmer this meat in four quarts water until it is very tender. Mince the meat and discard the bones. Add to the stock a crumbled bay leaf, a sprig of thyme, two sprigs of parsley, half a garlic clove, and a half-cup sherry. Simmer the stock for a few minutes longer, taste it for seasoning, strain it, and add the minced meat.

Transfer the *daube* to a casserole or serving dish slightly deeper and larger than the meat. Pour the prepared minced meat and stock over it, and set the casserole in the refrigerator overnight. The stock will form a firm and tender jelly, and the *daube glacé* can be sliced for serving, jelly and all.

## OYSTER AND SWEETBREAD PIES
### from Helen Duprey Bullock

Quantity for 18:2 pounds sweetbreads,
1 quart small oysters.

Put the sweetbreads in a pan with enough cold water to cover, add the well-washed leafy tops of celery, 1 bay leaf, 2 tablespoons mild vinegar, some sprigs of parsley, salt, and some white pepper. Bring slowly to a simmer and simmer about 15 minutes. Drain and plunge into water with ice in it to make them firm. Let stand in the ice water about 15 minutes, then remove the outer membrane and tubes. This may be done the morning of the day they are to be served. Just before time to serve them, pull the small clusters apart and sprinkle them with flour and mild paprika. Sauté them in a heavy pan in a generous amount of butter until a very delicate brown. Sift flour over them and blend it lightly. Then pour in rich milk or thin cream, and stir until the flour is cooked and blended and you have a delicate cream sauce. At the last add your oysters and their liquor, and cook gently until the petticoats on the oysters have curled. Have ready individual pie shells of rich pastry, preferably made in fluted patty pans. These should be warmed in a moderate oven. Place the shells on a large platter and fill with the creamed mixture. The secret of this dish is its delicacy—forget wine, dominant seasonings, etc.—and let it speak for itself. The platter should be garnished with parsley, and in a separate fine silver shaker there should be mace. Use one with pepper-sized sifter top. Mace should be of choice quality and very fresh—this should be passed, although it was frequently cooked in the sauce and sprinkled on top for a garnish.

## BAKED CELERY WITH ALMONDS
### from Helen Duprey Bullock

Use two stalks of green celery. Scrape and slice into about ½-inch slices. Put on to boil in salted water with some of the well-washed celery tops. When tender remove tops. Strain, reserving 1 cup of celery water. Make a rich cream sauce and thin with 1 cup celery water. Butter a flat shallow baking dish and add the celery alternately with a layer of sauce, a generous sprinkling of blanched almonds cut in long slips, and sauce at last. Dot generously with butter and crumbs, and sprinkle with additional blanched almonds. This may be made in the morning and reheated until thoroughly warmed and the almonds on top are lightly toasted.

## SALLY LUNN
### from Helen Duprey Bullock

Dissolve one yeast cake in a cup of warm, not hot, milk. Cream a half-cup butter and one third of a cup of sugar, beat in three eggs. Sift in four cups of flour, one teaspoon of salt alternately with the milk and yeast. Let rise in a warm place until double in bulk, then beat well. Pour into a well-buttered iron or earthen Turk's Head mold and let rise again until double in bulk and bake in a moderate oven about 30 minutes.

## SPOON BREAD
### from Eleanore Ott

To two cups boiling water salted with one teaspoon salt add two cups yellow corn meal and cook to a stiff mush. Add two eggs well beaten together, two teaspoons baking powder, two tablespoons butter, one and a half cups milk. Beat all together most thoroughly.

Place in a well-buttered and heated baking dish and bake in a moderate oven for 35 minutes. Serve from baking dish with spoon.

## CRACKLING BREAD
### from Eleanore Ott

| | |
|---|---|
| 1 quart corn meal | 1 cup finely chopped cracklings |
| 1 teaspoon salt | well-greased baking pan |
| 1 pinch soda | hot but not boiling water |
| | to make a stiff batter |

(Cracklings are bits of crisp browned pork fat.) Blend the meal, salt, soda, and cracklings with enough hot water to make a rather stiff batter and bake in a moderate oven.

## BATTER BREAD

| | |
|---|---|
| 1 pint sweet milk | 1 pint boiling water |
| 1 pint white corn meal | 1 teaspoon lard |
| 2 eggs, beaten | a bit of salt |

Pour half the meal into the boiling water, pour in the milk, the remainder of the meal, and the eggs. To this work in the melted lard. Have a deep dish greased and heated, and pour in the mixture, then bake.

## CORN BREAD

| | |
|---|---|
| ⅔ cup buttermilk | 1 teaspoon soda |
| ⅔ cup sweet milk | lump of lard |
| ½ pint white corn meal | |

The lard should be melted, the eggs beaten, and the mixture placed in a pan for baking.

## SOUTHERN JOHNNY CAKE
### by Eleanore Ott

To one pint of meal add a half teaspoon of salt and scald with boiling water to make a rather thin batter. Bake on top of the stove, turning as you would a batter cake on a hot buttered griddle.

## LADY BALTIMORE CAKE

2 cups sugar
1 cup butter
3½ cups flour

2 teaspoons baking powder
1 cup milk
1 teaspoon rose water
whites of 6 eggs

For the filling: Beat stiffly the whites of two eggs, adding confectioners' sugar until smooth. Add a half-cup chopped, seeded raisins, a cup of chopped pecans, and a half-teaspoon of vanilla extract. Figs may be used if desired.

## BEATEN BISCUIT

1 quart flour
½ teaspoon salt
1 teacup cold lard

Sift the flour into a bowl, cut the lard into little bits, add it and also salt. Use ice water to make a stiff dough. Place the dough on a flour-covered slab or block and give the traditional "hundred strokes, no more, no less," with a rolling pin or mallet. Continue folding when the dough becomes thin, using flour to keep it from sticking, and thus work air into the dough. Make little round biscuits about a half-inch thick, touch lightly with a fork, and bake.

## DOLLY MADISON CAKE

12 egg yolks
1 pound brown sugar
1 pound butter
1 pound floured citron
2 pounds floured currants
12 egg whites

1 teaspoon allspice
1 teaspoon cinnamon
2 grated nutmegs
1 pound cake flour
1 teaspoon cream of tartar
1 teaspoon baking soda
1 gill of molasses

Mix sugar with butter, combine egg yolks with mixture, then add the other ingredients, except for egg whites, then gradually fold them in, and bake.

## LOUISIANA SWEET POTATO PIE

4 eggs
1½ cups sweet
   potatoes, boiled and mashed
⅓ cup sugar
2 teaspoons honey

½ cup crushed pecans
⅔ cup milk
⅓ cup orange juice
1 teaspoon vanilla
pinch of salt

Beat the eggs until they are light, then combine with potatoes and sugar, beating thoroughly. Stir in the other ingredients and place the mixture in a pastry shell, baking at 450°F. for about 10 minutes. Lower to 350°F. and continue for about a half-hour longer. After the pie is cooled cover with whipped cream; an interesting addition is a mixture of grated orange peel and nutmeg.

## WASHINGTON PIE

2 eggs, lightly beaten
1 cup confectioners' sugar
1⅛ cups flour

2 teaspoons baking powder
vanilla
⅓ cup water

Combine eggs and sugar. Add baking powder to 1 cup flour and sift several times. Add half of the mixtures, then water, the rest of the flour and vanilla to taste. Use two baking tins. For filling use cream or custard or jam, and sprinkle powdered sugar over the top.

## MORAVIAN CHRISTMAS CAKES

1 quart Puerto Rico molasses
1 pound brown sugar
½ pound lard
½ pound butter
2 tablespoons cinnamon

1 tablespoon cloves
1 tablespoon ginger
1 tablespoon soda
flour to make a stiff dough
(about 3¾ pounds)

Add the sugar to the molasses and mix well. Add lard and butter which have been melted and cooled. Sift the spices and soda with a little flour and add to the molasses mixture, stirring in well. Then add the rest of the flour until you have a stiff dough. Let stand overnight. Roll very thin on a floured board, cut in shape with cookie cutters, and bake on greased tins in moderate oven (about 350°F.). This recipe makes about six pounds.

## STRIETZ—GERMAN CAKES

| | |
|---|---|
| 4 cups sugar | 4 eggs |
| 1 quart milk, scalded | 3 teaspoons salt |
| 1 quart yeast | 2 pounds raisins |
| 6 quarts flour | 1 cup chopped almonds |
| 2 cups lard | 2 tablespoons cinnamon |
| | ½ pound citron |

Mix well together all ingredients except raisins, nuts, and citron, and make into a dough. Let stand overnight until it doubles in size. In the morning add the other ingredients. Work it into loaves, then bake, as for bread.

## TIPSY PUDDING

Take a loaf of sponge cake, cut it into large pieces, put these in the bottom of a glass dish. Stick almonds into the cake. Pour half a pint of wine over this, then make a boiled custard and pour it over all. Top with a meringue made of three eggs and three tablespoons of powdered sugar, brown lightly in the oven, and serve cold.

## MARTHA WASHINGTON BONBONS

| | |
|---|---|
| 1 cup granulated sugar | ½ cup evaporated milk or light cream |
| 2 cups light brown sugar | 1 teaspoon vanilla |
| | 1 tablespoon butter |

Slowly cook the milk and sugar until mixture reaches the soft-ball temperature (234°F.). Pour into buttered bowl, and when cool beat in the vanilla and butter, and mix until creamy, then knead until firm into ropes about an inch in diameter, and chop into bonbon-size pieces. Decorate the individual candies with pieces of citron, nutmeats, cherries, coconut shreds, *dragées*, chocolate chips, and shaved chocolate, and dip some into hot melted chocolate and decorate.

## CALAS-AU-RIZ, CREOLE RICE CAKES
### from Miss Jeanne Roubion

To a pound of cooked rice, add sugar to taste and a little salt as well. Roll the rice into small balls, coat them in flour, and fry in deep fat (390°F.) to a golden brown. Serve at once.

## PRALINES
### from Miss Dolly Veters

Combine 1 cup brown sugar and 1 cup white sugar with half-cup water or cream. Cook, stirring, until the sugar is dissolved and the mixture begins to boil. Add 2 tablespoons butter and 1 cup pecan meats, and continue to cook until a little of the mixture dropped into cold water forms a soft ball and the syrup registers 236°F. on the candy thermometer. Remove the pan from the fire and beat the candy until it is somewhat thickened. Drop the pralines by the spoon on waxed paper and let harden.

## CAFÉ BRÛLOT
### from Miss Dolly Veters

Cut a large orange in half. Only one half of the orange is used in this recipe; reserve the other half and any juice for another purpose. Turn the orange inside out and put it in the bottom of the *café brûlot* bowl, pulp up. Add to the bowl 3 cubes of loaf sugar and 2 or 3 cloves for each serving. Add also 2 sticks of cinnamon, broken into several pieces. Pour over the inverted orange enough cognac to cover it generously. Ignite the cognac, and with the *brûlot* ladle stir the flaming liquid, dipping it up and letting it pour back into the bowl. Meanwhile hot coffee, preferably made by the French drip method, should be added slowly to the bowl. Serve in *brûlot* cups while the cognac is still burning.

# Acknowledgments

This book has grown out of a long interest in the subject of Christmas in the Southern United States; out of travel which has taken me back and forth over a period of years about my native region; and, not least, out of the generous and painstaking assistance of many people in each of these states. As a result, my files have been thickened by several hundred letters, folders of documents, microfilm and photostat material, together with dozens of pages of bibliographies and suggestions from friends in scores of places. Only through such kind help could I have hoped to accumulate a large body of data on the subject, much of which has not previously appeared in book form or in print.

Frank Dobie of Austin, Texas, beloved authority on the Southwest, made recommendations and loaned material for my Texas passages. Thomas G. Clark, author of *Pens, Petticoats and Plows*, was no less helpful with data relating to the post-Confederate South; and T. Winston Coleman, Winburn Farm, Lexington, loaned rare pamphlets and related data.

Vergil Bedsole, archivist of the Louisiana State University Libraries, Baton Rouge, Louisiana, called my attention to the striking Christmas diary of Mahala Roach, which appears in print for the first time in practically its full length.

Colonel Allen P. Julian, of the Atlanta Historical Society and president of the Atlanta Civil War Round Table, gave prompt response in tracking down remote references; as did Peter Brannon, Montgomery, director of the Alabama Department of Archives.

Grace Siewers, archivist of the Moravian Archives, and Mrs. Kate Pyron, librarian, Salem College, Winston-Salem, North Carolina, aided me in gathering scattered material on observance in that city.

Robert M. Maxwell, S. Vance Sellers, and Howell Stroup, Cherryville, North Carolina, loaned me several pounds of papers, photographs, and other background data on the New Year's Shooters of that state.

Mrs. Esther L. de Vazquez, San Antonio; Florence Johnson Scott, Rio Grande City, Texas; and Mrs. H. Welge Lewis, Fredericksburg, Texas, contributed data regarding Southwestern observances.

Herbert Knust of Bavaria, recently of New Orleans, assisted in translations and explanations of German customs. Roger Baudier, Catholic authority of Louisiana, generously shared his knowledge of Creole life and Christmas. On classic Christmas customs, considerable data were obtained from Mrs. Percy Leahmon McGehee, Chicago; Caroline Coleman, Fountain Inn, South Carolina; Daisy Poole, New Orleans; and Mrs. David Terry, Little Rock, Arkansas.

Senator George L. Radcliffe, president of the Maryland Historical Society; Mrs. Ferdinand Latrobe; Frederick Stieff; and Kate Savage, all of Baltimore, helped in Maryland research. Mr. and Mrs. Victor Baker gave Austrian and German background data.

Mrs. Ruth Woods Luderbach, Bay St. Louis, Mississippi; Mrs. Juanita Tucker, Christmas, Florida; Mrs. Merill Parrish Hudson and Clark Porteous of Memphis, Tennessee; Mrs. Evelyn Miller Crowell of Dallas, Texas; and Frank Garett, authority on Atlanta history, drew on their impressions and recollections of their home scenes.

H. C. Nixon of Nashville set down some of his own observations of country-store days in the recent South. Lon Tinkle, literary editor of the *Dallas News*, and Frank X. Tolbert, author and columnist, assisted with memoranda and suggestions.

In Williamsburg, Thad W. Tate, Jr., assistant director of research; Rose K. Belk, librarian; Van McNair, Lucius Battle, Donald J. Gonzales, and others of the staff, went to unusual pains to answer many questions. Mrs. George Coleman of the Tucker House and her daughter, Dr. Janet Kimbrough, helped me re-create the original Christmas-tree scenes in their famous residence.

Mrs. A. H. Toma, the executive director of the St. Louis Christmas Carols Association, provided prompt help; as did Irving Dilliard and Mrs. Fay Profilet of the *St. Louis Post Dispatch.*

Floyd Shoemaker, executive of the Missouri Historical Society, Columbus, helped settle many uncertain points; and equal aid came from Louis B. Nourse, librarian of the St. Louis Public Library; Dorothy B. Neuman, chief of the art department; Clarence E. Miller, librarian, and Elizabeth Tindall, reference librarian, St. Louis Mercantile Library Association; and Mrs. Eileen Cox, reference librarian, Missouri Historical Library, St. Louis, Missouri.

Mrs. Warren Reynolds, my sister, did yeoman service in tracking down library items and checking and rechecking the manuscript in many stages. Mrs. W. J. Kane and Anna Kane gave additional help.

Mrs. David B. Thompson, Charleston, South Carolina, contributed a striking series of memoranda on family observances, as did Mrs. Camilla Mays Frank of New Orleans, Mrs. Orleana Twichell Miller, and Mrs. Maud O'Bryan Ronstrom, want-ad columnist for the *Times Picayune States,* New Orleans, who helped in locating aspects of Creole observances.

In Richmond Randolph Church, state librarian; Milton Russell, head of the reference department; W. Edwin Hemphill of *Cavalcade* Magazine, responded to many inquiries. Resourceful help came, too, from India Thomas, house regent, and Eleanor S. Brockenbrough, assistant house regent, Confederate Museum; Mrs. Ralph Catterall of the Valentine Museum; Virginius Dabney, editor of the *Richmond Times Dispatch;* and Lamar Wallis, librarian of the Richmond Public Library.

Miss Essae M. Culver, executive of the Louisiana State Library, provided considerable bibliographical assistance. Charlotte Capers, director of the Mississippi Department of Archives and History, directed me to additional sources.

David Mearns, chief of the manuscript division of the Library of Congress, and Dr. C. Percy Powell, research director of the Lincoln Sesquicentennial Commission, aided me in locating previously inaccessible data. Similar help came from Hudson Grunewald of the *Washington Sunday Star* and Mrs. Glendy Culligan of the *Post* and *Times Herald*.

In Baltimore Miss Elizabeth Litsinger of the Maryland Room, Enoch Pratt Free Library, and Miss Martha Ann Peters, her assistant, tracked down considerable data, past and present. I am also indebted to James W. Foster, director of the Maryland Historical Society; Francis Haber, former librarian; Garner Ranney, assistant librarian; Miss Eugenia Calvert Holland, assistant curator; and Alice Kriete and A. Hester Rich of the staff.

Mrs. Dorothy Lawton, reference librarian of the Howard Tilton Library of Tulane University, handled a large volume of interlibrary loans, with the assistance of Betty Miles, Mrs. Marthy Robertson, and Mrs. Beverly Perry. Garland Taylor, general librarian, and Robert Greenwood, circulation librarian, were similarly helpful, with Mrs. Camille Jones, Mrs. Laura Hope, Mrs. Molly Eustis, Mrs. Margery Ohlsen. In other departments I received particular assistance from Mrs. Berthe Baker and Mrs. Aline Richter Stevens.

John Hall Jacobs, librarian of the New Orleans Public Library, and George King Logan, assistant librarian, gave unusual help, with Ruth Renaud, Margaret Ruckert, Gladys Peyronnin, Mrs. Alice V. Westfeldt, Mrs. Ellen Tilger, and Ruth Schuermann of the staff. James W. Dyson, librarian of Loyola University at New Orleans, gave frequent assistance.

Mrs. Sam McMeekin and Mrs. Willie Snow Ethridge, Louisville; Robert Molloy, New York; and David Westheimer, Houston, answered several requests for data unavailable in other sources.

In Dallas James D. Meeks, library director; Marie Stanley, of the Texas local history and genealogy department, made many photostatic copies, located music and other material.

In New York I was helped by Earle MacAusland, publisher of

*Gourmet* magazine; Robert Meyer, Jr., of Festival Information Service; Vernon Spencer; and Mavis McIntosh.

Others who gave assistance included Miss Ruth Blair, formerly of the Atlanta Historical Society; Mrs. Medora Perkerson, the author; Frank Daniell of the *Journal-Constitution;* Karen and Bob B. McCracken, Corpus Christi, Texas; Donald Page; Mr. and Mrs. W. E. Mays, and C. W. Bartlett, all of Anson, Texas.

John Jacob Niles, Lexington, Kentucky; Mrs. Gay White and Pressly Phillips, Sarasota, Florida; Tip McKenzie, Mexia, Texas; Mrs. Dagmar Renshaw Le Breton, New Orleans; George Hatcher, Sunday editor, *Journal-Constitution,* Atlanta; Mrs. A. J. S. Harmanson, New Orleans.

Mrs. Albert F. Storm, Bluff Plantation, Moncks Corner, South Carolina; Lucia M. Tyron, librarian, Pensacola Public Library, Florida; Very Reverend W. T. Dillon, S.J., Guadalupe Church, San Antonio, Texas; James A. Service, librarian, College of William and Mary, Williamsburg; Paul Hudson, curator, Jamestown, Virginia.

Mrs. Elmer Diess, Lexington; Mrs. Edith Amsler, Houston; James Murfin, Hagerstown, Maryland; Mrs. Lucelia Henderson, librarian of Carnegie Library, Rome, Georgia; and Mrs. J. T. Willis, Rome; Mrs. Samuel G. Stoney, Charleston; Mrs. Lillian T. Ray, Palm Beach, Florida; and Henry Biederman, editor, *The Cattleman,* Fort Worth, Texas.

Julien Martin, Wilmington, North Carolina; Dick Banks, *Charlotte Observer,* Charlotte, North Carolina; Tom Robinson, *Charlotte News;* Miriam Rabb, Raleigh, North Carolina; William S. Lacy, Jr., editor, *The Commonwealth,* Richmond; James Wharton, Weems, Virginia; Geoffrey Birt, Montgomery, Alabama; Barry Bingham, Louisville, Kentucky.

Caldwell Delaney, Mobile, Alabama; Cameron Plummer of the Haunted Bookshop, Mobile; William Fountaine, Fountaine Library, Columbus, Ohio; Mrs. Fidelia Anding and Mrs. Marian Harris of Anding Bookstore, New Orleans; Ralph Newman of Abraham Lincoln Bookstore, Chicago; P. M. Camack, Wilmington, North Carolina; Julia Estill, Fredericksburg, Texas; Roy Bird Cook, Charleston, West Virginia.

Ruby Parker and Mrs. Mary Herbert of Pensacola; Mrs. E. I. Smith, Athens, Georgia; Richard Walser, Raleigh, North Carolina; and June Buchanan, Caney Creek Community Center, Pippa Passes, Kentucky; Mrs. St. Julien R. Childs, Charleston, South Carolina.

Mr. and Mrs. C. T. Hooper, Brownsville, Tennessee; Mrs. Julia Preston, Winston-Salem, North Carolina; Mrs. Yvon du Quesnay and Mrs. Yvonne du Quesnay, Miss Dolly Veters, Judge Anna Judge Veters Levy, and S. Sanford Levy of New Orleans; Sidney S. Field of New York; Mrs. Mary Alice Bookhart of Jackson, Mississippi; James Ricau of New York; Stanley Horn, Nashville, Tennessee; Mrs. F. M. Robinson of McAllen, Texas.

Mrs. John D. Britton, Kingstree, South Carolina; Miss Edna H. Fowler, Los Angeles, California; Mrs. Kay Brady, Pass Christian; Louis Azrael, columnist for the *Baltimore News Post;* Charles G. Hays, West Palm Beach; David M. Cochran, Luling, Texas; Mary Lasswell, Austin, Texas.

Mrs. Walter C. White, Gates Mills, Ohio; Mrs. Shackelford Miller, Louisville; Mrs. Edith Wyatt Moore, Natchez, Mississippi; Mrs. Ruby Donahey, St. Petersburg, Florida; Aycock Brown, Manteo, North Carolina; Depew Meredith, Birmingham, Alabama; William S. Leinbach, Greensboro, North Carolina; Sherwood Canada, Charlotte, North Carolina; Mrs. Jessie Smith Young, Cartersville, Georgia.

The Reverend Mr. George Pardington, rector of St. Matthew's Episcopal Church, Houma, Louisiana; John Gordon, editor of Houma *Courier;* Clara S. Haupt, librarian, Terrebonne Paris Library, Houma; Nelson M. Cole, Montgomery, Alabama; Harry Golden, Charlotte, North Carolina; Louis Engelke, San Antonio, Texas.

Lucille Bostdorff, reference librarian, Petersburg Public Library, Petersburg, Virginia; Norah Albanell, chief of public services, Columbus Memorial Library, Pan American Union, Washington,

D.C.; Mrs. Mary Louise Holzapfel, librarian, and Mrs. Reba Sponcler, reference librarian, Washington County Library, Hagerstown, Maryland.

Anne Fisher, librarian, De Soto, Missouri, Public Libarry; C. R. Graham, director, and Mrs. Norman L. Johnson, acting head of the reference department, Louisville Public Library; H. G. Jones, state archivist, State Department of Archives and History, Raleigh, North Carolina; Florence Bethea, assistant director of libraries, Florida State University, Tallahassee; Mr. Irwin Sexton, librarian, Public Library, St. Joseph, Missouri; Morris Sauer, librarian, Public Library, St. Genevieve, Missouri.

Virginia Rugheimer, librarian, Charleston Library Society, Charleston, South Carolina; Vivian Branch, humanities librarian, University of Georgia, Athens; John C. Settelmayer, director, and Isabel Erlich, first assistant reference librarian, Atlanta Public Library.

Joe Templeton, director, and Mrs. E. W. Harris, Southern historical department, Public Library, Mobile, Alabama; Georgia Clark, reference librarian, Fayetteville, Arkansas; J. H. Easterby, South Carolina Archives Department, Columbia, South Carolina; Mrs. Virginia H. Taylor, state archives, Austin, Texas.

Mrs. Phyllis S. Burson, librarian of La Retama Public Library, Corpus Christi; Louise Crawford, librarian of City-County Memorial Library, Bay St. Louis, Mississippi; Mrs. C. A. Service, librarian, Sarasota Public Library, Sarasota, Florida; Charles E. Stone, librarian, Public Library, Greenville, South Carolina; James H. Renz, librarian of Florida Collection, Miami Public Library; Florrie B. Jackson, librarian, the Berry Schools, Rome, Georgia.

Emerson Greenaway, director of Free Public Library of Philadelphia; Doris C. Wiles, administrative assistant, St. Augustine Historical Society, Florida; Dorothy Dodd, state librarian, Florida State Library, Tallahassee; Llerena Friend, librarian, Barker Texas Center, University of Texas, Austin.

Mrs. Kathryn P. Arnold, historical librarian, Chattanooga Public Library; Margaret D. Mossiman, head of adult services,

Charleston County Free Library, Charleston, South Carolina; John Wyatt Bonner, Georgiana Collection, University of Georgia, Athens, Georgia; Betty E. Bell, Nashville Public Library, Nashville, Tennessee; Neal F. Austin, chief librarian, Public Library, High Point, North Carolina.

Fant H. Thornley, librarian, Birmingham Public Library; Mrs. W. W. Griffith, librarian, Wallace Library, Fredericksburg, Virginia; Cornelia Davis, librarian, Chestertown, Maryland; Margaret Burkhead, director, Little Rock Public Library, Little Rock, Arkansas; Mrs. Mollie Huston Lee, librarian, Richard B. Harrison Public Library, Raleigh; Esther Ann Manion, librarian, National Geographic Society.

Mrs. Forman Hawes, librarian, Georgia Historical Society, Savannah; Elizabeth Hodge, Geraldine Le May, and Joy Trulock, Savannah Public Library; Elizabeth Hooks Kelly, librarian, and Erin Murphy, staff member, El Paso Public Library, El Paso, Texas; Georgia H. Faison, reference librarian, general services division, North Carolina State Library, Raleigh, North Carolina; Mrs. Mildred B. Turnbull, librarian, Warder Public Library, Springfield, Ohio; Omar A. Bacon, librarian, Huntington Public Library, Huntington, West Virginia.

Pauline Weedon, librarian, Tampa Public Library, Tampa, Florida; Claude L. Settlemire, director, Roanoke Public Library; Mrs. Betty Giles, history department, City of Roanoke, Virginia; David Harkness, division of university extension, University of Tennessee, Knoxville.

HARNETT T. KANE

# Index

# Index

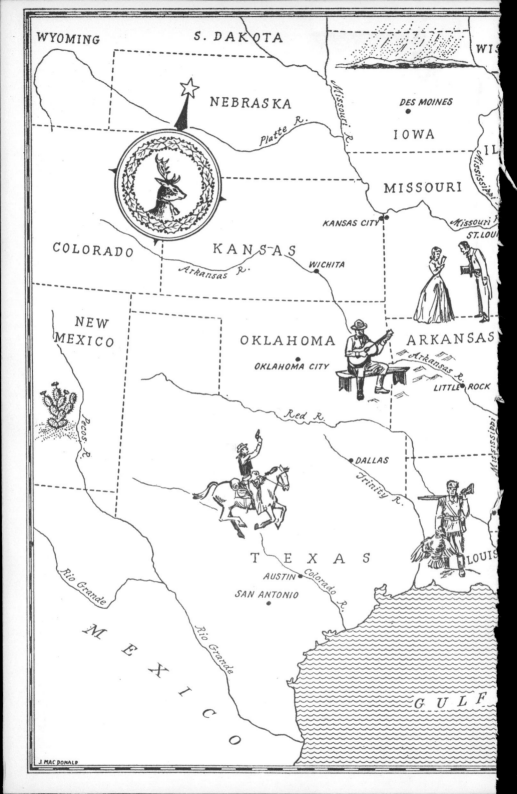